ONE WEEK LOAN

The Miller Method®

of related interest

The Complete Guide to Asperger's Syndrome
Tony Attwood
ISBN-13: 978 1 84310 495 7   ISBN-10: 1 84310 495 4

Asperger's Syndrome
A Guide for Parents and Professionals
Tony Attwood
Foreword by Lorna Wing
ISBN-13: 978 1 85302 577 8   ISBN-10: 1 85302 577 1

Autism, Play and Social Interaction
Lone Gammeltoft and Marianne Sollok Nordenhof
Translated by Erik van Acker
ISBN-13: 978 1 84310 520 6   ISBN-10: 1 84310 520 9

Practical Sensory Programmes for Students with Autism Spectrum Disorder and Other Special Needs
Sue Larkey
ISBN-13: 978 1 84310 479 7   ISBN-10: 1 84310 479 2

The Miller Method®
Developing the Capacities of Children on the Autism Spectrum

Arnold Miller

with

Kristina Chrétien

*Forewords by Diane Twachtman-Cullen
and Stuart G. Shanker*

Jessica Kingsley Publishers
London and Philadelphia

Extracts from Miller, A. and Eller-Miller, E. (1989) *From Ritual to Repertoire: A Cognitive-Developmental Systems Approach with Behavior-Disordered Children.* New York: John Wiley.
Reprinted with permission of John Wiley and Sons, Inc.
Case study on p.201 is adapted with permission from material originally published
in *Autism Spectrum Quarterly.*
Every reasonable effort has been made to trace all copyright holders of reprinted material. The author apologises for any omissions and is happy to receive amendments from copyright holders.

First published in 2007
by Jessica Kingsley Publishers
116 Pentonville Road
London N1 9JB, UK
and
400 Market Street, Suite 400
Philadelphia, PA 19106, USA

www.jkp.com

Library of Congress Cataloging in Publication Data
Miller, Arnold, 1927-
  The Miller Method : developing the capacities of children on the autism spectrum / Arnold Miller with Kristina Chretien ; forewords by Diane Twachtman-Cullen and Stuart G. Shanker.
    p. ; cm.
  Includes bibliographical references and index.
  ISBN-13: 978-1-84310-722-4 (hardcover : alk. paper)
  ISBN-10: 1-84310-722-8 (hardcover : alk. paper) 1. Autism in children--Treatment. 2. Cognitive therapy for children. I. Chretien, Kristina. II. Title.
  [DNLM: 1. Child Development. 2. Cognitive Therapy--methods. 3. Autistic Disorder--rehabilitation. 4. Child Development Disorders, Pervasive--rehabilitation. 5. Child. WM 203.5 M647m 2007]
  RJ506.A9M55 2007
  618.92 85882--dc22

                                        2006033570

British Library Cataloguing in Publication Data
A CIP catalogue record for this book is available from the British Library

ISBN-13: 978 1 84310 722 4
ISBN-10: 1 84310 722 8

Printed and bound in the United States by
Thomson-Shore, Inc.

I dedicate this book to Eileen Eller-Miller
1928–2004
wife and colleague for 45 years

As promised, the work continues.

Acknowledgements

Many hands and minds have worked to make this book readable—without sacrificing depth—for the parents and professionals who will draw on it to help children on the autism spectrum.

As I wrote this book I often had the feeling that my late wife and colleague, Eileen Eller-Miller, was with me—helping to find a better way to express key developmental concepts and strategies. Her gentle spirit pervades this book as it did in our earlier work *From Ritual to Repertoire.*

This book has been enriched by the down-to-earth chapter on how to be with the children written by Kristina Chrétien. Kristina courageously overcame her anxiety about writing in English (Swedish is her first language) so that she might share her wealth of knowledge and experience with others. I am very grateful to Kristina for the splendid result of her efforts.

Two mothers of autistic children with whom I worked over the years—Dr. T.C. Smith and Rebecca Sperber—gave generously of their time in reading and rereading each and every chapter. They complemented each other nicely. Dr. Smith has a flair for "good, juicy sentences" while Rebecca Sperber constantly viewed what was written through the eyes of parents and professionals who were dealing with these developmental concepts for the first time. The efforts of both mothers were invaluable in highlighting the need for crisp examples of concepts. I am also in debt to Dr. Smith for the time she spent carefully going over proofs.

Other important readers who critiqued various parts of the book were my colleague Dr. Paul Callahan, and indefatigable parent, and Language and Cognitive Development Center board member, Dr. Bruce Auerbach. Early in the development of this work, Dr. Cheryl Bragg made a number of valuable comments, as did Sonia Mastrangelo. I also wish to acknowledge the uncanny ability of Dr. Stephen Shore as he carefully "depixillated" the manuscript and helped resolve gaps in continuity.

Michael Kowalski, Principal of Crossroads School, Westfield, New Jersey was instrumental in making available—with the support of parents—photographs of the children as they went through different aspects of the Miller Method® program. Skilled Crossroads staff members Barbara Kolski and Amy Wilson graced this book with photographs of themselves with the children as has Maurya Farah during her tenure at Oak View School. I would also like to recognize the contribution of parents Tami and Randy Barmache as well as Teresa and Bruce Auerbach for their readiness to share photographs of their sons as they worked on and off the Elevated Square.

My son, Loren Miller, helped with the "nuts and bolts" of getting the many photographs and figures to our editor in good order. I also wish to acknowledge the efforts of my niece, Jennifer Hofert and her husband, Stephan, for their role—in the midst of demanding schedules—in tracking down difficult- to-find references.

Finally, I wish to acknowledge the important role of editor Jessica Stevens, who gently but persistently detailed missing figures and references, tactfully challenged some of my assertions, and worked hard to make this book the best possible account of the Miller Method®.

Contents

List of Figures

List of Tables

Foreword

An earlier work by Arnold Miller and his late wife, Eileen Eller-Miller, *From Ritual to Repertoire: A Cognitive-Developmental Systems Approach with Behavior-Disordered Children*, captured my attention in the early 1990s. I found its theory-into-practice approach both intriguing and fascinating. This new work by Dr. Miller builds on the core view regarding the education and treatment of children on the autism spectrum expressed in his earlier book, and does so in a manner that is even easier to understand and implement than previously. Indeed, Dr. Miller has created a work that is at once scholarly and practical.

Comprehensive in scope, *The Miller Method*® offers "a complete package" for parents and professionals. Its four parts clearly cover all of the bases. Part I explains, and gives numerous examples of, children's systems, and it does so in a manner that makes the concept crystal clear. Part II describes treatment and gives a supporting rationale for how it serves to develop both social capacity and communication. Part III tackles education, and focuses on establishing competence and "teaching to the children's reality". So, what could possibly be left for Part IV, you ask—research, an area that allows the reader to take a critical look at the methodology.

While some of the terms used to explain common features of autism are unique to the Miller Method®, all of them are explained in great detail. In addition, the vast number of examples and illustrations supporting the text give an "I can do that" sense to the reader. Other approachable features of this book are its comprehensive chapter summaries and its glossary.

There is much to celebrate in this excellent work, but space constraints limit a recounting of them. So I shall "cut" to the book's core. *The Miller Method*® is a book that is eminently respectful of the child with autism. The methodology espouses following the child's lead; "intruding" ever-so-respectfully into the child's world; and enticing him or her into ever-expanding social realms. Unlike other methods, it seeks to put the child in the important role of initiator. Perhaps most importantly, the Miller Method® meets the child where he or she actually is!

Diane Twachtman-Cullen, Ph.D., CCC-SLP
Editor-in-Chief, Autism Spectrum Quarterly

Foreword

The systems model of autism that that Dr. Miller presents in this book is internally related to the therapeutic program that he outlines: that is, his model of autism informs the principles and techniques employed in the Miller Method®. On this model, autism spectrum disorders are seen as the downstream effect of initial biological or processing challenges that constrain the child's capacity to regulate or process his sensory impressions and/or to control his movements, thereby impairing his capacity to differentiate between himself and others. The child may have trouble achieving any sense of stability at all, or he may settle on behaviors that enable him to maintain a sense of order at the cost of further development.

One of the basic tenets of systems theory is that developmental transitions occur during periods of increased instability, which lead to the formation of more adaptive patterns. This is very much the guiding principle in the Miller Method®. After establishing the nature of the systems that the child brings to new situations, the therapist carefully introduces elements of disorder in order to extend the range of challenges that the child is able to cope with. As the reader will see in the following pages, the goal here is not to produce the mere appearance of meaningful functioning but, rather, to effect a genuine developmental transition: one that enhances the child's capacity to interact with people and objects, to adapt to change, to learn from experience, and to engage in sustained co-regulated interactions.

Stuart G. Shanker
York University

Preface: Beyond Compliance

Profoundly disordered children on the autism spectrum are often intimidating to both the parents who live with them and the professionals who try to help them. Faced with the range of behavior the children present, professionals often ask themselves, "Where do I start?" Complicating things further, the child is often very appealing, perhaps beautiful, but behaves as if the people around him or her do not exist. The felt need is to elicit some kind of response—a fleeting glance, a smile—anything that communicates that one is more than wallpaper for that child. But the child often does not permit this. As one parent put it, "You knock…but no one answers."

The common second reaction to these children is to rationalize the disorder. It is painful to confront aberrant functioning in a child—one wants to make it go away. As a result, many professionals and parents rationalize the child's difficulty with change or following directions as simply "being stubborn," and resistance to including others in their play as being due to the child's "independent" nature. Sometimes, pediatricians— asked by anxious parents about their child's failure to communicate—are told not to worry and that "After all, Einstein didn't speak until he was four."

Children at the more severe end of the continuum echo commercials from radio and television, flap their arms and twiddle their fingers in front of their faces, run in circles or from wall to wall in a room, flick lights on and off, flush toilets, line things up, and get lost finding their way to the bathroom. Often, too, they demonstrate poor reactivity to pain, clumsiness, and an uncertain sense of their bodies.

We have dealt with these challenges for over four decades. To be effective we found that it is essential to see the children as they are—not as we would like them to be. Crediting the children with more capacity than they have is a serious error because it results in their beginning a treatment program that is beyond their reach, with the consequent waste of precious time.

WHAT ARE AUTISM AND AUTISM SPECTRUM DISORDER AND HOW HAVE THEY BEEN TREATED?

Autism is a bioneurological disorder of unknown origin which affects the child's ability to process information from his or her own body or from his or her surroundings. It also interferes with a child's ability to initiate functional or communicative behavior. First described in its "pure" form by Leo Kanner (1943, 1971)—emphasizing the impairment of the ability to make human contact or to communicate—the syndrome has been extended by the terms "pervasive developmental disorder" or "autism spectrum disorder" to cover children who show some but not all of the features initially described by Kanner. The term "spectrum" also implies that the disorder ranges from relatively mild to severe. Currently, about 65 children in every 10,000 (Wing and Potter 2002)—with four times more boys than girls affected—acquire some form of the disorder.

The first approach to autism in the 1950s was from a psycho-analytic perspective and assumed that unresponsive "refrigerator" parents were responsible; a proponent of this was Bruno Bettelheim (1950). In the early 1960s his discredited rationale for the disorder was supplanted by a behavioral approach derived from learning theory and based on experimental psychologist B.F. Skinner's findings in animal experimentation. Ivar Lovaas (1987) was and is one of the foremost proponents of the applied behavior analysis approach. At about the same time, we introduced our cognitive-developmental systems approach with its roots in Heinz Werner's developmental theory (Miller 1991, 2005; Miller and Eller-Miller 1989, 2000). Our approach is now most often referred to as the Miller Method® (MM).

Psychoanalytic approaches assumed that maternal deprivation was the major source of the disorder—probably because some of the autistic behaviors superficially mirrored findings with the emotionally deprived and withdrawn infants reported by Renee Spitz (1945–46). These children rapidly improved when they were provided with regular nurturing. Seeing some of the same kinds of behavior among autistic children, psycho-analytic therapists sought to treat the disorder by addressing the assumed deprivation. (I well remember a prominent psychiatrist—at the center at which I worked for a number of years—feeding candy to children with autism from his "breast pocket" to treat the assumed oral deprivation of the children.) In recent years, post-mortem studies (Sousa 2001) have found that people with autism "tend to have a proportionately smaller cerebellum than normal." Dysfunction or damage to the cerebellum may result in deficits in

Coping in everyday life requires flexibility. If a stranger offers a hand to a child, we do not want the child to compliantly take that hand. We want the child to discriminate between hands offered by special caregivers and those offered by strangers. Beyond this, we want the child to be able to cope with change. Some children with autism are compliant as long as the requests made of them follow a familiar, predictable course. However, an unexpected change in the familiar routine can trigger a catastrophic tantrum. This may occur when Mother changes from wearing long- to short-sleeved dresses, or takes a slightly different route to the store; or it may occur when a new child comes into the classroom.

We want the child to be able to cope with these everyday changes without distress. Excessive emphasis on compliance may work against the child coping with change. But there is another issue of concern: Requiring children with autism to behave and respond *as if* they were typical children ignores the important, bioneurologically based differences which the children present.

Children with autism exhibit an array of sensory and motor planning or sequencing issues (Bogdashina 2003). Sometimes they find being in a noisy classroom so painful that they need to cover their ears. Other children find it distressing to be touched. Some children, while having perfectly normal hearing, seem completely oblivious to spoken words or even loud sounds. Sometimes, some children may fall and skin their knees or bump their heads and yet fail to cry or locate the source of the injury.

These behaviors indicate either impaired transmission or impaired interpretation of sensory impressions from various parts of the body to the brain. These same transmission problems appear to limit the children's ability to use their bodies adaptively. For example, they may not have a clear sense of how one side of the body differs from the other and, as a result, may be unable to climb over a fence; or they may have difficulty integrating the upper with the lower part of their bodies and therefore cannot easily learn to ride a tricycle or how to swim. These difficulties indicate a striking lack of body awareness; the children may try to cope with this by generating self-stimulatory body activity and by seeking "edge experiences" to help define themselves. If this interpretation is correct, then requiring such children to remain seated for extended periods of time may deprive them of needed sensory input and contribute to increased self-stimulation or even explosive behavior.

sensorimotor functioning, low muscle tone, movement coordination, flat affect, and lowered physical endurance (Gilman and Newman 1992). The work of Schmahmann (1994), suggests that the structures of the cerebellum govern higher order behavior and learning as well as language.

The behavioral approach makes no assumptions about the sources of autism or the inner life of the child. Workers simply address the aberrant behavior which the children present, using the tools of learning theory—"reinforcing" with rewards of, for example, food or praise for desired behaviors and attempting to "extinguish," with "turning away" or "time-out" or aversive procedures, those behaviors viewed as unacceptable. Behaviorists assume that if they can get the disordered child to *behave* like typical children, then, indeed, that child will be typical. Since typical children learn from a teacher while seated at a table, behaviorists assume that children with autism also need to sit at a table and look at the therapist before they can be taught.

HOW DOES THE MM® COMPARE WITH APPLIED BEHAVIOR ANALYSIS?

The MM contrasts sharply with applied behavior analysis (ABA). Where ABA requires the child to remain seated to learn, the MM assumes that children with autism learn best through action; where ABA emphasizes "turning away" from tantruming or acting-out children, the MM emphasizes turning toward and engaging the child; where ABA tries to divert or "extinguish" aberrant behavior, the MM attempts to transform these behaviors into functional, interactive exchanges. ABA establishes compliance with the help of rewards, but the MM establishes repetitive rituals (systems) which are systematically expanded, complicated, and interrupted (disrupted) to elicit spontaneous initiatives from the children. Finally, unlike ABA, the MM specifically teaches the children how to generalize their functioning, to shift comfortably from one location to another, and to use transitions to acquire symbolic capacity.

BEYOND COMPLIANCE

While the ABA approach often achieves the child's compliance with its methods, its emphasis on compliance seems at odds with the child's need to cope in an inconstant world and—equally important—with the kinds of bioneurologically based challenges these children experience.

Our core view about treating and educating children with autism spectrum disorder remains what it was when we published our first book *From Ritual to Repertoire* (Miller and Eller-Miller 1989). We still maintain that there is a basic drive in all children—no matter how withdrawn or disorganized they may be—to find a way to cope with a confusing and inconstant world. Children with autism express this drive in spite of major challenges with experiencing their bodies and how they relate to the world. Our task is to help these children use every capacity or fragment of capacity to achieve this goal of coping. This becomes possible when we introduce both order and carefully gauged disorder into their lives. As described in Chapter 1, introducing order helps cohere the children's fragmented functioning while introducing carefully gauged disorder helps them cope with change.

We offer one caveat for parents and professionals working with special children. Do not settle for the mere appearance of meaningful functioning. Some professionals say—as they refer to the performance of a special child—"If it quacks like a duck and walks like a duck, it *is* a duck." In other words, if the child displays the outer forms of typical functioning behavior, speech, or reading, then that child understands what he or she is doing, saying, or reading. Unfortunately, we have seen far too many special children who *seem* to be acting appropriately, using perfectly articulated speech, or "reading," without having a clue as to what they are doing, saying, or reading, to accept the duck simile. In MM programs we insist that the children unambiguously demonstrate their understanding.

This book for parents and professionals, like our previous book, describes the theory and practice of the MM, which has evolved from over four decades with hundreds of children with autism spectrum disorders and their families. Our approach continues to be based on cognitive-developmental systems theory and stresses the need to both build on and add to the children's existing capacities. This book should be more readable and is certainly less expensive than our previous one. We intend it to provide ready access to the theory and methods we have found most helpful in working with the children. We hope the journey you take with us will result in your celebrating with us the gains that these challenging but wonderful children achieve as they realize their potential as human beings.

Arnold Miller
Newton, Massachusetts

Part I

ABOUT CHILDREN'S SYSTEMS

Chapter 1

What Makes the Miller Method® Unique?

The single most unique and important aspect of the Miller Method® (MM) is its work with systems. But what is a system? By *system* we mean any organized behavior with an object or event that the child produces. Even "upsetting" behaviors—such as throwing or dropping things, opening and closing doors, or lining things up—are systems, although they do not seem to others to serve any particular function.

We are interested in such behaviors because they are directed, are organized, and lead to some outcome—all parts of what we look for in functional behavior and in communication. If we can find a way to help the child modify or transform these repetitive action systems so that they become functional and interactive, then we have contributed to the child's development. For children who show little or no organized systems—even maladaptive ones—our first task will be to find ways to help them form systems.

When the nonverbal or limited-verbal child is involved in an action system, the child's reality *is* that action system. Nothing else exists for that child. Further, if someone interrupts or disrupts that system the child will need to restore or maintain it. Often it is the child's drive to restore "broken" action systems that provides us with the opportunity to communicate about restoring them.

Systems are in play in various ways: *Body systems* coordinate sensory capacities with motor capacities in the service of a particular function such as picking up an object, climbing over a fence, walking, riding a bike, swimming, and so forth. *Social systems* concern how two people interact with each other, whether by working together, turn-taking, competing, or bonding. *Communication systems* involve the integration of words and actions around objects in relation to another person. *Symbolic systems* involve the way in which a child organizes the relation between symbols and what they represent.

Systems may be viewed as organized "chunks" of behavior, perception, or thought. The 15-month-old child at the beach who repeatedly fills up his pail with sand and then dumps it into the ocean only to repeat it again and again is engaged in an action system; the autistic boy who, seeing my glasses perched at the very end of my nose, must reach over to push them higher on my nose where they belong is reacting to a disrupted perceptual system; the child who engages in "make believe" play to the exclusion of all else is involved in a system, as is the Asperger child who can only talk about airplanes. All are dominated in varying degrees by particular systems.

However, before one can apply understanding of systems to intervention with special children, it is necessary first to recognize what systems look like when they are forming, when they are fully formed, and when they are disrupted. Once parents and professionals understand the dynamics of systems they gain access to a powerful tool for dealing with every aspect of a child's life. In this chapter I will describe systems as they appear in all areas of human functioning—including social and communication—as well as their relevance for "meltdowns." But first, let's consider the role systems play in the order and disorder of everyday life for children with autism.

ORDER AND DISORDER

If we look at our lives we find both order and disorder—with *order* referring to predictable systems and *disorder* referring to the disruption of those systems. In fact, one might argue that an important part of living concerns coping with unpredictable disorder and trying to impose some order on it. (When I look at my desk it becomes clear that I have a way to go in this regard.) Both ordered and disordered systems have an important place in teaching children on the autism spectrum.

Used properly, the introduction of both ordered and disordered systems helps children make important progress that they would not make if only imposed order were the rule. Some children with autism—those we refer to as having *system-forming disorders*—are quite scattered and have trouble ordering (systematizing) and making sense of their immediate surroundings and the people in it. Another group of children—referred to as having *closed system disorders*—become over-preoccupied with routines (systems) and objects to the exclusion of people. They tend to live in isolated "bubbles" of repetitive activity with one or more objects.

The importance of ordered systems

For both kinds of children, developing daily routines (ritual systems) in therapy and in school sessions are important—but for different reasons. For scattered children with system-forming disorders, the repetitive and predictable routines of being greeted by therapist or teacher, putting their clothes in cubbies, knowing where everything belongs, helps to organize a safe, predictable setting. For children with closed system disorders, these predictable routines may at first be helpful because they guide them from their over-preoccupation with small "chunks" of the environment in therapy or classroom sessions to a broader experience of their surroundings. These routines also promote a bond between the children and their therapists and teachers. For these reasons it is desirable at first to establish and emphasize rituals (systems) in therapy and classroom.

Limitations of ordered systems

However, if the daily ritual systems continue unchanged for too long, they limit the children's potential for new learning, exploration, and development. In other words, the children will not learn to cope with the changes that new places or new people bring into their worlds but will, instead, become confused or distressed by new situations. To help the children learn to cope, therapists, teachers, and parents need to introduce different amounts of change into their predictable ritual systems. Obviously, if the changes are too great, too soon, the children will "fall apart." The challenge for therapists, teachers, and parents is to introduce small amounts of disorder within the children's everyday systems so that the children begin to develop the toughness they need to cope with more dramatic changes in the world outside the therapy and school sessions.

Introducing system expansions as "mild" disorder

When a child is engaged with the usual way of doing things, it is important after a time to carefully vary those routine systems. In therapy sessions routine systems are systematically varied by changing various aspects of a task such as pouring water into a can. The therapist's movement of the can to another location (*location expansion*) introduces a "mild" disorder which the child pouring water copes with by having to follow the new location of the can so that he or she can continue the water-pouring system. Similarly, when the therapist offers the bottle from different positions (*position expansion*), the child adjusts to these changes. A therapist can also offer bottles of different shapes and sizes resulting in ability to generalize (*object expansion*). And finally, although the child has grown accustomed to always receiving the bottle from one person, he or she can learn to tolerate the disruption produced by a new person offering the bottles (*person expansion*). Clearly, the child who can tolerate and eventually enjoy these mild changes is further along in development than the child who clings desperately to a fixed pattern. Additionally, the child gains a true understanding of the object by experiencing its *form* rather than just memorizing a single instance of a particular *type* of bottle.

In similar fashion, teachers, while keeping certain aspects of the daily routine stable, may systematically vary others. For example, the table at which the children sit and work may be varied in its location from day to day as can the chair in which each usually sits. Similarly, the order of events scheduled for the day may be changed. Cubbies should remain constant because they provide children with a "security station" while other things in the child's environment change. Care should be taken that only one aspect of the child's environment at a time is changed. If a change is too upsetting for a particular child, a lesser amount of change can be negotiated.

Interrupting task systems as "moderate" disorder

Once the child can tolerate and cope with the "mild" disorder implicit in the expansions described above, he or she is ready to cope with "moderate" disorder introduced by interrupting the various systems (tasks or activities) with which the child is engaged. "Moderate" disorder can be introduced by momentarily taking the bottle out of the child's hand just as he or she is ready to pour from it, or dropping the slide just as the child was ready to slide down; or it may be introduced by sitting in the child's path in a way which interferes with his or her access to a desired toy; or it may involve the teacher who is working with the child on the Elevated Square (a device to increase awareness and focus which is discussed in Chapter 5) suddenly "changing his or her mind" and requiring the child to go in the opposite direction to that to which he or she was accustomed.

If we apply the same concept in the classroom, the teacher, noting when the children are "captured" by a particular activity system such as scribbling with crayons, may suddenly interrupt the scribbling to shift the child to rolling play dough only to interrupt the play dough activity to return the child to the scribbling.

In all these situations, the child accustomed to a certain order must cope with the change induced by interposing another activity system before the child can return to the first activity system. Once the children can cope with both expansions and interruptions, they are ready to cope with more dramatic disorder.

Dramatic disruptions of familiar systems

From time to time, therapists working with children who have become completely familiar with the standard structure of the Elevated Square will completely dismantle the structure before the child's therapy session begins. Then, the child's need to restore that familiar structure (see Figure 1.1) results

Figure 1.1 An autistic child helping his therapist restore the disrupted Elevated Square. Photographed with permission from Crossroads School, Westfield, New Jersey

in cooperative efforts with therapist or with another child to repair it. In the classroom a similar procedure can be used.

Another example is as follows: One morning, as the children walk into their familiar classroom, they find everything "topsy-turvy." Tables and chairs are capsized, crumpled paper as well as cups, saucers, bottles, and kitchen utensils are strewn over the floor, mixed up with blocks and other toys. Everything is in complete disarray. Teachers—who created the mess after the children had gone home the day before—express dismay to the children, saying something like, "Oh my, look at this terrible mess. We have to fix it!" Then, as they "struggle" to right a table, the teachers turn to different children and say, "Help me pick up the table!" or "Help me clean up this mess!"

Some of the children (those with closed system disorders) spontaneously start to help clean up the mess while others need guidance about where to put things. Usually, the trash in the wastepaper basket is easiest for them, while helping someone move or lift something is more difficult. Still others need to put the toys and blocks on the shelves where they belong while others need to put the kitchen utensils in their proper compartments. One child may be very upset about the mess and begin to cry. A teacher needs to encourage that child to see that he or she can help put everything in its proper order. With support, the classroom is usually put together in 15 minutes.

Gains from "dramatic disruption" show themselves in a number of ways: First, the children feel more competent having used their bodies to lift and push fairly heavy things into their proper places. Second, they become more aware of the layout of the room and where different things go as they put back blocks and toys on their shelves. As they do this, they literally expand their awareness of their immediate surroundings. Receptive language is enhanced as children hear the teachers narrate what they are doing *while* they are doing it. Equally important, the children have started to learn how to work with someone else to restore order and, in doing so, establish a framework for cooperative interactions with children and adults. In short, dramatic disruption provides the conditions for interaction for the many children who are unable to initiate it spontaneously.

Why is dramatic disruption effective?

Dramatic disruption as a strategy is effective because it follows a previous predictable order. Without the well-established layout of routine systems there would be no basis for expecting the children to put things right. In short, it works because there is a drive in all children—but particularly among those on the autism spectrum—to restore disrupted systems. By exploiting this need we achieve a new ability to cope with disorder, whether it be dealing with the confusion of a department store, coping with a noisy, festive occasion, or simply learning to tolerate Mother taking a different route to the store.

Now that we have shared some notions as to how system concepts are applied in therapy and in classroom sessions, it will be useful to discuss more precisely the nature of systems.

WHAT ARE THE CHARACTERISTICS OF SYSTEMS?

Once it has been constructed, each system tends to maintain its coherence. This means that when a child's system is interrupted or disrupted, the child feels compelled to restore it through some kind of compensatory action. As is the case with the "dramatic disorder" introduced in therapy or classroom, these compensatory actions—whether action, gesture, or utterance—provide a basis for developing various kinds of functional or communicative behaviors. When a disrupted system cannot be restored, many children will have a major "meltdown."

The compulsive aspect of systems is evident in the child at the beach we mentioned at the beginning of this chapter who "has to" keep filling up and dumping his pail of sand: stopped from doing this he might tantrum until allowed to continue. Prevented from adjusting my glasses, the autistic boy might become very distressed. The Asperger child "needs" to inflict his airplane knowledge on anyone who would listen. The nonverbal child with autism who is lining up blocks resists any intrusion as he compulsively continues his lining-up-blocks system. Such children, unlike typical children, are literally unable to spontaneously shift from one system to another. This means that part of our treatment—explained in Chapters 5 and 7—is designed to help the children learn how to shift from one system to another without distress.

How do children's systems differ from each other?

Children's systems differ from each other in three ways: In terms of their *rigidity*, their *complexity*, and their *distance from reality*.

System rigidity refers to how urgent the child's need is to maintain a system unchanged. For some children even mild expansions are threatening and can trigger major tantrums. Other children find expansions less threatening and can, therefore, more readily tolerate modifications of their systems.

System complexity refers to whether the system is simple (a minisystem) or more complex (an integrative system). Minisystems involve only one kind of action, while integrative systems combine several smaller systems in service of a particular goal. Minisystems include picking up and dropping an object, opening and closing a door, flushing the toilet, flicking a light switch on and off, and so forth. However, if, for example, a child picks up an object to give it to someone, if the door is opened in order to let someone in, or if the cupboard is opened to put something inside, then we are dealing with integrative systems since more than one step is involved in order to achieve each particular goal.

Integrative systems are also evident when a child climbs a ladder to go down a slide. Here, we note the integration of several components—going up the ladder, sitting down, hitching forward, going down the slide, and then repeating the process. Integrative systems are also in play in basic problem solving or causal systems as when a child learns that pressing down on the pedal of his tricycle causes it to move forward or that pulling and turning the doorknob will open the door.

Systems also differ in the *distance from reality* dimension—the extent to which children substitute symbols for direct physical contact with a person, object, or event. For example, where communication is concerned, the child learns that instead of an action system of pulling Mother by the hand toward a desired object, the *come* gesture by itself brings her closer. Similarly, in developing symbolic capacity, the child learns to re-enact systems— previously performed with real objects—on miniature replicas of these objects. In each case, the developmental advance requires that the child learn to substitute symbolic systems for direct action systems with people or objects.

Do disordered children on the autism spectrum differ in the forming and maintenance of systems?

Yes, children on the autism spectrum often differ dramatically with regard to the forming and maintenance of systems. As we saw in the example of the disrupted classroom described earlier, these children differ in the intensity of the need to repair disrupted systems. The children seem to emphasize one of two ways of dealing with objects and people in their immediate surroundings. One way—characteristic of those children we refer to as having a closed system disorder—entails their becoming so preoccupied with one or more objects that they totally ignore people, and have difficulty with transitions. Left to themselves, such children may spend hours lining up blocks or toy animals or flushing toilets, or opening and closing doors. Some become very distressed if the usual way of going from one place to another is altered. These closed system children would be those who show the most compelling need to put the "messed up" classroom together as rapidly as possible.

Another group of children on the spectrum—whom we refer to as those with system-forming disorders—have not reached the point where they can become involved with objects. Instead, their behavior suggests that they are "driven" by one stimulus or another but are unable to engage these stimulating objects. Instead, they tend to flap their arms, toe walk, or twiddle their fingers in front of eyes. When they are required to address an object—such as a puzzle—there is often a "disconnect" between their eyes and hands with the eyes looking one way while the hands fumble with the puzzle piece.

Table 1.1 indicates that system-forming challenges may stem not only from the children's disposition to be "driven" by stimuli (referred to as Type B in the table) but by impaired body coordination (referred to as Type A) that interferes with their development. The table also shows that the closed system disposition can be very restrictive (as described in closed system Type A) or less restrictive (as shown in Type B).

Table 1.1 Contrasting children with closed-system and system-forming disorders

Disorder	Children	
	Type A	*Type B*
Closed system	Minimal executive functioning and few systems. Poor shifting/scanning. People excluded from systems.	Executive functioning with many object systems. Ability to shift from one system to another. People excluded from systems.
System-forming	Minimal executive functioning. Poor sensory-motor coordination limits system forming.	Little executive functioning. Salient properties of many sources induce repeated orienting, but not engagement.

Of the two kinds of children, those who tilt more toward the closed system type respond to treatment more rapidly than those with system-forming disorders. The reason for this is that those with closed system disorders, while they are "captured" by their systems, demonstrate a degree of organization with objects which, although aberrant, can be built on and eventually transformed into functional behavior. In contrast, those with system-forming disorders have first to be taught to build coherent systems before they can learn to expand them into functional behavior.

In the next chapter I will discuss further the distinction between children who are victims as opposed to masters of their systems.

SUMMARY

This chapter explained the systems concept and its important role in all facets of human functioning. Rituals are systems which, when developed properly, can help autistic children move from aberrant to more typical functioning. Systems are organized "chunks" of behavior, with each system having a causal dynamic. Once the system is formed, the child needs to maintain it. Interrupting or disrupting a child's system induces the child to produce a compensatory behavior to restore it.

Order and disorder in everyday life are related to the concept of systems, with "order" implying organized and predictable systems, while "disorder" refers to the disruption of systems.

Two kinds of autistic children—those with closed system disorders and those with system-forming disorders—have different system needs. "Scattered" children with system-forming disorders require organized, highly structured settings in order to help them organize their functioning and experience the world in predictable terms. Children with closed system disorders may initially need ordered settings but then require the challenge that disorder introduces. As children learn to cope with disorder, they are also learning to cope with change and to explore their surroundings.

Interventions with systems may vary from "mild" to "moderate" to "dramatic." The introduction of "mild disorder" is evident when the teacher or therapist expands a system by changing the location of the object, the person involved in the system, the objects used in the system, or the position with which the child deals with the object. Moderate disorder refers to the interruption of systems in a way which induces a compensatory reaction on the child's part to maintain the system. Finally, dramatic disorder refers to a substantial disruption of the child's immediate environment in order to have the child restore it.

All three system interventions have positive effects on the autistic child—with the child's repair of dramatic disorder contributing to his or her sense of competence as he or she restores the disrupted surroundings.

Systems are defined in terms of their rigidity, their complexity, and their distance from reality. Rigidity refers to the child's difficulty transitioning from one system to another; complexity refers to whether the child is dealing with a simple minisystem or a more complex integrative system; and distance from reality refers to the extent to which a system has a symbolic component.

Chapter 2

Children as Victims
or Masters of Their Systems

Asked why he repeatedly flapped his arms, Mike, a 12-year-old autistic boy, replied, "It helps me to think."

As we compare the involvement with various systems of autistic children with that of typical children, it becomes clear that while typical children are generally in charge of their systems, autistic children are generally dominated by them. The following vignettes of three children (one typical, two autistic), who were observed after being given a pile of assorted blocks, illustrate the point.

1. Jack, a typical three-year-old who integrates various systems

As soon as Jack received the pile of assorted blocks, he began to build a connected structure of ramps and towers. He picked up each block, examined it, selected a place for it in the block structure, and inserted it carefully.

Needing a block of a particular size, he scanned the blocks and spotted an appropriate one near the foot of the observing adult, about six feet away. He looked at the adult, pointed at the block, and exclaimed, "Block, please!" After receiving the block, he smiled at the adult, added the block to his structure, and took another block. Next, while making "rmm" car sounds, he "drove" his block up the ramp and around the block towers. Finished with car-block play, he got up and set off for something else to do.

2. Damon, a three-and-a-half-year-old boy with closed system disorder who is dominated by his systems

Damon, seeing the pile of blocks, immediately began to build a connected structure. But, unlike Jack's construction, his structure consisted only of a row of rectangular blocks carefully placed so that each block abutted the previous one. He paid no attention to curved or triangular blocks, and he did not make the sounds that other children made as they played.

Damon worked with rapid intensity, regularly scrambling from the end of the row of blocks to get another block so that he could continue extending the structure. At no time did Damon acknowledge the existence of the adult seated nearby. When the adult tried to hand him a block, Damon rapidly turned his body so that his back was between the adult and the blocks.

When the adult removed one block from the row, Damon screamed, then frantically sought another block to close the gap in the structure. Damon continued to extend the row of blocks until it reached the wall. Confronted by the wall, he made a right angle with the next block and continued placing blocks along the wall until there were no more blocks. Then he began rocking back and forth while twiddling his fingers in front of his eyes. Except for his scream when the adult altered his block structure, he uttered no sound.

3. Brian, a three-year-old boy with system-forming disorder driven by salient aspects of systems

Presented with the blocks, Brian was momentarily drawn to the clattering sound they made when they were placed in front of him. What Brian saw and heard, however, seemed quite disconnected from what his hands were doing. Even though he picked up a block, it soon slid from his hands, forgotten, as he was "caught" by the movement and sound the adult made as she seated herself in a nearby chair.

When the adult offered him another block, he seemed not to notice it because he was now turned toward the sound of a bus starting up outside the building. At no time did Brian spontaneously explore his surroundings or examine the manner in which blocks stacked or things worked. Instead, time and again, he turned toward or began to move toward a stimulating object or event only to be diverted by another new stimulus, which "drove" his behavior.

AN ANALYSIS OF THE CHILDREN'S SYSTEM FUNCTIONING

Although both Jack and Damon produced systems, their systems differed dramatically. Jack, the typical child, had a complex, integrative system composed of action with towers, ramps, and cars. As Jack played with the blocks, it became evident that he experienced himself as the executive or master-builder with an inner plan to which both the blocks and the adult contributed. This allowed him to form a complex, integrative system with the blocks (towers and ramps) that he could exploit in different ways. He could, for example, turn a block into a car and move it, car-like, up and down the ramps. He could also turn away from the main block structure to request a block from an adult and turn back to his structure without losing touch with his goal. In carrying through his plan, Jack demonstrated that he could integrate several smaller systems into a larger one.

In contrast, Damon, the autistic child with closed system disorder, had a single minisystem composed of lining up blocks. Damon's system was not driven by any inner plan but by the way the rectangular end of each block signaled the need to abut the next one. He changed the structure only when the physical barrier of the wall required such a change. This change, however, came about not through any executive decision on Damon's part, but because the wall required the change. Finally, there was no decision to stop connecting blocks; Damon stopped when he ran out of blocks. When this occurred, he had no means of directing himself to a new activity. Apparently, the only means he had of filling the void left by the end of the block-connecting system was rocking and hand twiddling.

Brian, on the other hand, because of his tendency to be driven by various diverting stimuli, never reached the point where he could become involved with and form a block system. His fragmented response to various stimuli illustrated another way in which autistic children can be dominated by their surroundings.

The different ways the children related to the observing adult indicates the extent to which they dominated or were dominated by their systems. Jack, needing a block to complete his block structure and seeing a block near the adult, was able to detach from his block system to turn toward the adult and ask for it. In doing this, he creatively brought together the world of relationships with people with his world of objects. In contrast, for Damon, the observing adult did not exist except as a momentary threat (when removing one of his lined-up blocks) to the integrity of his lining-up-blocks system. Clearly, his system involvement precluded people from being part of his system.

WHAT DETERMINES WHETHER A SYSTEM IS PRODUCTIVE OR COUNTERPRODUCTIVE?

Systems are productive when the child or adult is in command of them. They are counterproductive when the systems seem to dominate the child or adult. As executive function—the ability to make choices and problem solve—emerges, the child is able to govern his or her various systems. Think of a pianist weaving a medley of tunes. The pianist, while creating the medley, is able to choose and shift from one song (system) to another. As the examples just discussed have showed, when systems are functioning properly in service of chosen goals, they provide a basis for adaptive action, problem solving, social interaction, communication, and symbolic functioning. However, when systems dominate, they restrict the child's ability to explore or find meaning in surroundings or to shift from one system to another. The emergence of executive function—and the nature of the child's body/self —determines whether the system or the person dominates.

WHY ARE MANY AUTISTIC CHILDREN DOMINATED BY THEIR SYSTEMS?

Or, put another way, what is there about typical children that is largely lacking among autistic children?

Briefly, I suggest that autistic children—particularly those of the closed system type—are dominated by their systems because, once engaged, they do not have a means of disengaging. To disengage or detach from an ongoing system requires specific awareness of the body's existence as a separate entity. Only then can the child deliberately detach his or her body from an ongoing system, engage with another system, and return in the manner that Jack, the typical child, demonstrated.

This lack of a body/self was recently documented by a report about Tito (Blakeslee 2002), an autistic boy who, although nonverbal, had learned to share his experience in writing.

> "When I was 4 or 5 years old," Tito wrote while living in India, "I hardly realized that I had a body except when I was hungry or when I realized that I was standing under the shower and my body got wet. I needed constant movement, which made me get the feeling of my body. The movement can be of a rotating type or just flapping of my hands. Every movement is a proof that I exist. I exist because I can move."

Body/self awareness is impaired among children with autism because of the faulty transmission and/or interpretation of sensory impressions from the body to the brain. This results in their "not hearing" when addressed and often not feeling pain or being able to locate the source of hurt on their bodies. Since it is the processing of these sensory impressions that teaches the child his or her body, and since in the case of an autistic child this is impaired, it follows that a poor sense of the body and how it relates to the world is the result. To be able to shift rapidly from environment to body sensations requires the child to "pick up" changes in the environment and to act accordingly. However, if, because of faulty transmission or inadequate interpretation of sensory impressions, the child cannot do this, then we find the kind of behavior Damon was described as exhibiting.

If there is little or no awareness of the body or body/self as a separate entity independent of what the body is engaged with, then the child becomes so captured by the ongoing body–object system in play at that time that he or she cannot spontaneously detach from the ongoing system. Only as the child develops the notion that his or her body and its parts have an existence independent of the object or event system with which he or she is engaged can the executive function emerge (which makes possible a child's spontaneous expansion of his or her systems). In other words, body–world polarity is a prerequisite for executive function.

Among typical children, this capacity emerges gradually in the course of the first two years of development. For example, by six months of age, the child has achieved sufficient differentiation between his or her body and others to demonstrate a clear preference for Mother over others. Between six and nine months of age, the child is able to relate to (establish systems with) either a person or an object. By nine or ten months of age, the child can relate to another around an object (child–object–person system) as evident in the ability to give an object to a caregiver on request (Trevarthen and Hubley 1979). And, of course, by 18 to 24 months of age, the child becomes self-consciously aware of his or her ability to accept or refuse requests.

Children whose development has been compromised often fail to achieve these basic body–object–other capacities. For example, they may not differentiate between one person and another, and they may not be able to give an object on request. They remain fixed in a "single track" involvement with a particular property of an object or event and show striking difficulties in relating their bodies to people and objects in their surroundings.

Good clinical evidence finds serious deficiencies in body–world awareness which makes it difficult for the autistic child to resist the "pull" of systems. Consequently, such a child cannot deliberately detach himself or herself from one system to engage another.

Impaired body–world relations are apparent in every area of autistic children's functioning. This impairment seems to account for most of the difficulties the children have in coping with their systems and in communicating their intentions. The following examples illustrate this:

> After much work, eight-year-old Andrew had finally learned to ride a two-wheel bicycle. Soon, however, his parents noted that, while he could do well on a flat surface, as soon as he reached a slight incline he would stop and get off the bike. His parents also reported that he could ski and maintain his balance while going down a slope but could only stop by crashing into a snow bank.
>
> Andrew's problem riding his bike up an incline came from his inability to rapidly relate the change in his immediate environment (from flat to incline) to what his body needed to do to compensate. Feeling the change in the bike's performance while going up the hill, but not knowing exactly when or how to adjust his body to the incline by leaning forward or standing up while pedaling, he could only stop pedaling and get off. Similarly, when he reached the end of the ski run, Andrew, unable to rapidly relate that end point to the required body adjustment (turning and edging both skis at just the right moment), could only stop by crashing into a snow bank.

> Sam, an eight-year-old autistic boy, would echo with perfect articulation sentences addressed to him but was quite unable to express his own intentions through sentences.
>
> Echoing a sentence is an automatic unthinking response that does not require awareness of body/self and other. Nor does it require conscious awareness of the mouth as a source of utterance under the child's control. However, to *deliberately* initiate a sentence directed to another, both body/self–other and mouth–sound awareness are essential. Only then might Sam be able to spontaneously express himself to another.

Sometimes, as in the following example, a child develops a partial sense of the body/self–other relation:

> Meg is able to point to *her* nose, mouth, ears, and so on, on request but is quite unable to point to these features on either her mother or another person.
>
> Meg is a child who has developed sufficient body awareness to locate her own body parts. However, the absence of sufficient awareness of the distinction and similarity between herself and her mother makes it impossible for her to relate her body parts to her mother's. This, in turn, must interfere with her ability to communicate with her mother and other people.

WHAT ROLE DOES EXECUTIVE FUNCTION PLAY WITH REGARD TO SYSTEMS?

Executive function emerges when a child has developed awareness of his or her body as a distinct entity separate from others and from his or her surroundings. It is this awareness that enables the child to select, detach from, or modify existing systems. Early examples of executive function may be seen when a child decides that he or she no longer wishes to go down the slide in the sitting position but prefers, instead, to slide down on side, back, or belly, for instance. These *spontaneous expansions* of the going-down-the-slide system are possible because of the newly emerging awareness of the body as an entity that can be arranged in different ways. These changes in body position are choices that presage executive capacity. With this capacity children are able to choose one system over another, to alter systems, or to combine previously developed systems in new ways, as evident in Jack's performance with the blocks.

Perhaps the best known indication that body–world separation has resulted in executive function is when the typical two-year-old responds to his or her mother's request to pick up toys with a defiant "No!"—a statement that marks both awareness of self and other and the notion of choice.

The failure of this shift to fully occur among developmentally challenged children accounts for many of the dramatic differences in behavior between typical and compromised development.

INTERVENTION WITH SYSTEMS: MAJOR STRATEGIES

The Miller Method®—as you will find in later chapters—uses three major sets of strategies to restore typical developmental progressions:

- *The first set of interventions* involves systematic body work to improve awareness of the body and its relations to others. This entails "rough and tumble" play with therapists and parents as well as systematic work on the Elevated Square.

- *The second set of interventions* deals with the transformation of children's aberrant systems (lining up blocks, flushing toilets, or driven reactions to stimuli, etc.) into functional behaviors on elevated structures or on the ground.

- *The third set of interventions* entails the systematic and repetitive introduction of developmentally relevant activities (called spheres or spheric activity) involving objects and people to fill in developmental gaps.

These strategies help the children learn to hear, and to make transitions from one system to another without distress. They also help them achieve symbolic functioning by making transitions from the "here and now" to representations of their immediate realities.

The next chapter, "Searching for Capacity," describes how to assess the capacities (systems) a child brings as well as to determine how well he or she can assimilate the introduction of new ways (spheres) of doing things.

SUMMARY

In this chapter three children—Jack, a typical three-year-old; Damon, a three-year-old with closed system disorder; and Brian, a three-year-old with system-forming disorder—were considered in terms of whether they were masters or victims of their systems.

Jack, the typical child, demonstrated mastery of his systems by his ability to spontaneously combine different systems to serve his car play system—driving a make-believe car through a series of ramps and tunnels he built. His mastery was also evident in his ability to shift from his car play system to request a block from an adult and then return to his car play system.

Damon, the boy with closed system disorder, demonstrated "victimization" by his systems; this was evident in his need to build and maintain a lining-up-block system in which each block had to abut precisely with the preceding one. He could not tolerate any variation from or intrusion within this system and could not deliberately detach from it.

Brian, the boy with a system-forming disorder, was victimized by his need to react to every salient event that occurred. As a result he had an inability to form systems and a disconnect between what he was looking at and what his hands were doing.

Analysis of the children's functioning led to the inference that their victimization occurred because they lacked the body awareness and executive function which would have allowed them to detach from, combine, or complicate their systems. This lack of body awareness is thought to be due to problems transmitting sensory information to the brain, or interpreting this sensory information. Since executive function depends on body awareness, its absence accounts for the system limitations of the children.

Chapter 3

Searching for Capacity[1]

Our task is to help the children use every capacity or fragment of capacity to cope with a confusing and inconstant world.

Our search for children's capacities is essentially a search for the kinds of systems a child brings to a situation: we need to know to what extent a child is dominated by his or her systems. Is there enough body–world separation to permit the child to explore his or her new surroundings? We need to know about the relative rigidity of these systems, their complexity, and the extent to which they can be altered. We also need to assess the child's relative emphasis on whether he or she is engaged exclusively with action–object systems, with people systems, or with both.

In the following we show how these issues are assessed with the help of the Miller Umwelt Assessment Scale (MUAS) (Miller and Eller-Miller 1989) and the Miller Diagnostic Survey as shown in Appendix B.

With these instruments we try to determine how the child experiences and interacts with the world around him or her. In doing so, we examine the nature of the systems the child brings to a new situation by first examining his or her behavior in unstructured situations where the child has access to both people and a variety of objects, but where the adults are passive. We also examine the child's ability to become engaged in new systems (spheres or spheric activity) that the examiner introduces.

---

1   Material in this chapter is taken from the *Miller Umwelt Assessment Scale*, copyright © Arnold Miller 1989. Used with permission.

THE MILLER UMWELT ASSESSMENT SCALE
Unstructured session

The introduction of the child to this unstructured situation is the first part of the Miller Umwelt Assessment which includes both unstructured and structured situations. The term "Umwelt," coined by von Uexküll (1957), refers to the "world around the child" or the world as perceived through the child's eyes. In this setting there is—in addition to parent and examiner—a step-slide which has been set up, climbing equipment, a soccer ball, and a large plastic car, as well as a large red ball suspended on a rope from the ceiling to the child's eye level. There is also a box of wooden blocks placed under the slide. How does the child deal with this novel, unstructured situation?

We know what typical three- to six-year-olds do in this kind of situation: They try out the different structures; examine the objects; push the suspended ball; and get into the large plastic car, drive it, and beep its horn. Periodically, they glance at the grown ups either for approval or to make certain they are not crossing any forbidden boundaries. In short, they eagerly check out the new place and quickly discover its varied possibilities. However, children with autism behave in quite different ways.

The child's action systems

A disordered child in this unstructured situation may simply run in circles or back and forth between one wall of the room and another. Alternatively, the child may fasten on one object to the exclusion of everything and everyone else. Our task in this unstructured setting is to observe the child's behavior in terms of the systems he or she produces. Do these systems exclusively involve objects or do they sometimes include people?

If the child engages in and persists with repetitive actions with an object, we view the child as *captured* by this involvement without knowing how to detach from it. With this mindset we can think as follows: "If the child is 'stuck' in a particular repetitive system, how can I help the child transform that system so that it becomes more functional, interactive, and communicative?"

No matter how delayed the child's development, the child will have some notion of the world around him or her. To help the child progress, it is useful to try to sort out what this world is like. Often we can infer this by noting what the child relates to and what he or she doesn't see or ignores.

When a child is very young, for him or her only those things exist which can be touched, tasted, smelled—things close to the body (Werner 1948). Things further away seem not to be part of the child's reality. The same thing is true for many autistic children. By carefully watching what the child does, we can determine what and how the child experiences the immediate surroundings and the people in it. The Systems Analysis form which we discuss later in this chapter provides guidance in observing the child's behavior during both unstructured and structured situations.

One of the goals of the Miller Method® is to assess each child's capacity to interact with people and objects, adapt to change, and learn from experience. During the assessment we are also interested in determining how close a child is to achieving the next step in development which is determined by the additional cues a child might require for success. We refer to this process as "testing the limits" but it is also known as Vygotsky's (1962) "zone of proximal development." In addition, we examine the child's resourcefulness in coping with objects in various problem situations and by using tools. Finally, we seek to determine the child's emotional resourcefulness in initiating and maintaining ongoing interactive systems with adults in the manner described so vividly by Greenspan (1997; Greenspan and Wieder 2000).

In summary, we examine three kinds of interaction with a particular child:

1. the child's response to unstructured situations (adults passive)

2. the child's ability to maintain an interactive system with the examiner when the examiner actively builds on the child's initiatives and so forth

3. the child's ability to accept and participate in examiner-initiated systems.

Table 3.1 captures the three different ways of examining the child.

Table 3.1 General strategies used during the Miller Umwelt Assessment

Assessment strategies	Adult stance	Child's task
Unstructured	Passive	Child to initiate without support.
Child-initiated	Interactive	Child initiates and cyclically builds on adult's response to his or her initiatives.
Adult-initiated	Directive	Child to accept adult-initiated interaction and expansions.

Since many circumstances, such as school, entail teaching the child from the adult's and not the child's agenda, the child's response to "examiner-directed" systems provides an indication as to how well the child will be able to "fill in" developmental gaps through teacher- or therapist-initiated systems (called *spheres*). Further, it will provide information about how readily the child can take in new academic work presented by the school teacher. In short, how the child responds to an adult setting up, expanding, and directing shifts from one system to another provides important clues about how well the child will function in school-related or similar situations.

Sixteen different tasks[2] from the Umwelt assessment help clarify the unique way in which each child with a disorder experiences reality as well as his or her adaptive potential.

Assessing the capacity to interact with a person and an object
The suspended ball task

Figure 3.1 illustrates the manner in which the examiner assesses the child's ability to form an interactive system involving an object and another person.

Figure 3.1(a) represents a child enjoying a repetitive pushing game (a child–object–adult system) in which adult and child push a swinging ball back and forth. The dotted lines to both ball and adult indicate that the child's system includes awareness of both the ball and the adult. Figure 3.1(b) reflects a more limited child–object system which includes the ball (which the child pushes whenever it arrives) but does not include the adult. Figure 3.1(c) shows an even more circumscribed system. Here, the child fails to react even when the ball bumps into him, and therefore the child lacks that object system.

Typical children as young as two years of age will behave interactively with ball and person as illustrated in Figure 3.1(a). Children with closed system disorders will interact with the ball but not with the person, as shown in Figure 3.1(b). Children with system-forming disorders may not respond—as shown in Figure 3.1(c)—because they have difficulty coordinating with the ball's trajectory.

2   All 16 tasks can be reviewed in Chapter 7 of Miller and Eller-Miller (1989) or by purchasing the Miller Umwelt Assessment Scale from www.cognitivedesigns.com.

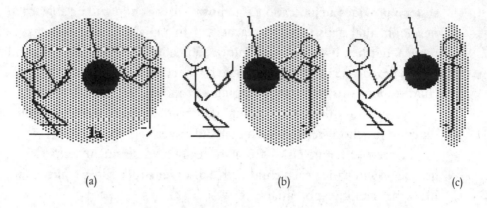

(a)   (b)   (c)

Figure 3.1 Assessing a child's ability to form an interactive system: (a) child–object–adult;
(b) child–object; (c) no object

Assessing the capacity to adapt to change

Stacking cups and bowls

Successfully coping with surroundings requires the child to adjust his or her approach to changing circumstances. To assess this capacity we first require the child to stack cups vertically in a variety of different ways. Figure 3.2, for example, shows "asymmetrical inversion" stacking in which a bowl is presented over right-side-up cups and a cup is presented upside down over right-side-up bowls. Once the children have established a mindset for stacking vertically, the format for stacking cups is changed. Now, instead of vertically stacking the cups given them, they are asked to place a cup in each of the six bowls spread out horizontally in front of them (see Figure 3.3). The examiner models this shift by placing one or two cups in bowls.

Even after the examiner has repeatedly modeled placing cups in the bowls, many children with closed system disorder persist in vertically stacking the cups. Some, however, with support and repetition, are finally able to make the shift from vertical to horizontal stacking.

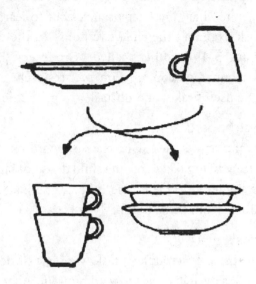

Figure 3.2 Asymmetrical vertical stacking

Figure 3.3 Breaking the stacking set

The next two tasks examine, although in different ways, the child's ability not only to adjust to changing circumstances but to learn from the experience.

One task examines the child's response to the elevated "Swiss cheese" board (Figure 3.4); another, called "Croupier" (Figure 3.5), examines the child's manner of coping with progressively more demanding tasks involving the use of rakes and obstacles to gain a desired object.

The "Swiss cheese" board

The child walks across the "Swiss cheese" board but may inadvertently step into a hole (care being taken that the child does not fall). On subsequent trials we observe the child to determine if he or she has learned from his or her "almost fall" to avoid these holes .

The "croupier" task

In the rake-obstacle ("croupier") task, we seek to determine if the child— shown pulling a desired object toward himself or herself—can learn to push it away from himself or herself through the gap and then toward himself or herself.

Often, the child persists in pulling the object toward himself or herself even though the barrier blocks access to the object. We then "test the limits" by placing the desired object closer and closer to the gap to determine at what point the child will understand the need to first push the object away before it can be brought closer. Once the child succeeds with support in pushing

Figure 3.4 "Swiss cheese" board: Assessing the child's ability to cope with variously shaped holes on an elevated structure

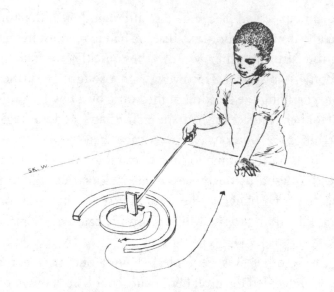

Figure 3.5 "Croupier": Child solves a multistep problem to get an object with a rake

the object through the gap, in the next trial we place a new object in the center of the horseshoe ring to determine if the child has generalized this understanding to the new object given or will revert to the original, unsuccessful effort to bring the object toward himself or herself.

In the following section we show how five-year-old Angela's functioning on the Umwelt illuminated her capacities and her prospects for development.

Angela's Umwelt Assessment[3]

Initial contact with Angela

We first met Angela in Toronto where we had conducted a workshop after which we briefly consulted with five parents about each of their children. Angela, one of those children, was a beautiful, blonde five-year-old who had been diagnosed with autism spectrum disorder and who was completely nonverbal. Even slight changes in the way a task was introduced induced tantrums during which she bit her hand, screamed, and fell on the floor.

During our first encounter before the Umwelt—which lasted less than an hour—we found two encouraging bits of systemic behavior. When we gave her a bottle with a slit in the top and kept feeding her discs, Angela

3   Angela's Umwelt assessment and her subsequent progress may be seen in the documentary *Where is Angela?* (Miller 2000).

began to anticipate and place one disc after another in the bottle. She even tolerated my turning the bottle so that she had to readjust her hand to get the disc in the slit. In other words, she quickly formed an organized disc-in-bottle minisystem. However, when I sought to further expand the system by changing the location of the bottle by a few feet, this change was too great for her. Her face flushed, she bit her hand, and she began to scream.

Searching for other ways to engage her, I started to blow up a balloon—pausing from time to time to catch my breath. Soon I noted that Angela was "caught" by the process of my making the balloon expand. Each time I paused from blowing, she would purse her lips and thrust her head forward as if by doing so she would magically cause me to make the balloon expand.

Angela's mother was very pleased with our brief contact with her daughter and decided to enroll her in our school. So, a few months later, we were able to continue our search for latent capacities in Angela's functioning with tasks from the structured part of the Umwelt. In the following, I focus only on those tasks that yielded important information about Angela's capacities.

The suspended ball task

As discussed previously (see also Figure 3.1), the most advanced level of the suspended ball task is when a child plays a game with the examiner by pushing the ball to him or her and expecting it to be pushed back. On this task, Angela performed at Level B as, with eyes averted, she pushed the ball away from her when it arrived, but never pushed it to the examiner.

Step–slide task

To succeed on this task, the child needs to integrate several components: He or she must climb up the steps, sit down, hitch forward, go down the slide, and return to the steps to repeat the cycle. We wished to examine how readily Angela could form an integrative system with the step–slide task and then expand that system. In other words, after she understood the basic system (going up the steps, down the slide, and returning to the steps), could she tolerate an expansion of this system by sending blocks down the slide before she went down?

Angela formed the step–slide system after only a few repetitions but added her distinctive quality to it. Each time she would arrive at the top of the steps she would jump up and down stamping her feet—as if in protest. She was able to expand the system by sending blocks down before she went down

but, instead of letting the blocks slide down, she insisted on throwing the blocks down the slide—another example of a spontaneous expansion.

The "croupier" task

As described earlier, this task involves problem solving and tool use at increasingly difficult levels. Angela did brilliantly on all the rake tasks demonstrating cognitive ability and excellent perceptual awareness away from her body. For example, when confronted with the cut-out rake (see Figure 3.6) and required to use it to retrieve a bit of cereal, Angela immediately flipped over the rake to its flat side so that it would not slide over the bit of cereal she sought to bring closer. When a barrier was interposed between her and the bit of cereal, she immediately used the rake to maneuver it around the obstacle. When the cereal was placed between two parallel boards (as shown in Figure 3.7), Angela immediately realized that she had to turn the rake on to its narrow side and place it behind the cereal bit if she were to be successful in pulling it out. So here we see many instances of ability to adapt swiftly to new circumstances suggesting again that in certain areas she was only marginally captured by her systems.

The cup–bowl task

As described earlier (and shown in Figures 3.2 and 3.3), this task tests the relative flexibility or rigidity of a child's systems. If we set up one way of doing things for Angela, could she adjust to a change in that system without a breakdown?

Figure 3.6 Child attempting to adapt to the cut-out rake in the "croupier" task

Figure 3.7 Solving the parallel boards problem

Angela's behavior was fascinating. First she stacked cups vertically in all variations, demonstrating that she could sort by category—cups with cups, bowls with bowls—even when a cup was presented over a bowl and a bowl over a cup. Then, we shifted the task so that it required a different mindset.

Instead of stacking vertically, Angela was now required to put a cup in each of the six bowls spread out in front of her. She did well at first, placing a cup in each of three bowls, but then, suddenly, reverted to vertical stacking—placing one cup on top of another. In spite of my repeated efforts I could not get her to stack a cup in each of the bowls. Instead she would look out into space and fumble the cup into a vertical stack. When I persisted, she dropped her head to one side so that she was facing the wall and I could not see her face.

Soon her mother lifted Angela's head and revealed Angela with an impish smile on her face which clearly suggested that she knew what I wanted her to do and was provocatively refusing to do it…Angela was teasing me! I will discuss the important implications of this teasing later.

Symbolic doll task

In this task the examiner shows the child the baby doll being fed a bottle and then being put to bed. When Angela was given the doll she introduced her own variation. She first pulled off the clothes of the doll so she could inspect it without clothes. She then took the bottle and pretended to drink from it before she gave the bottle to the baby.

Angela's mother leaves Angela with us

The last part of the Umwelt required Angela's mother to leave Angela with us. The intent here was to assess the bond between mother and child (mother–child system).

As soon as her mother said "Bye, bye" and left the room, Angela ran to the door, opened it, and pulled her mother back into the room. Then, holding on to her mother's hand, she walked around her, silently crying. Abruptly, while still crying and holding her mother's hand, she turned toward her mother, looked at her, and made an aborted striking gesture toward her.

Analysis of Angela's Umwelt

The Umwelt findings revealed that Angela had all the capacities needed for communication—except a conventional mode of communication. She had a profound bond with her mother, could express her distress when her mother "abandoned" her with us, had good perceptual and cognitive ability ("croupier" task), and demonstrated ability to integrate and expand systems (step–slide task) as well as an ability to spontaneously assert herself (stamping her feet, throwing blocks down the slide).

However, of the many things she did, most important for her future development was her ability to tease by playing a trick on me. To do this, and to conceal the fact that she was doing this by hiding her face, indicated awareness of me and what I might see if I saw her smiling face. She was literally anticipating my reaction to her provocation. Even without conventional language Angela had found a nonverbal way of playfully communicating with me.

Other capacities she demonstrated included her ability to size up a situation, and then to act appropriately in that situation ("croupier" task). She also demonstrated the profound bond she had with her mother and her ability to express feelings when she felt that her mother had abandoned her with strangers.

On the basis of her Umwelt we felt that in spite of her age (nonverbal children at age five are considered too old to be able to learn to speak and communicate, although we and other professionals have successfully taught nonverbal children as old as 12 to speak) we felt that she had an excellent chance to develop functional communication.

Here is Angela's mother's report on how her progress unfolded during her first four months at the Language and Cognitive Development Center (LCDC):

Angela's mother's report

During the first week [in the program] she would scream a lot and tantrum... With even little demands she would throw herself on the ground, bang her head, slap her face and bite her wrist... But in the second week of the program she made her first sign... I remember we were in the swimming pool and she was in the hot tub and she looked at me, smiled...and for the first time in her life she signed *come* to me. I immediately ran to her.

From that time—every day she would come up with a new sign she had learned in school: *come, go, plate, give, cup, glass*... About one month later she both signed and spoke her first words "come," "give," "plate," "juice," "drink." After three months and three weeks she could request in words—using simple sentences—"Give Angela juice" (or drink or apple). Or she would say, "I want juice... I want play... I want toys."

Once Angela started to sign and speak that was the turning point in her life... Actually, that was the turning point in *our* life... Our whole life changed because she became much happier. She tolerated changes much better... And, for the very first time in her life she could *wait* for things she wanted... She now understands what we say to her and she focuses much better.

Since we left the program I haven't seen her slapping her face or biting her wrist... Also, her tantrums and screaming have subsided... I would like to thank Mrs. Miller and Dr. Miller for implementing this program for Angela... And I would like to thank the exceptional teachers and therapists who were very gentle and caring and yet made a profound change in her life...and in ours.

One year later, six-year-old Angela returned with her mother, a nurse, and her father, an engineer, to LCDC to attempt the next step in her development—learning to read and write. During the next three months she achieved a basic understanding of sightreading sentences and moved on to phonics. Following her stay at our school, we were able to arrange videoconferencing with her school in Canada and to guide individual work with her with a gifted teacher. Subsequently, she was able to sustain herself completely in a regular class with typical children. We believe that one of the factors contributing to a good transition was the status Angela achieved when she demonstrated prowess in reading and writing beyond that of the other children.

What were the Capacities that Enabled Angela to Achieve Communication and Eventually Succeed in a Classroom with Typical Children?

Primary, we feel, was the awareness of body/self and other that she demonstrated in her playful teasing of me during her Umwelt. (Subsequently, she did the same kind of teasing with the shop teacher. In the middle of working on a wood project, she would suddenly smile and drop to the ground—requiring the shop teacher—a gentle, fatherly man—to lift her and bring her back to the project. A bit later, she would—while smiling—do the same thing again.)

Secondary factors were her rapid ability to "take in" a new situation and even modify it to express her individuality.

Note: For a complete presentation of all 16 MUAS tasks, see Chapter 7 in Miller and Eller-Miller (1989) or the MUAS kit available from www.cognitivedesigns.com.

SYSTEMS ANALYSIS

System Analysis, a guide to the observation of system functioning among disordered children, is designed to help parents and professionals gain relevant system information through observations of children with both closed and system-forming disorders.

Systems Analysis is an important skill to develop because it provides a basis for effective interventions with the children. It requires systematic observation of what a child is able to do with *objects* and *people* in both *unstructured* and *structured* situations in classroom, home, and clinic settings.

To do a Systems Analysis of a child's unstructured functioning it is necessary to observe the child in a setting which provides access to both objects and people for about ten minutes. During this period you should remain quite passive and respond only minimally to the child's initiatives. Following this period, you should be able to answer the questions outlined in the following Systems Analysis questionnaire. Encircle phrases that apply to the child being observed.

Unstructured

1. What aspects of the immediate environment engage the child?

    (a) *Objects:* Ball, car, opening and closing doors, pouring water, blocks to line up, throw, etc.

    (b) *People:* Mother, father, teacher, therapist, assistant, other children, strangers, etc.

2. What is the nature of the child's engagement with the objects and people in the unstructured environment?

    (a) *Object engagement:* Fixed, episodic, scattered, persistent and repetitive, exploratory, constructive, creative contact.

    (b) *People engagement:* Spontaneous initiatives toward people in his/her immediate environment are clinging, episodic, scattered, persistent and repetitive, exploratory, constructive, creative contact.

    (c) *Emphasis:* Assuming that the ten-minute observation period = 100 percent, what percentage of the time was the child engaged with objects vs. people? For example, 80 percent objects vs. 20 percent people.

    Note: Performing an unstructured systems analysis once each month can supply data with regard to the trend of the child toward more (one hopes) or less functional contact with people and objects.

Structured

3. How does the child respond when the adult initiates direct interaction with the child?

    (a) *To rough and tumble activity:* Avoids (runs away, cries), enjoys (laughs, giggles), seeks more.

    (b) *To face-touching and restabilizing:* Avoids (distressed, cries), enjoys (laughs, giggles), shows or does not show improved focus and eye contact.

    (c) *To chase game (I'm going to get you!):* Unresponsive, distressed (cries), enjoys, looks over shoulder, laughs with delight.

    (d) *Sudden interruption:* How does the child respond if, in the midst of exciting adult-initiated interaction, the adult suddenly interrupts the activity by "freezing?" Does the child immediately lose interest (wanders off) or approach the adult to try to get the interaction to continue?

4. How does the child respond to the adult interacting with the child around an object?

    (a) *When the child is engaged with that object:* Child resists (turns away) from adult involvement; allows minimal adult involvement; allows complete adult involvement (includes adult in his or her object involvement).

    (b) *When the child is not engaged with that object:* Resists adult interaction; accepts or does not accept it when it is repetitive, rapidly paced, or contagious in nature.

    (c) *What is the child's zone of intention?* Very close to the body (about a foot); varies from one to three feet; varies from one foot to twelve feet depending on interest in the object or person.

    (d) *How does the child respond to adult efforts to expand systems?* Child resists (tantrums, screams); accepts minimal expansions; accepts substantial expansions of systems.

5. Are the child's action systems influenced by signs or words?

    (a) Can the child's action systems be guided by spoken words? By gestural signs? By pictures? By combined spoken and signed concepts?

    (b) Can the child use spoken words, gestural signs, or a combination to influence the actions of another?

THE MILLER DIAGNOSTIC SURVEY

The Miller Diagnostic Survey (MDS) is a unique instrument for several reasons: First, the MDS is organized developmentally in that each category includes specific questions about behaviors from both earlier and later stages of development, ranging from 18 months to about seven years of age. The questions are based on observations which parents and teachers are likely to make in their everyday interactions with the child. In a few cases parents may not know the answer to a question from prior observation. In these cases, they are asked to set up a "simple experiment" so they can directly observe the child's response to the situation set forth in a particular question. They can then answer the question based on the child's actual performance.

Second, parents' responses to MDS questions provide an estimate of the child's functional capacities as well as an estimate of how aberrant the child's behavior is. The MDS uses these estimates to establish a Coping Score which is based on a ratio of functional to aberrant behavior with the view that only by taking both factors into account can one gain an estimate of how severely the child's atypical behavior compromises his or her ability to perform. The MDS also attempts to clarify the kind of autism a child's behavior reflects. For example, is the child's autism primarily a closed system disorder, a system-forming disorder, or some mixture of both?

Once a parent or caregiver transmits his or her responses to the questions by pressing a button after completing the survey, a computer program organizes the responses into a profile. Then, a senior staff member at the LCDC reviews both the profile and the responses, summarizes the results, and shares impressions about the child with the parent or caregiver. With parents' permission the data are then added to the results of other MDSs submitted by parents. This group data, treated statistically, provide the basis for the present study's effort to determine overall program efficacy. Results from the MDS given to parents of 71 children on the autism spectrum are presented in Chapter 11.

The MDS presents 107 questions (see Appendix B) to parents. As the reader views these questions, it will become apparent that they cover a broad range of functioning—including the child's disposition toward closed system or system-forming disorders.

Designed to be completed by parents at the beginning and end of the academic year (with a gap between responses of 10 to 12 months), the responses provide information needed to accurately assess the child's capacities and to determine what, if any, changes in program emphasis should be made. Such an assessment is helpful to the child's teachers and therapists in tailoring a program to the child's needs.

Rationale for Parents Completing the MDS

There are several compelling reasons for having parents or caregivers completing the MDS rather than the teachers or other professionals who are concerned with a particular child. First, parents or caregivers who live with the child continuously are, we maintain, more fully aware of the child's capacities and challenges than any professional who deals with the child for at best a few hours a day during the school week. Second, when gains which are first generated in school or clinic become apparent at home, this demonstrates that new learning has been generalized by the child beyond the confines of school and clinic. Finally, the probing questions which are part of the MDS may have the positive effect of helping parents look more closely at exactly what the child can or cannot do. That, in turn, may help them develop a more realistic view of the child's capacity and contribute to more focused and meaningful intervention.

Areas Covered by the MDS Questions

- *Sensory reactivity.* Does the child fail to react to a nasty fall or to locate or touch the injured part? Similarly, does the child possess normal hearing, yet either fails to respond to a loud sound or is excessively responsive to such sounds?

- *Body organization.* Does the child know how to use his or her body to climb over a fence or to pick up things? Is the child able to peddle and steer a tricycle? Does the child have difficulty traversing the space from bedroom to bathroom or from downstairs to upstairs or from outside to inside the house? Can the child stack blocks while attending to their balance? Does the child use pincer movements to pick up small objects?

- *Problem solving and tool use.* Can the child perform simple tasks such as picking up overturned chairs, getting an out-of-reach object on a shelf by climbing a stool, or with a stick, sliding a bolt to open a door, or open a two-turn jar?

- *Social contact.* What kind of bond does the child have with his or her mother or caregiver? Does he or she show poor eye contact, understand the distinction between mine and yours, and play with other children? Is he or she able to take turns?

- *Communication: Receptive and expressive.* Can the child follow one- or two-step directions by word or gesture both near and far from the body? Does the child have the ability to express intentions through gesture, word, and sentences and to communicate events that happened elsewhere and/or will happen?

- *Symbolic functioning.* Does the child have the ability to recognize and be guided by pictures, to draw, to participate in make-believe play, to count, to give required quantities of things, to add and subtract, to make changes, and to read and write?

We will now examine reports based on the MDS of two children. One child, Randy, scored high on closed system disorder while Monte scored high on system-forming disorder:

MILLER DIAGNOSTIC SURVEY REPORT: RANDY

Written by Arnold Miller, Ph.D.
Date of birth: August 16, 1999
Age: 4 years and 2 months
Report sent: October 18, 2003

General impressions

Randy seems to fall within the group of children on the moderate range of the autism spectrum. His communication is limited to his immediate surroundings. In other words, he can only refer to things he can see, hear, and touch.

Sensory reactivity, body organization, problem solving/tool use

Randy's sensory reactivity is entirely appropriate as is his ability to use his body in an organized manner. Except for toilet training—which is not quite established—he functions quite well on an action level. He understands spatial relations and can find his way home even when the house is out of sight. Randy's fine motor activity is somewhat lagging. For example, when stacking blocks he seems to have some difficulty keeping in mind that he has to keep them balanced while he stacks them.

He shows good problem-solving ability and understands the function of basic tools as an extension of his reach to get out-of-reach objects.

Social contact

Randy has a strong bond with his mother. He certainly knows to whom to go when he is hurt or needs the security of her presence. His mother reports that Randy sometimes has a buddy, but, still, he rarely plays with other children. He delights in peek-a-boo as well as vigorous "Get you!" games. He can play a reciprocal ball game and is starting to "catch on" to the notion of turn taking. He already grasps the concept of "mine" vs. "yours." There is also an indication that he is starting to grasp the notion of competing with someone to get a desired object.

Factors which may be interfering with his social play with others are his decided preference for objects over people, his poor eye contact, and his difficulty putting himself in the position of the other—as when he allows a door to close in the face of the person following him.

Communication (receptive, expressive, nonverbal)

It is somewhat surprising to find a child as competent as Randy in problem solving having such a limited grasp of the way spoken words relate to their objects. He certainly understands and can define familiar body parts (nose, mouth, etc.) on himself, on another, and on a picture. And he will give an object in front of him to a person requesting it. However, there is a drop in his capacity as soon as he is asked to give an object that is a few feet from him. This same drop in capacity is evident when he is asked to bring a specific object from another room. It becomes even more pronounced when he is asked to get an object in another room when that object is in an unfamiliar place, or to get two objects.

What this suggests is that Randy has not yet internalized spoken words and their meanings in a way that lets him "carry" the meaning outside their usual context. Children who are on the cusp of achieving this will often repetitively mutter the word as they look for the object it represents in another context. The muttering or "self talk" allows them to keep in mind what they are looking for. This suggests that part of Randy's problem with communication is learning how to detach words and their meanings from their usual settings and carry them internally so they may be used everywhere.

This same dependence on words in their familiar contexts accounts for Randy's difficulty expressing himself through words. He can sometimes initiate single words and can always complete a sentence when most of it is given to him. However, Randy rarely initiates a sentence on his own. Even when he does, he never varies the sentence (verb + noun or subject + verb). Further evidence of Randy's dependence on the "here and now" is his inability to use words to refer to events that happened elsewhere, had happened, or will happen.

Examining the quality of Randy's communication further, we find that he frequently echoes what is said to him, and he comes out with "air words" that have nothing to do with the other person. He also consistently refers to himself as "you" instead of "I".

However, the good news is that Randy's nonverbal communication is quite good and can be drawn on to help him maintain meaning outside of familiar contexts. He can signal his intentions with gestures, can pull a person by the hand to a desired object, and can sometimes point at a desired object and share his pointing with another. This suggests that incorporating manual sign language into his program should help him improve his receptive and expressive language by grounding spoken word meaning with the help of gestures. The

Sign and Spoken Language Program (to be discussed in Chapter 10) can be of help in this regard.

Symbolic functioning

Except for scribbling and make-believe playing (which he varies), Randy shows little inclination to get involved with symbolic activities. He rarely matches pictures to objects and seems not to understand that pointing to a picture can get him the object represented in that picture.

System functioning

Over the years we have found that children on the autism spectrum seem to emphasize one of two ways of dealing with objects and people in their immediate surroundings—closed system disorder and system-forming disorder (see Chapter 1).

Randy's behavior clearly fits with the closed system disorders. Our experience with such children is that they can often make rapid progress in all sectors if there is a knowledgeable therapist available to help the child expand and complicate systems and learn how to make transitions from one place to another.

Summary

It seems that the further Randy gets from active physical involvement with objects and events, the more difficulty he has. Clearly, one of his major issues is how to cope with a world that is largely unseen but that can be represented in a variety of ways. Randy has many strengths but clearly needs help making the transition from things to representations of things. This shows itself in his communication and in his difficulties with representations... Promising, however, is his ability to represent reality—and to vary it—in his make-believe play.

Recommendation

I strongly recommend that Randy be introduced to manual sign language. This means that each verbal direction would be paired with a manual sign related to the object or event. Our experience with the Sign and Spoken Language Program is that there is a rapid increase in the child's ability to process spoken language. It also results in the child communicating more effectively with both signs and spoken words. For Randy, sign language should be viewed as a temporary expedient, to strengthen his understanding and use of words. You can view a description of this program on www.cognitivedesigns.com.

The next MDS report is on Monte, a two-year, seven-month-old nonverbal autistic child with system-forming disorder.

MILLER DIAGNOSTIC SURVEY REPORT: MONTE
Written by Arnold Miller, Ph.D.
Date of birth: October 15, 2002
Age: 2 years and 7 months
Report sent: May 26, 2005

Overall impressions

Although he shows strengths that can provide a framework for developmental gains, Monte's current functioning places him within the group of children on the more severe range of the autism spectrum. Below I describe the major issues which seem to be interfering with his development.

Monte's system-forming disorder

Monte's behavior tends to be scattered. He reportedly flaps his arms, toe walks, or twiddles his fingers in front of his eyes. When addressing an object—such as a puzzle—there is often a "disconnect" between Monte's eyes and his hands, with the eyes looking one way while the hands fumble with the puzzle. This "disconnected" quality affects Monte in every area of functioning.

Sensory reactivity and body organization

The "disconnect" between Monte and his surroundings is evident in how he responds to stimuli and how he copes with simple problem-solving situations. For example, Monte's uncertain response to stimuli is evident in the fact that he only "sometimes" reacts to a loud noise or to a "hurt" that he has sustained.

Because of Monte's limited body organization he is not only uncertain about finding his way from one place to the other within his home, but he is also stymied by using a doorknob to open a door or by opening a two-turn jar. (Both of these tasks require the child to master a two-step sequence: To use a doorknob the child must learn to both pull and turn at the same time. Similarly, to open a two-turn jar, the child must keep in mind the two-step procedure of turning the lid, lifting his or her hand, and starting over.)

Other basic problem situations which dramatize Monte's limited understanding of how his hands work is evident in his inability to "right" turned-over chairs, or to manage a bolted door. In addition, he only "sometimes" can use a stool to get a desired out-of-reach object on a shelf. Monte is also unable to use a string or stick to bring a desired object closer.

Social contact

In spite of the above, there are features of Monte's social functioning which suggest a basis for successful intervention. I refer to the finding that Monte has a strong emotional bond with his mother (or primary caregiver). He wants to be near her, goes to her to "make it better" when he is hurt, and seems to draw on her as a source of security enabling him to venture into the world. Also positive is his ability to respond to vigorous "Get you!" games.

However, even in this area, Monte's limited eye contact, preference for objects over people, and lack of understanding of "turn-taking" and "mine" vs. "yours" concepts severely compromise his ability to play with other children.

Communication: Receptive, expressive, and nonverbal

The quality of Monte's communication becomes clearer as we examine different facets. Receptively, he has difficulty distinguishing between his mouth and the mouth of another person. He can give a requested object from three feet away but rarely from six feet away. He has never succeeded in getting a requested object from another room… Sometimes, his mother reports, he responds to "Come!" and "Stop!"

Monte has no expressive utterances. However, he does demonstrate good pre-communicative skills on a nonverbal level. Monte's ability to pull his mother toward desired objects, to point, and to share joint attention around an object are important precursors of functional communication. These capacities suggest that, with the systematic use of gestural signs in combination with spoken language, his ability to understand what is said to him will increase substantially, as will his ability to communicate his intentions.

Recommendations

ACTION–OBJECT SYSTEMS

To help empower Monte and—at the same time—teach him how his hands work, he needs to be introduced "hand-over-hand" to a variety of activities common to children aged from 12 to 18 months. He needs to learn how to pick up and drop objects, to squeeze water out of sponges, to push over blocks, and to carry relatively heavy objects (taped phone books are fine) from one place to another. While he is doing these things, his parent or therapist should be narrating the behavior, for example "Monte picks up and drops!" (Leave out the "good jobs," they are a waste of time.)

Once Monte can perform these activities for one person he must do them for others and perform them in different locations.

SOCIAL GAMES

Start with vigorous "rough-and-tumble" games involving tickling, then graduate to "chase games," peek-a-boo games, and rocking-chair games (periodically stalling them to see if he initiates a wish to continue).

While the MDS is extremely helpful in providing hypotheses about a particular child—and in forming a preliminary developmental profile—it is not a substitute for direct observation of the child. Only by observing and working with a particular child can one determine what resources the child has, as well as how close he or she is to the next step in development. Direct contact with the child also provides an opportunity to determine what kinds of supports are effective in helping a child move forward. In recent years, we have first been using the MDS to develop preliminary hypotheses about the child, and then testing this in a face-to-face assessment using the previously described Miller Umwelt Assessment Scale.

Chapter 4, "Getting Started with the Miller Method®," draws on insights gained from the MDS and MUAS in providing relevant interventions for different children.

SUMMARY

This chapter presented two ways of assessing the capacities of children on the autism spectrum: The MUAS and the MDS. Each contributes to understanding in a different way: The MDS is a questionnaire—filled out by parents—which taps a broad range of functioning including sensory reactivity, body organization, problem solving, social contact, communication, and symbolic functioning. The MDS also assesses the child's aberrant functioning and, by establishing a ratio between a child's overall performance and his or her aberrant functioning, yields a coping score which reflects the extent to which a child's performance is adversely affected by aberrant functioning.

Two sample reports on different kinds of autistic children have illustrated how data from the MDS permit a multidimensional view of the children's functioning.

The MUAS, on the other hand, is a face-to-face assessment of the child in which the child's behavior is examined in unstructured, interactive, and structured situations. During the structured part of the assessment, examiners introduce various tasks to study different facets of the child's functioning. These include, for example, a suspended ball test to examine a child's capacity to interact, a stacking cups and bowls task to assess the child's flexibility, a "Swiss cheese" board task to examine a child's awareness of space near the body and the ability to learn from experience, a "croupier" or rake-object task to examine a child's problem-solving ability, and a separation task to examine the child's bond with the mother.

The case of Angela illustrates how the Umwelt contributes to understanding. Angela's mother's report of Angela's progress documents the dramatic gains she made during her six months in the program.

Part II

TREATMENT

Chapter 4

Getting Started
with the Miller Method®

"You knock but nobody answers."

"If I'm in his way he walks over me as if I am a piece of furniture."

"When he does look at me he seems to look right through me as if I'm transparent."

These are some of the poignant comments that parents have shared with us over the years. The challenge is to help the special child "come alive" or to "break through" so that when one "knocks," someone answers. But what does a "breakthrough" mean? It means several things. It means that the child responds to parents and familiar professionals with smiles and delight when they play with him or her, that he or she acknowledges other people's existence and returns affection, that he or she shows through behavior a preference for the parent or caregiver over strangers, and that he or she can play with and even tease others—all behaviors that show that he or she is becoming more conscious of the self in relation to others. In short, that the child is becoming "alive" as a person capable of independent action and choices.

This chapter will discuss how to begin applying the Miller Method® (MM) to achieve these goals. However, before describing work with these children, I would like to dispel certain unhelpful notions about the source of the child's disordered behaviors. The most misleading of these notions is the tendency to assume that the child is rejecting or not responding because of poor nurturing or handling or willfulness.

THE CHILD'S DISORDER IS NOT THE FAULT OF PARENTS

It is completely understandable for parents to take their child's unrespons-
iveness as a "rejection." However, it is important to get past this notion as
soon as possible for two very important reasons. First, the child's aberrant,
non-responsive behavior is *not* a rejection of parents or caregivers and the
child tends to behave like this with everybody. The distressing behaviors of
self-preoccupation, eye avoidance, and failure to respond to affection are part
of the child's bioneurologically based problem. The same is true if he or she is
a scattered child. The child's central nervous system does not allow him or
her to take in and process information the way typical children can. In other
words, the autistic child does not have the tools to respond to parents or
professionals *without assistance.* Second, if the child is viewed by parents as
rejecting, a natural, self-protective tendency is for them to "pull back." And
that can trigger more distressing behavior. The special child needs parents
and professionals to be emotionally available so that he or she may reach out
and make emotional contact with them.

THERE IS OFTEN A BOND EVEN WHEN THIS IS NOT IMMEDIATELY APPARENT

Parents and professionals need to know that even though a child might not
be able to demonstrate feelings in the usual way, this does not mean that those
feelings are not there. That bond will often show up indirectly when a new
baby comes along, or the teacher becomes involved with another child. We
have many times gotten reports that after a baby was born and the mother
became preoccupied with nursing and caring for it, the special child
suddenly became very distressed, aggressive, or self-abusive. One mother
reported that after the birth of a new baby she couldn't even go to the
bathroom or answer the phone without her special child becoming upset and
often developing a major tantrum. Another mother, driving a car with her
special four-year-old child in the seat next to her (and her new infant in a car
seat in the rear), turned to attend to the infant and was suddenly attacked by
her special child "for no apparent reason."

Sometimes, however, there is not even that indirect expression of
a bond. For example, one father reported that when he came home
from work his daughter leaped into his arms while his three-year-old son
kept endlessly turning little animals in his hands and behaved as if the
father weren't there—leading this father to report with obvious distress
that he "had absolutely no relationship with his three-year-old son" (this

is shown in the video documentary *A Small Awakening* available from www.cognitivedesigns.com).

CAN A BOND BE BUILT BETWEEN MOTHER AND CHILD WHEN THERE IS NONE INITIALLY?

The answer to that question—based on the many such children with whom we have worked in our center—is that it can. Even among those children who show no apparent relationship with a parent, we have found that many can—with help—learn to establish such a positive relationship. In Chapter 5 I describe strategies that have been helpful in establishing or strengthening the bond between parent and child. There are, however, "ways of being" or styles that parents and professionals have with special children that work for and against forming a bond.

FOUR COMMON "SUPPORT/DEMAND" STANCES TOWARD SPECIAL CHILDREN

As we will examine in the following pages, there are many ways to establish mutually satisfying contact between parents and their special child. All of these strategies, however, build on an underlying stance. That stance is that neither the parent nor the professional should be overly respectful of the child's neurologically driven tendency toward isolation, self-preoccupation, extreme passivity, or scattered behavior. I recommend a very active, supportive, but carefully intrusive approach toward the special children with whom we work. I refer to this as a *high support/high demand* stance, which we teach our staff and the parents with whom we work. Over the years we have found that those who achieve this stance are most successful in helping the children reach their full potential.

Approaches which work against the emotional and developmental "breakthrough" we seek are the "high support/low demand," the "high demand/low support," and the "low support/low demand" stances. Perhaps, as I briefly describe them, you will recognize your attitude in some of them. Awareness of one's own stance is an important part of working with special children.

High support/low demand

A parent or professional who carries the child when the child is capable of walking, who dresses the child "because it's quicker," and who would much rather keep the five-year-old child in the grocery cart than risk having the child *push* the cart is expressing a "high support/low demand" stance. When we are assessing their child, such a parent will often dart in and "do for the child" what we are trying to assess. The underlying feeling that drives a mother to behave in this way can be paraphrased as follows:

> My child is disabled…injured in some way. Those who would make demands of him are likely to add to his injury (or make his limitations too painfully evident to me). My task as his mother is to protect my injured child (and myself) by helping him avoid demands and by keeping him close to me.

Among professionals this stance shows itself in their "over-supporting" the child by doing too much "hand over hand" so that there is little opportunity to determine what the child can do on his or her own.

High demand/low support

The opposite stance to high support/low demand—is often adopted by fathers who cannot tolerate the thought of their child being disordered. The thinking behind this might be phrased as, "There is not a damn thing wrong with my child… I will see to it that my child does everything the other kids do!" The regime such fathers impose often does not take into account the child's needs and results in a well-meaning but unfortunate "bullying" of the child to try to do things that are often beyond his or her reach. Often this stance induces the child to withdraw further.

Among professionals, this stance is evident among "tough" teachers who insist on imposing a curriculum on children independent of its relevance to them—and in spite of the fact that it is clearly not getting through to the children. Such a teacher might insist on going through the days of the week or the seasons of the year when the child is unable to anticipate what is going to happen during the next five minutes.

Low demand/low support

The saddest stance is one in which one or both parents—depressed or overwhelmed by the demands placed on them by the apparently intractable behavior of their child—have pretty much given up. Their attitude can be paraphrased as, "There is nothing you can do with that child…so I just let her sit in front of the TV… If she gets too wild I leave her in her room." Among professionals this used to express itself in a "Don't make waves" attitude. "The kid is not making any trouble by herself so I just leave her alone." Fortunately, this attitude is less and less prevalent in classrooms.

High support/high demand

In sharp contrast, the high support/high demand stance we recommend avoids the errors of "overprotectiveness," "bullying," or "*laissez faire*" inherent in the other stances. It implies a vigorous, supportive, playful, carefully intrusive, somewhat challenging attitude. This attitude shows itself in an intolerance of the child "disappearing." Such withdrawals can be combated by "getting in the child's face," by cautiously "aggravating" in a variety of ways—by putting the child's shirt half on so he or she has to struggle to find where the arms go, by putting one sock on the child and "forgetting" to put the other on, by "forgetting" to give the spoon the child needs to eat the soup, by "getting in the child's way" or "accidentally" bumping into him or her as he or she tries to walk past or over the parent or professional, and so forth. This attitude, we suggest, in concert with appropriate interventions, is most likely to lead to substantial gains in all areas.

TWO WAYS OF APPLYING THE MM

In working with autistic children using the MM, two sets of strategies are employed. One, transforming systems, is used when the child has pre-existing although aberrant systems; the second, creating systems, is used to establish new systems. Transforming systems means that one takes the disordered systems that the child brings to the situation and attempts to transform them into more functional activities that serve a particular goal. Creating systems, on the other hand, refers to a set of interventions designed to "fill in" developmental gaps in the child's functioning.

Transforming systems

The general mission with this set of strategies is to find ways to channel the energy used by children with autism to maintain their rituals into systems which are both flexible and interactive. When this succeeds, the child develops a repertoire of new ways to interact with people. This new repertoire—combined with the high support/high demand attitude—on the part of caregivers and professionals, enables the child to move closer to typical functioning. However, before the child's systems can be transformed, the parent, teacher, or therapist must view the child's disordered behavior differently. This means that even the most disordered behavior must be perceived in terms of its potential for becoming functional. If one studies the various behaviors the child produces, one may find that the drive and energy that the child puts into them may be channeled or transformed into interactions with another person and the object in a way that leads to functional behavior and communication.

Autistic systems

There is an entire array of autistic systems which have within them a causal dynamic that can quite readily be transformed into interactive systems. These autistic systems include repetitively rocking, flapping, dropping things, opening and closing doors, flicking on and off light switches (or TVs), repetitively flushing the toilet, and performing other similar activities. To transform these autistic systems it is necessary first to assess the causal dynamic that captures the child and then to find ways to cast that dynamic as part of an interactive and flexible system.

We will now examine common systems of autistic children and how you might change them.

Rocking

Rocking back and forth either standing or sitting is a typical autistic behavior, with the child demonstrating little or no awareness that anyone else exists. However, if *you* introduce rocking behavior with your child instead of waiting for him to produce it as part of his autistic system, then you may be able to transform rocking into an *interactive* system in which the child starts to develop some awareness of the distinction between him and you, and his ability to influence what you do.

Try the following with your habitual "rocker." Sit on a stool or in a rocking chair with your child sitting astride your legs, facing you. You are supporting the head and back of your child. This is necessary so that, as you rock by moving from a tilted-back position to a leaning-forward movement, the rocking motion does not interfere with eye contact. Start rocking slowly, then gradually build up the tempo until—when the moment is right—you abruptly interrupt the motion.

The right moment to interrupt the rocking is when your child shows signs that he is beginning to anticipate the rocking motion. When you see or sense this, interrupt the rocking at the point when you are sitting straight. If your child responds to interruption by seeking to continue the rocking sequence—showing this with intense eye contact, and large or small but urgent rocking motion of his body—then he is indicating a need for you to continue rocking and, when you respond to this need, you begin to communicate with him about the rocking. Equally important is that, when he initiates this rocking behavior, he is having the opportunity to experience himself as the independent source of that motion. You can repeat this rocking game 10–12 times. Remember to discontinue the rocking while your child still wants to continue.

Flapping

A behavior in autistic children that is closely allied to rocking is repetitive flapping of the arms and hands. Recently, after carefully observing the arm–hand flapping motion made by a five-year-old child at the center, we suggested that his teacher provide him with cymbals (one for each hand). When this was done, the child's flapping motion resulted in the cymbals clashing together with a resonating metallic sound to the child's great delight. With help the child began to be able to modulate the sound by producing both loud and soft cymbal sounds. He now uses his cymbals in a small rhythm group with other children. Recently, he has added rubbing sandpaper bars (one in each hand) to create another interesting sound. His flapping movements have diminished dramatically.

Repetitive dropping or throwing things

Just as typical infants at nine or ten months of age delight in picking up things on their tray and dropping or throwing them, so do many children on the autism spectrum. The difference is that after the nine- or ten-month-old child—over the course of a few weeks—finishes with his or her experimenting with releasing things and noting how they fall, his or her need to keep doing this disappears. In contrast, the special child seems never to have finished the experiment and doesn't know how to stop. Our task is to help the special child complete the experiment so that it becomes part of his or her repertoire.

One of the few systems that Robert, the "scattered" child, has is expressed by his throwing everything near him. The therapist, Amie, places a pile of blocks near him, which he promptly begins to throw. Amie then guides the throwing in different directions by gesturing where Robert should throw the blocks. She then tries to have him throw the blocks into different containers. She may set this up by catching one of his thrown blocks in a can so it makes a loud metallic sound, or in a bucket of water where the splash sound is quite different. Robert looks up to see what new event has interrupted his usual system. Once he is "caught" by the intriguing new sound feedback, Amie shifts the locations of can and bucket so that he has to track them. Then she has him pick up and drop variously sized blocks into the can and then the bucket. Next, she begins to throw blocks with him: She tries to get him to take turns saying, "First Robert then Amie!" and holding his throwing or dropping arm when it is her turn.

She repeats this each day for five or ten minutes not only with blocks, but also with different objects. She also narrates what is happening while Robert is doing this and while she is doing it: "Robert is dropping the big dog in the water bucket! Now Amie is dropping the giraffe in the water bucket!" and so forth. Soon Robert waits for Amie to throw or drop something before he does—clearly indicating that his previously autistic throwing or dropping has transformed into an interactive system involving another.

Opening and closing doors

A child's compulsive opening and closing of doors can also be transformed. In this case, because the doors are fixed in place, the therapist must immediately work to make the experience interactive. The example of Robert and Amie illustrates how this can be done:

> First, Amie narrates what Robert is doing: "Robert is opening…and closing the door." Then she joins Robert and as both open and close the door she narrates: "Amie and Robert open…and close the door!" Next, Amie turns the door interaction into "peek-a-boo" with herself on one side and Robert on the other. Each time Robert swings the door open, Amie is there saying, while tapping her chest, "Here is Amie!" Then, when Amie opens the door and discovers Robert, she says, while patting him on the chest, "There is Robert!" The same game is played with other doors around the house and with other people until Robert has a sense that behind every door he opens there may be a person. As this notion takes hold the door opening and closing becomes less perseverative and more explorative.

Since the drive behind this system concerns opening and closing, it can readily be expanded to opening and closing a whole host of things including boxes, the refrigerator, jars, and so forth. In this way, not only does the system become interactive, but the concept of open and close becomes generalized to many different items that can be opened and closed.

Flicking on and off light switches or TV sets

This behavior can be particularly annoying if you are watching a good program or doing something that requires light and your child starts to turn things on and off. You can cope with this first by alternately turning the light on and off with the child while saying "On!…Off!" and then guiding her to other devices—such as a pen flashlight—that she can turn on and off, with you and she taking turns in doing it without plunging the room into darkness. The principle guiding all such transformations is that we add an interactive component, flexibility, and a sense of capability to what the child has previously been able to achieve only as a ritualized behavior.

Repetitively flushing toilets

If you watch a child with autism repetitively flushing the toilet it becomes clear that what fascinates him is his ability to make the water swirl around and carry items along until they disappear. Again, the first task is to make the toilet flushing system interactive. So, first the child and then the therapist (or teacher) alternate flushing the toilet while the therapist narrates ("Mike flushes!" etc.).

The next task is to develop other causal systems that give the child some of the same dynamic feeling he gained from toilet flushing and to make these spin-off systems interactive in the same way. You and he might, for example, take it in turns to press the lever of a drinking fountain so that he can see how both of you are able to produce an arc of water. From there you may move him to alternating with you in pouring water over a waterwheel and watching the motion induced by the pouring. If the toilet-flushing system is very powerful it may be necessary to reduce its compulsive force by moving him from the toilet-flushing system to three, four, or even five water-related causal tasks before returning him to flushing the toilet. Ultimately, as the child tolerates more causal and interactive systems being introduced between one toilet-flushing cycle and another, the toilet-flushing system loses much of its power to "capture" him.

Transforming an "attack"

At times a special child—for no apparent reason—will strike out, or slap the teacher, therapist, or parent working with him or her. Sometimes, but not always, this occurs when the teacher is attending to the child next to him or her. It is often useful to view the "attack" as an effort by the child to make human contact. An effective strategy when the child "attacks" is to hold up both hands as in the "Patty Cake" game and have the child hit both your hands. Periodically, during the day, before the child initiates an "attack," hold up both your hands so that he or she can pat them. After a time, attempt to get the child to alternate patting your hands as in the Patty Cake game.

Transforming screaming and stamping protests

From time to time a child, confronted by the various demands that the introduction of new systems triggers, will scream and rapidly stamp his or her feet in a rather impressive display. An effective strategy for dealing with this is for the therapist, teacher, or parent to reproduce the behavior and then to tell the child to do it again. After two or three such cycles, the adult says, "One more scream, then send cars down ramp" (or whatever the new system is).

Variations of this procedure are to have the child scream loudly and then softly. It is interesting to see a child attempting to scream softly. Children treated in this way become more aware of their behavior and show less need to produce it in demand situations.

Lining things up

For Damon, the three-and-a-half-year-old captured by the lining-up ritual system to the exclusion of the rest of the world, the goal is to expand the ritual behavior so that he can tolerate variations in it and ultimately tolerate another person playing with him in context of his ritual system. The more he can tolerate such expansions of his original lining-up blocks system, the more readily will he tolerate expansions in other contexts and the more teachable he becomes.

Begin by bringing out additional blocks of the same kind that the child is using in his line up. Hand him a block to see if he can accept it and add it to his other blocks. If he cannot, simply place your block near his line-up. After he has taken a few blocks, start placing them in front of your face so that as he takes the blocks from you he inadvertently looks at you and takes you into his lining-up-blocks system. Then, move about a foot or two away from his block line-up so that he has to go further to get his blocks from you. If he can tolerate that, gradually move three, then four, then five feet away. If he has a problem with this, move closer.

As another variation, try adding one of your blocks to the child's line up and see if he can tolerate this. If he accepts this, try altering the way his blocks are lined up by moving one block a half-inch out of line with the others. If he runs to "fix it" allow him to do so. Repeat this by slightly disrupting his "line-up-blocks" system again but this time, just before he scrambles to fix it, look at him and "fix" it yourself as if you have just understood his concern. Repeat this several times with different "adjustments," correcting each one while nodding knowingly to your child about what he wants you to do. Gauge the level of his distress during these interruptions and try not to go too far beyond his comfort level.

Following this—particularly if the child is getting upset because you have "messed up" his action system—set up a row of blocks parallel to his. Set it up close enough to the child's line-up system for him to notice your construction, but not so close that he is seriously threatened by it. Then, alternate adding to your row of blocks with occasionally offering him a block for his row. When this has gone on for a while, ask him for a block for your row by tapping your hand and saying, "Give!" If he gives you a block for your row, repeat the process, sometimes giving him a block from your pile and sometimes asking for one from his pile. (If he does this, then you have already expanded his ritual lining-up-block system to include an interactive element—a function which is critical for the development of communication.)

If this is successful, you might try walking with your fingers across your "road" to determine if the child mimics your actions. If he doesn't but seems interested, try walking with your fingers on *his* road. If he protests, retreat to your road and try again, later, to walk with your fingers on his road. If that succeeds, take a small car and "rmm" it along *your* row of blocks. Offer the child a small car and see if he does the same. If he does, risk connecting your row of blocks with his, drive your car briefly from your row of blocks to his, and then rapidly drive back to your row of blocks.

See how your child takes this incursion into his "turf." If he accepts it, invite him with gesture to drive with "rmm rmms" from his row to yours until there is two-way traffic across both rows. After a time, as your child drives his car from his road, try putting your car in front of his. Does he go around your car, back up, get distressed? His reaction and what he does tells you how far you can go with your next intervention with him. For example, you might consider adding ramps to your blocks and send one car after another down the ramp. Then see if he can send cars down your ramp or construct a similar ramp at the end of his road. Continue to carefully introduce new play variations and determine what he can accept. Reduce your intrusiveness if he gets too distressed. Once you understand completely what you are trying to accomplish, all kinds of variations will occur to you to help your child expand and transform his ritual into interactive play with you.

The child who can tolerate these kinds of interventions clearly demonstrates that he is not so "captured" by what he is doing that he cannot interact with you around it (once you carefully intrude). This suggests that he will be responsive to many similar interventions that, step by step, teach him how to play more creatively with toys and with you. The child that cannot tolerate rapid shifts in the level of intrusion might learn to tolerate smaller intrusions. You need to gauge what *your* child can tolerate and not go too far beyond this in any one session.

These interventions can, with modifications, be applied to a range of other rituals (systems) that the child performs. The principle involved in all work with solitary rituals is to expand them so that:

1. they involve interaction with you

2. they incorporate variations

3. they become less rigid and more like creative play.

Study each ritual carefully before you attempt to work with it. The work described with the lining-up ritual is illustrative of the kind of work you can do with all such rituals.

Summary for child "captured" by a "lining-up" ritual

1. Offer the child a block for his line-up-block system.

2. Hold block in front of your face so that the child inadvertently looks at you as he gets his block.

3. Vary the location by moving further away from the child's block line up so that he has to chase you to get his blocks.

4. Try "adjusting" his blocks and then "fix" them before he does so in response to his need for the row to remain the same.

5. Build a parallel line up of blocks near his line up.

6. Offer his an occasional block for his line up, then ask him to "Give!" a block to you on request. Continue alternating between giving and receiving a block.

7. Walk with your fingers on your line up of blocks and then attempt the same with his.

8. Introduce a car to "rmm" along your line up. Then, offer him a car to see if he will do the same with his.

9. Connect the two "roads" and attempt to drive on his road. Invite him to drive on your road.

10. Set up a traffic jam (cars facing each other) and note how he copes with it.

11. Add a ramp at the end of your road and send a series of cars down your ramp.

12.   Offer him cars to send down your ramp. Offer him a ramp and try to send your cars down his ramp.

13.   Introduce other complications as appropriate. Repeat for 20–30 minutes on consecutive days.

CREATING SYSTEMS

Transforming behavior, by itself, is not sufficient to move children with autism forward. What is also needed is a way of dealing with developmental gaps or lags. The children need to develop an array of systems that are common to typical development. These may include body systems, such as how to hop or skip; or object systems, where the children learn how, for example, an inclined plane works, or how tools work as extensions of the body. To build these systems, you will often have to use some "hand-over-hand" with the child until the system catches.

In our terminology, we refer to the introduction of such activities as *spheres* or *spheric activity*. Spheres are characterized by repetition and a gradual "taking over" or conversion of the sphere into a system by the child. Our goal is to turn spheres introduced by parent, teacher, or therapist into systems that become part of the child's repertoire. The next section shows how different children on the autism spectrum accept spheres and convert them into systems.

Three Children on the Autism Spectrum

These three children showed different system dispositions and varied levels of reactivity to their surroundings: One child, Damon, three and a half years old, we have discussed in terms of transforming his lining-up-blocks system (see Figure 4.1). But, for Damon, transforming his systems is not enough. He needs help filling in developmental gaps through the creation of new systems. Jim, six years old and diagnosed autistic with system-forming disorder, seems oblivious and completely unresponsive to his surroundings. He sits there picking at the space between his toes. His Umwelt, therefore, seems not to extend beyond his body. The third child, Robert—another child with system-forming disorder—is three and a half years old. He has no language, and is so easily stimulated by different aspects of his surroundings that he is quite "scattered." Robert is excited by all the objects around him and scrambles first toward one, and then another, but never gets involved with any of them. Clearly, these three different children need

Figure 4.1 Transforming a child's perseverative "lining-up-block system" into interactive play. Photographed with permission from Crossroads School, Westfield, New Jersey

different interventions to help them form new systems. In the section below, we describe how one might begin working with these children. Before intervening, it is desirable to observe the child for about 15 minutes of unstructured time.

The interventions illustrated are by no means an entire program for each child. They merely suggest how to get started applying MM strategies with different children. Variations of these interventions can and should be made when the children are ready for them. We will get into more comprehensive interventions later.

Damon, a child with closed system disorder

Giving an object on request

While typical infants learn to give an object on request when they are as young as nine or ten months of age, many special children become so involved in their repetitive systems that they fail to do so even when the requested object is right next to them and the parent or therapist is tapping an outstretched palm and saying "Give!" The following strategy is effective in helping children like Damon respond to such requests.

The first step is to have the child throw the object with which he is involved in a box. With a child like Damon, this can be done by the therapist starting vigorously to throw blocks in the box and then giving him blocks to throw. Continue giving him blocks until it is clear that he is now deeply involved with the throwing-blocks-in-box system. At that point, abruptly interpose your hand, so that, as the child drops the block in the box, you catch it momentarily, and then immediately flick it into the box.

At times the child will try to avoid your hand so he can put the block directly into the box himself. If so, allow him to throw a few blocks before again interrupting the system by placing your hand in his path. After a few trials, during which you say "Give!" while you tap your outstretched palm with your other hand, the child will accept your hand on top of the box and begin to place the block in your hand instead of trying to avoid it. When this happens immediately drop the block into the box so that the child can experience your action as an extension of his.

When the child can do this, start to push the box out of his reach while placing your extended hand in front of the box while continuing to tap your hand and saying, "Give!... Give!" When you get the block immediately dump it in the box, which should now be out of the child's reach. On subsequent trials, move your hand progressively away from the box, so that it is clear to the child that when you say "Give!" he is to put the block in your hand no matter what its position is relative to the box.

EXPANSIONS

Once you have succeeded in establishing "Give!" as an imperative term, it is important that the child learn to give objects to anyone requesting them from him. After several persons have succeeded in this with him, then it is important to perform the same task with different objects (pegs, cars, trains, balls, etc.) at home and elsewhere.

Summary for establishing "giving an object on request"

1. Establish a repetitive throwing/dropping block-in-box system.

2. Interpose and tap outstretched hand in front of box while urgently saying, "Give!"

3. If the child avoids your hand allow him to do so for a few trials before again interposing your hand.

4. When you receive the block immediately drop it in the box.

5. Push the box out of the child's reach while your hand remains where the box was as you continue to tap your hand while saying, "Give!... Give!"

6. Once this succeeds, change position of your hand with respect to the box so that the child gives you blocks no matter what position your hand is in.

7. Periodically, allow the child to drop a block in the box without you intervening.

8. Continue same procedure with other objects and with different people in other locations.

Jim, a passive child with system-forming disorder

During the entire 15 minutes of unstructured time, Jim has been surrounded by various attractive objects and, facing his mother, has remained quite passive, never looking around. He has spent the time picking at the skin between his toes. Our first goal, therefore, is to move him from his passivity into some systematic involvement with objects and with his therapist. To do this the therapist intrudes within his Umwelt by placing three or four blocks in Jim's lap and then waiting to see what he does with them. Does he push them off? Great! Then the therapist starts a pattern of repeatedly dumping blocks on Jim's lap so that he can push them off. As he does so, the therapist says, while making a pushing gesture from Jim's orientation, "Jim is pushing the blocks!" (Narrating with word and gesture what the child is doing *while* he or she is doing it is an important technique to help develop receptive understanding, since it helps him or her connect the gestures and words he or she sees and hears to what he or she is doing.)

The therapist keeps adding more blocks and, unexpectedly, alternates that "game" with some tickling or "rough-and-tumble" play.

Afterwards, while repeatedly putting blocks in Jim's lap, the therapist unexpectedly pauses (system interruption) just before she places the blocks in Jim's lap to see if he expects the blocks by lifting his arms to push them off his lap (an indication that he has formed a pushing-block-off-lap action system). When you do this with your child, try to gauge the blocks-in-lap and rough-and-tumble activities so that they stay within his or her comfort level. If your child gets too excited, speak softly and reduce the pace and intensity of the activity.

If Jim does not respond to the blocks being placed in his lap, the therapist drops a few blocks in his shirt next to his skin. The placing of the blocks next to the child's skin often requires the child to do something about them—such as taking the blocks out of his shirt. If the child takes the block out of his shirt, you should hold your hand palm upwards, and tap your palm sharply, saying, "Give!" If he hands over the block, then next time present the hand at a slightly different location so that he has to "chase it" to get the block into your hand. Periodically, introduce pauses followed by tickling and rough-and-tumble play.

With these simple interventions "passive" children like Jim begin to improve their awareness of and ability to interact with the therapist and with the blocks. Equally important, they begin to attach spoken words and gestures to their actions in a way that will eventually allow the therapist as well as teacher and parent to use the actions to guide the children's behavior and advance their receptive understanding. In the activity the therapist also guides the child—as he gives her the blocks or pushes them off his lap and expects new ones—into simple but important communication patterns that involve interaction with her around an object.

Jim's ability to respond to these simple interventions tells us that he has the potential for interacting with many such object systems. It also tells us that he needs help in constructing these object systems before he can interact and communicate independently about them.

We recommend that this procedure be repeated with your special child on subsequent days for 15–20 minute intervals. Stop the intervention each day while he or she is still interested in continuing.

Summary for suggested work with a passive child with system-forming disorder

1. Intrude by placing blocks (or something similar) in the child's lap.

2. If he knocks them off, add more so he can knock them off again—perhaps eventually getting a "game-like" interactive system going.

3. If he ignores the blocks, put two or three inside his shirt next to his skin. (If he has difficulty getting them out, help him.)

4. As the child takes each block out, hold your hand out palm upwards and tap it firmly with your other hand as you say, "Give!"

5. Intersperse this activity with some tickling or "rough-and-tumble" activity to keep the child engaged, then resume the activity with the blocks.

6. Try to expand the activity by moving your hand to the left or right to see if he "chases" it.

7. End the activity while the child still wants to continue it.

8. When your child has assimilated this system, introduce new ones. Useful systems might include:

    (a) knocking over stacks of blocks
    (b) using a squirt bottle
    (c) sending objects down a ramp
    (d) putting discs in a slit on top of a bottle
    (e) pouring water into a bucket.

Robert, a "scattered" child with system-forming disorder

From observing three-and-a-half-year-old Robert's behavior during an unstructured period, we found that he didn't know how to engage with objects. He might look at one object and start to move toward it but then get diverted by the next thing he saw or heard. Or he might look one way while his hands were feeling an object near him. His eyes and hands tended not to work together.

With such a child, the first role the therapist or parent should assume is that of eye–hand–object coordinator. Start with a simple task—picking up a block and dropping it onto a metal pan (to provide the child with the feedback he needs in order to realize that the sound came from *his* act of dropping the block in the pan). Take your child's hand and help him pick up the block. Then guide his hand until it is over the metal pan. If his head is averted from his hand, gently guide his head so that it is facing his hand. (He needs to see how his hand works in releasing the object.) Then, help him drop the block in the pan. (You do this by gently pressing his knuckles with your hand until his hand opens and drops the block). This technique is illustrated in Figure 4.2.

You use the pan to magnify and dramatize the effect of the child's dropping action. But if the noise of the block dropping in the pan is too loud and he starts holding his ears, drop a towel over the pan to muffle the sound.

Repeat this process a dozen times or until you feel that the child is starting to "take it over:" in other words, that a dropping-block-in-pan system is starting to form. Then, begin to move the pan slightly to one side (location expansion) so that the child has to visually check the new location of the pan. Keep moving the pan from his left to his right side and then, bit by bit, to other locations further away from his body. If he "loses" the pan or becomes distressed, bring the pan closer. Note whether or not your child is beginning to search for the pan in its different locations. Repeat the dropping activity

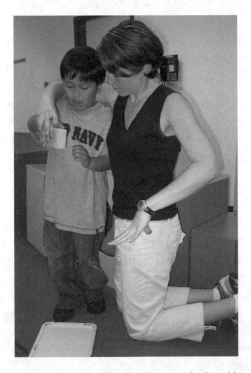

Figure 4.2 Teaching a child to release an object by pressing the knuckles. Photographed with permission from Crossroads School, Westfield, New Jersey

with different objects. Stop the session before your child wishes to stop. Devote about 10–15 minutes to this task. Then repeat it on following days until your child, when he sees the blocks or other objects next to the pan, will pick up the blocks or other objects and begin to drop them into the pan without any support.

With this activity you have begun to teach the child how to coordinate his vision with his hand function and you have taught him that he can make things happen in a way that produces a discernible effect (noise). You have also given him a simple system for engaging with the blocks or with other objects. The relevance for communication is this: as your child learns to influence what happens by using his hands, he develops the framework for eventually understanding that he can use signs and words to influence what others do.

Summary for a "scattered" child with system-forming disorder

1.   Start with a simple, causal task, such as dropping an object into a metal pan.

2.   If the child is sound-sensitive, throw a towel over the pan.

3.   If the child looks one way while his hands are holding the object, gently guide his head so that he is looking at what his hand is doing.

4.   Help the child release the block into the pan.

5.   Repeat a dozen times or until the child starts to "take over" the task.

6.   Then move the pan to one side or the other so that the child has to extend his hand to make the object drop in the pan.

7.   Interrupt the activity by hiding the pan behind you and observe to what extent the child searches for the pan to drop his block into it.

8.   A useful cue in determining what new tasks to introduce can be gained by noting the things he turns toward but doesn't engage during the unstructured period. You can then help him become fully engaged with these objects.

9.   Repeat on consecutive days for 10–15 minutes each day with many different objects so that the child more fully understands the capacity of his hand to hold and release different objects.

These simple interventions demonstrate some of the ways that you can begin to help the children create new systems. As you note the children's improved functioning, you may begin to think of other simple causal systems that he might learn to establish.

Chapter 5 will add to your understanding of your child's developmental status and suggest new interventions.

SUMMARY

This chapter dispels the notion that autism is the fault of the parents. It suggests that there is often a bond between child and parents, and that, even when there is not, a bond can be built.

Four common stances toward autistic children have been discussed: High support/low demand (where the parent or professional is overprotective), high demand/low support (where the parent or professional denies the child's disorder and insist on the child performing as if he or she were typical), low demand/low support (where the parent or professional has "given up" on the child), and the high support/high demand stance emphasized in MM programs and considered to favor the child's development.

The MM has two major strategies to help autistic children: *transforming* their aberrant systems into functional ones, and *creating* new systems to make up for developmental lags.

Examples have been given of transforming autistic systems such as rocking, flapping, compulsive throwing/dropping, opening/closing doors, flicking lights on and off, toilet flushing, attacking, screaming, and lining things up.

Ways of creating new systems for three different children have also been explained. Ways of teaching a closed system child to give an object on request were described, as well as ways to move a passive child with system-forming disorder from passivity to interaction. Finally, a method was given which enables a "disconnected" child (system-forming disorder) to coordinate his or her vision with hand function as he or she learns how to deliberately release an object.

Chapter 5

Elevating the Special Child: Creating an Enhanced Reality

"I stand there screaming my lungs out 'Stop! Stop!' but he keeps chasing those birds right into the traffic. Finally, thank God, somebody grabs him and brings him to me!"

"Another time he's gotten himself all wet and dirty splashing in a puddle not 20 feet from me. I say 'Mike, come! Come to Mommy!' but he just ignores me."

Incidents like those cited above are typical of the reports which mothers of some special children have shared. Sometimes mothers attribute their child's failure to respond to deafness (only to find that the child's hearing is normal), or to the child being "willful," "obstinate," or "stubborn." But for a child to be "obstinate" or "stubborn" implies that he or she has the consciousness of self which would allow him or her to oppose a parent's wishes. Typically, however, we don't find evidence for such self-awareness in nonverbal children. If it is the result of neither "deafness" nor "stubbornness," how can we explain the child's failure to respond when Mother calls? To understand "word deafness" it is useful to consider the unique way in which some autistic children process reality.

"Word deafness" stems from the fact that, for children like Mike, spoken words are not relevant to what is engaging them at the moment. When Mike is chasing birds into traffic his reality consists only of that engagement; when he is splashing water, that activity and the sensory feedback it provides *are* his reality. The sounds of words directed to him are simply not part of the moment in which he is living. The question we must ask in relation to Mike and children like him is, "How can we make spoken words relevant for him?" Or, put another way, "How can we create a reality for him in which spoken words and gestures assume significance and the ability to guide his behavior?"

Our response has been to create an enhanced reality for Mike and children like him by simultaneously elevating the children on an Elevated Square and focusing their actions, so that the words they hear and the manual gestures they see become directly related to what they are doing moment by moment. But before going further into this, I would like to share with you the rationale for elevating special children.

WHY IS THE ELEVATED SQUARE IMPORTANT?

The Elevated Square (see Figure 5.1) is important because it contributes to a different, more "grounded" psychological state for the child. On the floor, many children on the autism spectrum toe-walk, flap their hands and twiddle their fingers in front of their eyes, or simply wander aimlessly. On the Elevated Square these otherworldly behaviors diminish markedly. For example, many children who toe-walk continuously on the ground walk quite normally on the Elevated Square. This change seems to occur because the children have moved from an *undefined* reality, in which they float along on their toes, twiddling or hand flapping with little body/self awareness, to a *highly defined* reality which requires their rapt attention as they carefully, and body-consciously, move one foot in front of the other to traverse the structure.

Figure 5.1 The Elevated Square with corner work stations

The properties of the Elevated Square help counter some of the significant challenges that children on the autism spectrum confront. One of these challenges is an uncertain sense of their bodies in space—or of space itself. It is this uncertainty which may account for the tendency of many autistic children, when introduced to a new setting, to run and collide with one wall of a room after another in an effort to establish the spatial extent of that room. Unable to process the room in purely visual terms, the children seem to need these collisions to help map the room for themselves. Some who don't collide with the walls and lack spatial boundaries simply run in endless circles in the center of the room.

Now, suppose that in the center of that room there is a well-defined structure (with colors that contrast with the space around it) that allows the child to walk along a 14-inch path 2.5 feet above the ground around a 5 by 8 foot structure. The structure stands out. It is both visually and proprioceptively salient: in other words, the repeated visual impression and body feeling the child gains as he or she repeatedly—and carefully—steps around and turns corners on the square vividly establishes that space and the child's body actions in that space.

Another reason for the square's effectiveness is the constraint it places on the actions of the child. The child can only go in one direction at a time. Random, scattered action is not possible on this structure; the structure demands focused and directed action as the child repeatedly walks around it. Soon the child begins to understand—as he or she walks around it—that continuing around the square will result in a return to the starting position.

The rationale for using elevation was derived from observing that children on the autism spectrum are driven to compensate for an uncertain sense of their own bodies. We refer to this drive as seeking an *edge experience*. "Edge seeking" is apparent when the child with autism squeezes his or her body through narrow spaces to feel the boundaries of the body better. Temple Grandin's "squeeze machine" (Grandin and Scariano 1986) expresses the creative way in which Temple accented her own body boundaries. Edge seeking is also evident in children who are drawn to heights. One five-year-old autistic girl we worked with used to hang by her fingertips from her third-story window, causing a crowd to gather until she was rescued. An associate of ours, Stephen Shore, author of the book *Beyond the Wall* (Shore 2000), tells about his life as a child with autism trying to experience his body (and himself) better by often climbing the highest tree he could find. Then, after climbing as high as he could, he would cling to a narrow branch, experiencing both fear and delight—as well as an enhanced sense of his own body—as he swayed back and forth 40 feet above the ground.

To help the special child find his or her "edges" I suggest that if, during a walk with the special child, you come across a low wall (two to four feet off the ground) on one side you allow the child to walk on the wall while you hold a hand. In the playground, once you are secure about your child's ability to climb and hang on, allow him or her to climb monkey bars and move from lower to higher levels. Sometimes a child will work to distinguish one side of the body from the other by walking with one foot on top of the curb and the other on the lower part of the curb. Hold the child's hand while he or she is doing this to insure his or her safety.

After observing many such spontaneous behaviors produced by children with autism—and noticing how much more aware of themselves and how much more focused they became while they were "working their edges"—we began, some 40 years ago, to elevate children at our center. We began first with simple planks placed between tables. These gradually evolved into a variety of elevated structures, of which the most important is the Elevated Square. (Although I will describe in detail our evolved Elevated Square, parents and professionals can accomplish many of the same goals with less elaborate structures as described in Chapter 7.)

Other features of the Elevated Square

The two-and-a-half-feet height of the structure places most three- to six-year-old children at or near eye level with most adults—making it easier to establish eye contact with the children. The short side connectors of the square are removable, making it possible for the therapist to stand in the middle in easy reach of the child. Removing a side connector also creates a U shape in which the child must make a detour in order to get to a desired person on the opposite side. The steps used with the Elevated Square are attached to each other with Velcro and—because they are designed to fit snugly in the channels of the Elevated Square—can be readily used as obstacles or small platforms placed around the square so that the child can respond to "Up!," "Down!," and "Around!" as well as "Get up!" and "Sit down!"

Finally, there are work stations at each corner of the square, which can be adjusted to the child's height to provide the best possible architecture for eye–hand coordination with the various tasks placed on these stations. The last piece of equipment is the slide, which connects to the square but can be readily removed.

The Elevated Square serves different purposes for different kinds of children. For easily "scattered" children with system-forming disorders, the square provides the external organization the children desperately require in order to function. However, for children with closed system disorders, the square provides the framework in which they can be taught to expand their systems, move from one system to another, and include people as well as gestures and spoken words within these systems. In the following vignettes, we illustrate the effect of work on the square first with Robert, a scattered child with system-forming disorder, and then with Damon, a child with a closed system disorder who is also "word deaf."

The Elevated Square with Robert, a "scattered" child with system-forming disorder

Preliminary work with Robert indicated that he had the following challenges:

1.   Scattered, easily distracted by extraneous stimuli.

2.   Little awareness of his own body (eye–hand disconnect).

3.   Limited ability to engage with and influence objects and events.

4.   Inability to follow spoken or signed directions.

Given the kinds of challenges Robert experienced, the major treatment emphasis for him was providing him with a sense of his own body efficacy while helping him form organized systems. The secondary emphasis was on guiding his behavior with spoken words and gestures. Until Robert could form coherent action–object systems, spoken words and gestures could not become part of what he was doing. Only when he had a greater sense of his ability to influence his surroundings with coherent systems could words and gestures become part of these systems and be capable of guiding his behavior.

The reader will recall from Chapter 4 that three-and-a-half-year-old Robert might look at one object and start to move toward it but would then get diverted by the next thing he saw or heard, or he might look one way while his hands were feeling an object near him. Once on the Elevated Square—which he climbed on without difficulty—a series of spheric (repetitive) activities were introduced to focus him, to help him become more aware of his body, and to help him "connect" with different objects.

Robert accepted the therapist's hand and climbed the steps to the square with little anxiety—perhaps because he couldn't fully assimilate the experience. To help him gain more of a sense of his body, and to keep him engaged, we decided to begin by having him push large blocks placed in the channels of the square; these provided him with some resistance and fell over when he pushed them. At the same time, we paced the activity fairly rapidly so that Robert didn't have time to become diverted from what he was doing.

Pushing large blocks
Large blocks—about three feet high—were placed on all four sides of the square. Robert's task was to push the blocks over as the therapist made a pushing gesture (from Robert's orientation) and said "Push!"

Pushing blocks/bowling pins over with and without sticks
After Robert directly pushed over the large blocks, the therapist used the word and sign *push* on the stations. By pushing both large and small blocks—those directly in front of him and those on the stations—Robert learned that his pushing action was effective with different objects. As Robert walked around the square, he was allowed to push some but not all of the objects on each station—leaving a few to induce him to return. First he pushed with his hand, then with a stick or small rake. He seemed pleased when the blocks or pins landed with a satisfying "plush" sound as they fell in a barrel of water, or with the brash sound they made when they landed in a metal pan. Robert repeated this a number of times.

The train
Now Robert experienced the sign/word *push* with regard to a "train" of large, fairly heavy blocks (formed by duct-taping a number of phone books together to make a stack and then lining up several such stacks) that moved when he pushed them. Robert—with some support—pushed the "train" to the end of the connector where the slide was attached. Small wooden blocks were placed on top of the larger stacks of phone books. Then, as Robert pushed, he craned his neck so he could see the effect of his pushing as one block of phone books after the other disappeared over the edge and traveled swiftly down the slide with the small wooden blocks adding clatter to the event as they toppled over. Both narration and celebration accompanied him as Robert pushed and saw the last block disappear from view with a satisfying tumult.

Interspersed with such big body actions were tasks designed to help him accent one side of his body over the other.

Parallel boards
Robert had difficulty moving forward on the parallel boards—revealing a problem distinguishing one side of his body from the other (see Figure 5.2). To remedy this, the therapist touched one foot and helped Robert lean to one side so that the other foot was unweighted and could slide forward. Then, the same procedure was used with the other foot. Through this intervention Robert learned to alternate his feet on both sides of the gap between the parallel boards. Obstacles were added to help accent awareness of his feet.

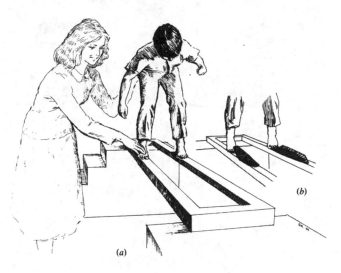

Figure 5.2 (a) Parallel boards used to help differentiate sides of the body; (b) obstacles added to help accent awareness of feet

Anticipation board

This fence-like structure was placed diagonally across the connector. The task for Robert was to climb over the structure to get to his mother, who was beckoning and calling on the other side (see Figure 5.3). It is called an anticipation board because the child has to anticipate that the space for his or her feet is getting narrower—and the board higher—and will soon prevent the child from crossing over unless he or she realizes this and crosses over sooner.

In climbing over the anticipation board, Robert—like many children with poor body awareness—showed confusion by leading with the wrong leg in a way which left him facing away from his mother as he finally climbed over the board. During one trial he got one leg over and was for a time stranded with one leg on each side of the board because he was not sure how to get the other leg over. With support and repetition using the anticipation board he soon learned how to bring the inside leg over before following with the outer leg. When we turned the board around so he had to address it with the other side of his body, it became apparent than he did better from his right side than his left. It was encouraging to see that repeated trials enabled him to reduce the difference between one side of his body and the other.

Mini-maze

Also helping Robert distinguish one side of his body from the other was a mini-maze set up on the square (see Figure 5.4). Blocks were set up in such a way that he had to go around them leading first with the left side of his body, then with the right, and then with the left. When the sequence was reversed, Robert had to lead right, left, right.

(a)   *(b)*

Figure 5.3 The anticipation board: Child (a) successfully crosses and (b) fails to cross over and reach the parent

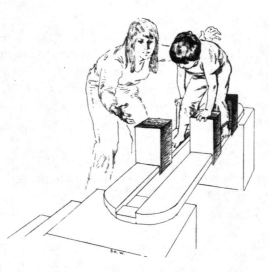

Figure 5.4 Child working his way through the mini-maze

"Swiss cheese" board

This board, substituted for one of the long connectors, presented Robert with another challenge. To cross the "Swiss cheese" board, Robert had to pick his way over a variety of free-form holes to get to the beckoning therapist or parent on the other side. Initially, he stepped in one of the holes and was caught before he could fall through. He clearly lacked the ability to scan the holes but had to, instead, explore each hole with an extended foot before he could work his way around it. (The child who can scan the holes and then step over them is further along in development than the child who needs to determine the existence of each hole by feeling it with an extended bare foot.) When Robert inadvertently stepped into one of the holes, he was allowed to experience the sudden drop but not to fall. Children who—after stepping in a hole—carefully watch their foot placement are demonstrating the ability to learn from their immediate experience. Robert needed to experience the sudden drop several times before it fully registered that he had to watch where he placed his feet (see Figure 5.5).

Figure 5.5 Child withdrawing foot from hole in the "Swiss cheese" board

Note: The need to carefully observe where children are walking (so they do not walk into open manholes on the street) generalizes nicely from the above exercises.

A variation used with this device involves placing balloons of different colors in each of the free-form holes. The task for the child is to press the balloon with his or her foot to force the balloon down and out of the hole. In doing so, of course, the child must become more aware not only of the hole but also of his or her effect on the balloon. You could attach strings to each balloon so that the child can alternate between pushing the balloons through their holes with his or her feet and pulling them out with the string attached to them. Another expansion entails attaching a new set of string to bottles filled with sand and placing them on the floor with only the string showing through the holes. Robert, with support, soon began to learn how to pull the bottles through the holes using both hands in a hand-over-hand maneuver. In working through this part of the task Robert developed more confidence in his ability to influence events through either pushing or pulling actions in a way which brought his hands to life.

Body flexibility

Another variation of the above set-up is placing blocks or beanbags *next* to each hole and requiring the child to alternately use first one foot and then the other to push the blocks into the adjacent hole. After this, the therapist touches the right foot and indicates by pointing that the child should push a beanbag into a hole next to the left foot and vice versa. In doing so, the child develops increased flexibility in using his or her feet and legs.

Carrying relatively heavy objects in repetitive tasks

Robert picked up, carried, and placed heavy objects (duct-taped phone books) to his mother or therapist at the end of one of the connectors. In this way, he began to integrate a person with the object with which he was engaged.

Home tasks

At home, a good task for Robert would be helping to remove groceries from the family car. Another good task would be assisting his father, who was building a wall, with moderate-sized stones: Robert could help load the stones into a wheelbarrow and with assistance wheel the stones to where the wall was being built and under supervision place the stones in the proper position. Any repetitive task which involves weight and has a clear outcome or result would be appropriate. In the house, Robert could be called on to move furniture from one location to another (even if his mother had to pretend that she didn't like the current placement of the furniture). Following this, she might decide she liked it better where it was, so Robert has to help move it back to its original site.

Following work on the Elevated Square—carried through in the classroom and at home—Robert became more focused and better able to follow directions. Having developed a number of functional systems, he became more responsive to following directions to perform certain actions, as long as the request related to objects near him.

Summary of steps to help a scattered child become better organized

Develop body efficacy through the following:

1. Have the child push relatively heavy objects so they fall over.

2. Have the child push smaller objects off stations, first with his or her hands, and then with a stick.

3. Have the child push a "train" of objects off the square (down the slide) so that the child can note the effect of his or her pushing.

4. To help the child distinguish between the sides of his or her body, have him or her walk on elevated parallel boards as well as climb over a fence-like structure and traverse the mini-maze.

5. Help the child cope with challenging spaces ("Swiss cheese" board) near the body.

6. Have the child carry and stack relatively heavy objects from one place to another.

An intervention case example: Damon

Damon, the three-and-a-half-year-old described earlier in Chapters 2 and 4, is a child on the autistic spectrum with a closed system disorder, Type A. His various challenges include the following:

1. Poor human contact. Won't look at people or include them in his systems.

2. "Word deaf." Does not seem to hear or follow directions.

3. Transitions. Damon has great difficulty shifting from one action–object system to another.

4. Communication. Pulls adult to desired object.

5. Symbolic play. Does not participate in make-believe play.

We felt that Damon's "word deafness" was directly related to his tendency to become so involved with what he was doing that spoken words and gestures were quite irrelevant to him. Consequently, for Damon, expanding his closed systems so that they might include spoken words and gestures was a primary goal of treatment, as was developing in him an ability to include people within his systems.

Improving body–other awareness
We began each of Damon's 45-minute therapy sessions with about five to ten minutes of big-body work. This entailed a combination of pleasurable rough-and-tumble activity, including Damon "scrunching" his knees against his chest with his feet on the therapist so he could feel himself push the other away as he straightened his legs, guided bouncing on a trampoline, and swinging Damon in a blanket.

To help Damon develop improved eye contact, we alternated gentle, mutual face-touching with subtle restabilizing (i.e., tugging his clothes front and back and left to right in an unpredictable manner which made it necessary for him to constantly "right" himself and to look at the therapist).

These procedures were introduced carefully and resulted in Damon smiling or laughing, with improved eye contact. Then, when certain big-body systems (jumping, swinging, rough and tumble) were interrupted, he sometimes indicated with the sign *more* (tips of fingers of both hands touching each other) a wish to continue the activity.

Helping Damon "hear" and respond to words

Damon, as described earlier, was "word deaf," which meant, for example, that he did not respond to spoken word directions such as "Come!" or "Stop!"—placing his life at risk if he was not constantly held or supervised.

To increase Damon's capacity to respond to spoken words, we followed the *principle of inclusion* (Miller and Eller-Miller 1989, 2000) which states that when a sign or word is repeatedly paired with a directed action, the child begins to experience that sign and word as part of his or her action–object experience. Then, when the word and sign are introduced *without* its action, the child experiences them as a "part-system" that requires him to perform the relevant action to complete the system. We applied this principle with various action words used with Damon: "Come!" "Go!" "Up!" "Down!" "Push!" "Pull!" "Around!" "Get up!" "Sit down!" "Pick up!" "Drop!" "Pour!" and many others.

We also supported Damon's behavior by narrating what he did with a vocal tone that expressed the delight we felt at his performance. We found this affective narration to be far more relevant to his development of receptive language than was using the term "Good job!" with its doubtful meaning to the child. From time to time we varied the intensity of our utterances so that sometimes they were loud and sometimes whispered. But now, let me describe our work with Damon on the Elevated Square so that the reader can follow, step by step, how he achieved his gains.

Following directions on the square

After the rough and tumble—including tickling—we sought to have Damon climb up the steps to the square. He balked at first and needed to go up and down the steps three or four times before he would venture further. Once on top of the square, he looked down at his feet and then at us as if asking, "What am I doing up here?" Because of his obvious uneasiness, we helped him settle into his mother's lap as she sat on one of the connectors on the short side of the square. His therapist sat on the same connector two or three feet away.

As Damon became more comfortable, the therapist held out her arms, beckoned, and said, "Come!" The linear quality of the board, coupled with her supportive beckoning and calling, soon induced Damon to gingerly come to her. She then briefly hugged him and turned him around to face his mother, who also said and signed "Come!" to which he promptly responded by swiftly going to her and settling in her lap. Bit by bit the space between mother and therapist was increased until Damon—now clearly enjoying himself—responded to being called back and forth across the short side of the square[1] without difficulty. (To insure safety an assistant on the inside of the square hovered near him.) Then, the same strategy of gradually increasing

---

1　At times changing the length of the connectors turns the square into a rectangle.

distance between his mother and the therapist was used on the long side of the square. Following this, Damon confronted a new problem.

"Turning the corner"

Turning the corners was initially difficult for Damon because—unlike walking along the "straight ahead" portion of the square—turning required him to make a decisive body shift of direction, which was difficult for him because of his limited body awareness.

The procedure followed was for Damon's mother to stand about two feet from the corner of the square while the therapist holding Damon stood two feet on the other side of the corner. Damon's mother said "Come!" as she held out her arms and beckoned to Damon as she had done on the straight part of the square. The first time Damon addressed the corner, the therapist gently guided him around it to his mother. Then, Damon, with only minimal support, successfully turned the corner from the opposite direction to get to his beckoning and calling therapist. Again, space was increased and support reduced until Damon was comfortably changing direction and turning the corner to go back and forth without support between his mother and therapist, guided only by the beckoning gesture and spoken word "Come!" As Damon mastered this he also learned about the nature of the square. After successfully turning the corner at one location on the square, Damon rapidly demonstrated his ability to turn his body at the other three corners.

Note: For some children, several sessions are necessary before they can achieve what Damon accomplished in one session.

Managing detours

During the second session, when Damon was able to follow directions around all four corners of the square going clockwise as well as counter-clockwise, a detour was set up by removing the connector on the short side of the square.

Damon was placed at one end of the short side opposite his mother on the other end. Mother beckoned and said "Come!" as she had done before.

Damon looked urgently at his mother, peered fearfully at the empty space separating him from her, and then scanned the solid remaining portion of the square. Finally, he reluctantly turned from his mother (trusting that she would still be there even when he was not looking at her) and began the long trek around the remaining U-shape of the square (see Figure 5.6)—until he reached her for a big hug and much applause. Damon's mother then exchanged positions with the therapist who held out her arms, beckoned, and called Damon to make certain that his successful solution was not limited to one direction. Then, when the long connector of the square was removed, Damon again successfully performed the detour in both directions.

Figure 5.6 An autistic boy beginning to solve the detour problem

As Damon solved the detour problem, he demonstrated that he had generalized his response to "Come!" with the beckoning gesture on both the short and long sides of the square, to making detours in both directions across the square and with both his mother and the therapist—a considerable achievement.

If a child, unlike Damon, cannot spontaneously solve the detour problem, the therapist gently orients the child's head away from her mother to help the child see and scan the detour. Often that is sufficient for the child to continue around the square to her mother. If it is not, the child is led around the remaining U-shape of the square by the therapist or the assistant until she reaches her mother.

During subsequent sessions, to further develop Damon's ability to follow directions, and to continue to address his "word deafness," new demands involving the spoken word, gesture, and action were introduced.

"Up!"..."Down!"

Blocks (about six inches high) fitting within the channels on the square were placed on all four sides of the square. The task for Damon was to go up and then down as the therapist or parent said the word and made the sign for *up* (finger pointed upward in front of Damon's face) and *down* (finger pointing downward in front of his face). As Damon achieved this, the therapist changed the rhythm by periodically requiring him to remain on top of the block, until he looked expectantly at the therapist or his mother for the next direction. When he looked at her, the therapist made the *down* gesture while saying the word "Down!" A few cycles later, the therapist altered the procedure by requiring him to remain standing in front of the block until he looked at her. Then, when the therapist made the *up* gesture and said "Up!" she required him to immediately go up the block.

Note: The stalling is not done on every cycle. Only once the rhythmic system of going up and down paired with spoken word and gesture becomes fully predictable for the child does the therapist, from time to time, stall for eye contact both before the child goes up on the block, and while he is standing on it, before he steps down.

"Sit down!"…"Get up!"

Following this activity, Damon was taught to "Sit down" and then "Get up" when he heard the words and saw the signs. From time to time, after he had come down from the block, the therapist would direct him with word and gesture to sit down and then get up. She repeated this several times until he responded smoothly and promptly to the direction. (The sign for *get up* required both hands moving upward—palms up—while the sign for *sit down* required both hands moving downward, palms down.)

"Block down!" "Damon down!"

The next sequence—involving blocks and the slide attached to the square— was designed to help Damon distinguish between himself and the blocks going down. It was also designed to further generalize the concepts of *up* and *down* to a different activity.

First, Damon was asked to sit down next to the slide. Then he was handed blocks to throw down the slide. He giggled and thoroughly enjoyed the clatter the blocks made as they landed on the metal slide. As that system was established the therapist and Damon's mother—one on each side of him—would hand him a block and then withdraw it so that he had to both reach for it and look at the person holding it. Once this was established, the block-down-slide system was periodically interrupted by one of the adults tapping Damon on the chest and saying, "Damon down!" After a number of sessions, Damon was able to perform the requested act without needing a tap on his chest or a pointed reference to the block to indicate whether he or the block should go down the slide.

In this way, Damon learned to look expectantly at the therapist for the next command and to be guided by the signs and words for *come, go, up,* and *down.* Once Damon developed the appropriate response to a command while on the square, the next step required him to generalize his response to these words and signs on the ground, in the classroom and at home, where he learned to respond to these directions from different family members located at varying distances from him.

Sign/word guidance to assist with motor planning

When we used sign/words in the context of the step–slide arrangement attached to the square, Damon began to hear and respond appropriately to them. A key aspect of the strategy was to first have Damon establish a step–slide system—the steps were at right angles to the slide—by repeatedly climbing the steps and then sliding down the slide (see Figure 5.7).

To make the implicit meanings of his activity explicit, the therapist began to introduce the relevant sign and word (pointing up and saying "Up!") as he went up and as he slid down (pointing down the slide while saying "Down!"). Subsequently, Damon's mother stood at the bottom of the steps and beckoned and said "Come!" as he returned to the step to repeat the process.

Gradually, as he began to anticipate what was coming next, Damon also became increasingly responsive to the signs and words which accompanied his actions. These were then generalized first within the step–slide set-up (with different people using these words) and then outside the slide set-up (location expansion). But, as we shall show in the next section, the opportunities to introduce new signs and spoken words exist not only in the child's therapy or playground but also in his or her own home and its surroundings.

Changing one's mind

Another variation used to further encourage Damon to attend carefully to what was being said and signed to him involved the therapist abruptly changing her mind. For example, while saying "Come…come!" she would suddenly change her mind and introduce signs and words for him to sit down or jump. The purpose here, of course, was to underscore for Damon his need

Figure 5.7 Testing for system-forming capacity on the step–slide sphere

to turn toward her and listen closely to what she was saying in order to know what to do next.

Summary of strategies for achieving sign/word-guided behavior

1. Improve body–other awareness and eye contact using:

    (a) rough-and-tumble activities
    (b) face-touching and restabilizing.

2. Teach *come* in varying spatial contexts:

    (a) from close to then further away from caller
    (b) when turning a corner
    (c) when managing a detour.

3. Pair signs/words with their relevant actions (*up, down, push, pull, get up/sit down*, and so forth).

4. Teach the child to distinguish his or her body/self and action from object and action (as with the example "Damon down!" vs. "block down!").

5. Generalize sign/word terms to another context (using *come, get up, sit down*) within a step–slide set-up and at home with different speakers uttering the words.

6. Improve the child's orienting to the speaker by having the speaker unexpectedly "change her mind."

The challenge of change for Damon

Children like Damon are typically and largely victims of their systems. Nowhere did this show itself more than in Damon's difficulty making transitions from one action–object system—such as pouring water over a water wheel—to another—such as putting cups on hooks. As indicated previously, to make spontaneous transitions a child must first be aware of his or her separate existence as well as the object or event system with which the child was engaged at a particular moment. Otherwise, the child becomes so captured by the ongoing body–object system in play that spontaneously detaching from the ongoing system is not possible.

Among typical children, the awareness of body/self and the world—including the ability to make choices—develops gradually in the course of the first two years. For example, by six months of age, the child has achieved sufficient differentiation between her body and others to demonstrate a clear preference for her mother over others. When the child is between six and nine months of age, she is able to relate to (establish systems with) either a person or an object. When the child has reached nine or ten months of age, she can relate to another person around an object (child–object–person system), which is evident in her ability to give an object to a caregiver on request (Trevarthen and Hubley 1979). And, of course, between 18 and 24 months of age, the child becomes consciously aware of her ability to accept or refuse requests.

Damon—and children like him—need help to learn to transition more easily and, at the same time, to become more in command of their systems.

One of Damon's most serious difficulties was his tendency to become so repetitively involved with a task, such as lining up blocks—as well as following and becoming obsessively entranced by any straight line—to the exclusion of all else, that he could not spontaneously shift to other tasks (systems). Without this ability he could not explore or learn to cope with changes in his surroundings. Often, when he was required to transition to another activity, Damon would become very upset and tantrum. Two strategies were employed to help him with transitions: One, disrupting his familiar Elevated Square; the other, using multispheres.

Disrupting the Elevated Square

Since the square had become a well-developed system for Damon, it was now time to present him with selectively disrupted aspects of it (see Figure 5.8). We felt that by experiencing disruptions—change in the status quo —and learning that he could cope with these disruptions, Damon was being prepared for the necessary disruption brought about by the need to shift from

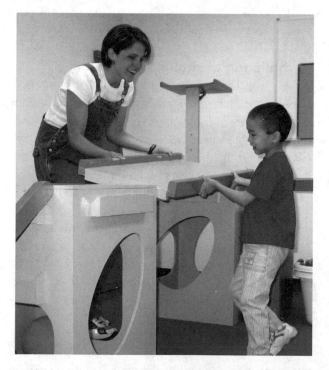

Figure 5.8 An autistic child helping to repair the disrupted square. Photographed with permission from Crossroads School, Westfield, New Jersey

one thing to another. We disrupted the square by turning over the steps, dropping the slide, or removing connectors or stations—so that Damon would need to "fix it." As he repaired these disrupted systems he learned that change did not have to mean disaster. An additional benefit of his repairing these disrupted systems was the increased sense of his own competence——and an enhanced sense of himself—that developed with each repair. In Chapter 6 I will discuss the social implications of helping to repair the square or other disrupted systems.

Using multispheres

To help Damon make transitions, we first had to establish compelling systems on each of the four corner stations of the Elevated Square. On one station we had Damon pouring water over a water wheel and then dropping the empty water bottle into a can as he waited for another water bottle; on the second station we had him sending small cars down a zig-zag set of ramps; on the third station, he placed discs inside a slit made on top of a transparent jar; on the fourth, he placed cups on cup hooks.

To establish the various systems, Damon went to each station and performed the task. At the first station the teacher or therapist handed him a small bottle of water and guided his hand repeatedly with a number of bottles until he was able to hold the bottle and pour water over the water wheel by himself. The same procedure of repeatedly helping him with the activity until he took it over was repeated with the other three stations.

After Damon became engaged with A (the first sphere, pouring water over a water wheel), we interrupted this system at the point of *maximal tension* (the point at which the child most needs to continue the activity). We inferred that when this was done, Damon experienced—in Lewinian (Lewin 1935) terms—a *tension state* related to the need to continue that activity. By maintaining that tension state while we helped him move to the second, entirely different system (B: sending cars down a zig-zag ramp), the first system continued to remain "alive" for Damon even while he became engaged by the second station.

Damon was "caught" by the first system and had difficulty leaving it when we interrupted it to take him to the second system. Guided from that first system he looked back longingly until he got caught in the "gravitational field" of the second system. (It is this duality of experience that begins to make it possible for the child to relate and soon easily shift from one sphere or station to another.) After a number of cycles involving two (AB), then three (AB and C: putting discs in bottle), and four (ABC and D: hanging cups on hooks) systems, Damon's resistance to leaving one system to go to another began to decrease. He seemed to be developing a sense that all was not lost when he left one system to go to another—that the system still existed after he left it and that he could return to it. After a few sessions with this multisphere procedure, he showed no more distress when his systems were interrupted.

But merely being able to shift clockwise from A to B to C to D systems, although it was important, was, by itself, not sufficient for Damon to cope flexibly with his surroundings. He needed to learn how to cope with less predictable transitions. At this point, we began to vary the systems. In other words, after A (the pouring water system), Damon expected to move from A to B (the car down the ramp). Instead, Damon—clearly unhappy—was guided past Station B to Station C (discs in bottle). At first he complained vocally about this change. However, as this process continued over a number of sessions, Damon learned to tolerate shifts from one station to another in all possible combinations—ACBD, DBAC, and so on—without getting upset.

Once Damon could cope with shifting in all possible combinations on the Elevated Square, stations were shifted to the ground. Here, without the support of the square, Damon soon demonstrated his new ability to shift to the various stations without upset. After Damon mastered this sequence, he was placed in a position where he could scan all the stations. He was then asked to choose which one he wished to go to. When he expressed a preference for one system over another by pointing, sign, or word, we had evidence of the emergence of new executive functioning.

At this point we learned from Damon's mother that he was no longer becoming distressed when she had to unexpectedly change her plans for going shopping or taking a different route to the store.

Summary of steps to treat transition challenges

1. After child has become comfortable with a particular system (Elevated Square) selectively disrupt parts of that system and support the child's effort to repair it.

2. Introduce multisphere strategies:

    (a) Establish four compelling systems in a square configuration— preferably on an Elevated Square.
    (b) Once established, interrupt the first system at the point of maximal tension and take the child to the second station.
    (c) Repeat process at second, third, and fourth stations in an A, B, C, D manner.
    (d) When the child is comfortable with the A, B, C, D arrangement, randomly change the sequence to A, D, B, C or C, D, B, A, etc.

3. When the child is accepting of these variations, have the child go through a–d on the ground.

In the next chapter, "Exploiting Systems to Develop Social Capacity," I discuss how to systematically advance the autistic child's ability to make contact with both adults and children.

SUMMARY

"Word deafness"—the child not responding to someone calling—is defined in terms of the child's single track investment in what he or she is doing at a particular moment. He or she does not, therefore, hear spoken words, because they are not relevant to the system engaging the child.

To create a reality in which spoken words are relevant entails placing the child on an Elevated Square—conceptualized as a "highly defined" reality that requires the child's rapt attention as he or she carefully and body-consciously traverses the structure. The Elevated Square appears to provide an "edge experience" for the children that enhances body awareness. It also contributes to improved eye contact and problem solving.

The manner in which the square was used with Robert, an autistic boy with system-forming disorder, contrasted sharply with how it was used with Damon, an autistic child with closed system disorder. Various tasks used on the Elevated Square—pushing blocks over, pushing a train of blocks, the parallel board, the anticipation board, the mini-maze, the "Swiss cheese" board, carrying heavy objects—contributed to Robert's improved body organization and improved responsiveness.

For Damon the emphasis was more on resolving his "word deafness" and body/self–other awareness. Signs and words were attached to functional activities on the square and narrated. To reach his mother Damon had to solve a detour on the square created by removing the connector between himself and his mother. Through the work on the Elevated Square Damon began to respond to a range of action signs and words, on the square, the ground, and at home.

Strategies for improving Damon's ability to cope with change included disrupting the Elevated Square so that he had to repair it, and the use of multispheres to teach him how to shift from one disparate object to another without distress.

Chapter 6

Exploiting Systems to Develop Social Capacity

A mother—knowledgeable about psychological issues—observed her four-year-old son carefully sawing an earthworm in half with a sharp piece of stone. Immediately, she worried about her child's sadistic tendencies and thought about therapy for him. As he completed the separation, he very softly started to speak. She leaned closer and heard him say, "There, now you have a friend."

Paraphrased from Shlien (1963)

Like the mother described above, we need to make certain that the inferences we make about our special children are accurate and not based on their surface behavior. For example, one visitor to the home of a four-year-old autistic boy was impressed with how "friendly" Jason was, because—after she had been with him for only a few moments—he sat on her lap and cuddled as if she were a member of the family. Jason's mother reported he was like that with everybody.

From our perspective, Jason was a child who—while expecting good things from people—may not have bonded with his mother in a way which made her a special person for him. In this chapter I discuss various ways in which systems thinking may be applied to establish social capabilities which were bypassed during an autism spectrum child's first years. Foremost among these issues is mother–child bonding as well as social exchanges with others.

MOTHER–CHILD BONDING

The failure of mother–child bonding to take place is one of the tragic effects of classical infantile autism as described by Kanner (1943). It is devastating for a mother to find that she is not a special person for her child. One mother, alarmed by her son's retreat and her loss of eye contact with him, consulted with me and then wrote to describe how it had changed her approach with her two-and-a-half-year-old child, Joshua.

> Thank you for your suggestions about making contact with Joshua. After I talked to you, we literally spent hours playing with Lego, reading books and playing. Whenever he would approach me to nurse I would draw his attention to my eyes and hold them there at any cost. It was really hard for him! It wasn't until today that I realized he's found a position to nurse in which he doesn't even have to acknowledge that I'm attached to my own breasts! When he tried to get into that position, I gently turned his face back to me and kept talking, or singing, or blowing air at him through a straw, or peering over my sunglasses, or sticking my tongue out, until he let me participate. I can't tell you how unbelievably good it felt to have him look at me. There's a look in his eye, the same look he had when he was a newborn baby, like, "Who are you, anyway?" I can't believe after all we've been through together over the last two years, I have to go back to square one!

The lack of mother–child bonding also shows itself when the child either will not go to anyone when in need of comfort or will go to *any* person. Typically, such children are reported to have been very "good," undemanding babies. Whereas other babies at six months would cry when passed over to a stranger, mothers of these children reported no such stranger response occurred with their children. One person was as good as another. Then, by the time they reached three years of age, the children showed no reaction when left with strangers but would, typically, become repetitively engaged with one object or another.

The Miller Method® (MM) therapist follows a three-step program to establish mother–child bonding. The first step entails teaching the mother how to physically engage the child; the second involves cataloguing the various action–object systems the child engages in; the third involves teaching the mother how to insert herself within the child's various object systems.

Physically engaging the child

The range of activities important for the mother to use during this phase—which were described in Chapter 5 in the vignette about Damon—include face-touching, restabilizing, tickling, peek-a-boo, chase games, "I'm going to get you..." as well as body games such as "getting" the child's nose, foot, arm, and so forth. Of these activities, mutual face-touching (see Figure 6.1) is particularly important since the rhythmic face- touching—abruptly interrupted by the adult blowing on the child's hands—induces both eye contact and enhanced interaction.

Also included in this group of activities are "interrupted rocking" (described in Chapter 4), rough and tumble, and interacting with the child while he or she is swinging. The intention here is to have the child not only become more aware of his or her own body but also begin to experience that body in relation to the mother.

Restabilizing—often alternated with mutual face-touching—consists of unexpectedly but lightly plucking at the child's clothes from left to right and front and back. By throwing the child slightly off balance this induces self-righting. Like rough-and-tumble play, restabilizing helps ground the child in his or her body.

Interrupted rocking with the child on your lap is an effective way of getting the child to respond interactively. Once you establish a rhythmic

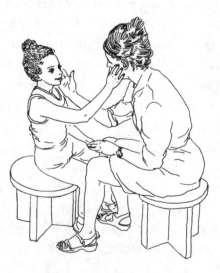

Figure 6.1 Mutual face-touching to induce eye contact and interaction

rocking motion, interrupt the rocking. Often the child will make a small decisive movement of his body with an urgent grunt to communicate the wish for the rocking to continue.

Swinging

After placing the child in an enclosed swing, his mother faces the child and begins to gently push the swing while saying "Mommy pushes David!" As the child becomes comfortable with the rhythmic motion of the swing, the mother unexpectedly stops the swing (interruption) to determine if the child in some way (gesture, word, body movement) indicates a wish for her to continue.

Expansions include varying the excursion of the swing, as well as telling the child that his mother is going to touch his foot, nose, hand, arm, etc. each time the swing returns. A positive sign is when the child starts to anticipate the touching by touching the designated body part before his mother does. Other variations include swinging the child in a blanket or raising and lowering the blanket and then pausing (interrupting) to elicit some expression from the child that he wishes to continue.

Noting the child's action–object systems

Autistic children who fail to bond with their mothers often have an array of action–object systems that exclude people. These may include lining up blocks, animals, cars, etc.; repetitive throwing of blocks or scribbling; endlessly pouring water from one cup to another; flicking light switches; flushing toilets; or opening and closing doors. Once the mother—with the help of a trained therapist—has catalogued the different action–object systems in the child's repertoire, the next task is to find ways for the mother to insert herself within these systems.

Becoming part of the child's action–object systems

The mother can become part of these systems in a variety of different ways. For example, if the child is engaged in lining up blocks, as we described in Chapter 5, the mother becomes the repository of all the blocks the child needs. In order to continue lining up blocks the child must come to her to get them. As the child reaches for the block, the mother holds it in front of her face so that the child inadvertently looks at her face as well as at the object. If the child is engaged in opening and closing doors, the mother arranges

to appear behind the various doors the child opens, and celebrates her appearance with tickles, hugs, and comments like "Here is Mommy!" If the child is engaged in scribbling, the mother begins to scribble on the same page.

Helping John bond with his mother

When John, a classically autistic nonverbal three-year-old, expressed his discomfort with his mother's intrusion in his scribbling by accelerating crying, she moved her scribbling toward the edge of the paper until his crying eased, but then began again to encroach on the space in which he was scribbling until he could tolerate her participation.

"Stealing" John's crayons also proved helpful. John would be contentedly scribbling at one of the stations on the square when the therapist would abruptly "steal" the crayon from his hand and toss it to his mother standing at another part of the square. John would yelp but then, as the therapist pointed to his mother holding the crayon in front of her face, he would very purposefully walk to his mother, peer at the crayon (and notably at her face), get his crayon, and then return to his scribbling system.

Following these and similar interventions over the course of a year, John was videotaped during an Umwelt as he had been at the beginning of the year. While the first Umwelt showed John totally ignoring his mother when she left the room, the second one showed him first trying to open the door behind which she had gone but then, failing that, going over to me to take my hand and lead me to that door. Then, facing me in front of the door, he made the *open* sign—clearly indicating that I should open the door. When I did so he possessively took his mother's hand to pull her into the room. His mother reported that these days John even got upset when she had to leave him momentarily to go to the bathroom!

Leaving mother

Once the child establishes a bond with the mother, it can be extremely difficult for the child to leave her. The following question by a parent and my response to it suggests how this may be handled.

My nonverbal four-year-old son (diagnosed PDD) always has a hard time separating from me, his mom, to go on the bus for preschool. Getting on that bus is like torture for the poor little guy. Any suggestions?

My response

It may be that your son feels that when he leaves you to get on the bus he will never see you again. In other words, he may not yet have gotten the notion that even though he leaves you he will eventually return to you. For him, it is

likely that when he is with you, the teacher at school doesn't exist, and when he is in school, you don't exist. If this is correct, then finding ways to help him connect his mom-at-home reality with the teacher-at-school reality should ease the problem.

One way to do this is to set up a picture sequence showing him going on the bus, going to school on the bus, getting off to go to school, being in preschool with his teacher, then leaving teacher and school to go on the bus, getting off the bus to be happily greeted by you. You should have one of these sequences and his teacher the other so you can show pictures of him going to school on the bus while the teacher can show pictures of him going home to you on the bus.

Another tactic that might help is giving him some item that he associates with you to take with him on the bus (a kerchief, a pin, etc.). At school the teacher can give him something from school to take home.

To further help him connect these two parts of his life have a large picture of his teacher at home (so you can call his attention to it) and a large picture of you at school so that his teacher can refer to your picture (and your continued existence) even when you are not physically present.

Summary of the process for establishing mother–child bonding

1. The mother can physically engage her child through:

    (a) face-touching and restabilizing

    (b) rough-and-tumble play with tickling

    (c) interrupted rocking

    (d) swinging

    (e) playing a chase game ("I'm going to get you!")

    (f) playing peek-a-boo.

2. Catalogue the child's action–object systems.

3. Become part of the child's action–object systems by:

    (a) becoming essential to the child's lining-up systems

    (b) becoming part of the child's repetitive rituals (appear behind the door the child opens and closes)

    (c) carefully intruding into the child's space during activities such as scribbling

(d) using pictures and transitional objects to establish the mother's continued existence when the child is in school or away from her.

While mother–child bonding provides the child on the autism spectrum—or any child for that matter—with a secure framework from which to launch an interaction with others, this, by itself, does not insure his or her success in relating to others. Mother–child bonding does not require the same level of sophistication—or awareness of self vs. other—that relationships with other children require. For example, in addition to well-established self–other awareness, the child must develop interactive skills which include the empathic ability to place himself or herself in the position of the other. In the following section, I shall discuss ways of achieving these capacities.

AWARENESS OF SELF AND OTHER

The fragility of autistic children's sense of body/self is suggested by the following question posed by a parent:

> My seven-year-old limited-verbal child [on the autism spectrum] becomes distressed in movie theatres yet enjoys watching television at home. When taken to SeaWorld and Disney World he becomes very upset when taken into a dark enclosure or tunnel and begins crying and stating "No! Out!" until he is taken back outside. Why does he react like this?"
>
> *My response*
> Many children on the autism spectrum have a "fuzzy" sense of their own existence. In the dark, enclosed settings you describe your son may become frightened because he loses visual contact with his own body (he can't see his feet, etc.).
> Such children (like many small typical kids) often need a night light at bedtime. A small pen flashlight that your son can shine on himself could be very reassuring to him in dark places.

There are many strategies which build the child's body/self awareness as well as awareness of the other. These include the following.

Collision

At the most basic level, nonverbal children on the autism spectrum become aware of others when they bump into or collide with them. It is for this reason that staff at MM schools are encouraged to never let an autistic child walk past them without getting in his or her way, ruffling hair, and so forth.

The "Grand Central Station" strategy

This strategy gains its name from the hubbub which occurs as groups of hurried people at the station work around each other to go to their different destinations (see Figure 6.2). Similarly, a child's awareness of other children can often be improved by dividing a class of six children so that three are crossing a 14-inch wide elevated board two and a half feet above the ground in one direction, while the other three children are trying to get past them to go in the opposite direction. In order to pass, the children going each way must notice the children trying to pass them. Initially, they try to pass without acknowledging the others. Later, as speech becomes available, they say "Get out of my way, please." With work these responses can be generalized to the ground in other situations.

Caution: Grand Central Station should not be attempted unless there is adequate staff to insure the safety of all the children.

Disrupting clothing or accessories

This next intervention helps establish awareness of the other. Some years ago, while consulting at a program for children on the autism spectrum, on a whim

Figure 6.2 Simulating "Grand Central Station" at rush hour

I put on a baseball cap cocked sharply to one side. Abruptly, a 14-year-old boy with autism who had been quietly rocking about 20 feet away dashed toward me, straightened out my cap, and then ran back to where he had been to continue his rocking.

In recent years, following the same principle, I have engaged profoundly withdrawn children by perching my glasses precariously on my nose in such a way that certain children (with closed system disorders) felt compelled to restore them to their proper and more secure position. Since then, a colleague has gotten children to restore his tie after he had flipped it over his shoulder. The notion guiding all such use of clothing and accessories is that the children develop a fixed expectation (system) as to how clothes are worn and accessories carried. When these everyday systems are disrupted, closed system children on the autism spectrum feel compelled to restore them to their proper place.

For one autistic boy, the need to keep his mother's clothing the same resulted in severe tantrums when, in the summer, she shifted from wearing long-sleeved dresses to those with short sleeves. The problem was finally solved by placing a strip of cloth around his mother's wrists at the same level as her long-sleeved dresses. As soon as the boy saw this, the tantrums stopped. Subsequently, we were able to reduce the size of the strips and finally eliminate them entirely.

In speculating why it was so important for this boy to have his mother continue to wear long-sleeved dresses, we felt that, for him, his mother's changing the sleeve from long to short meant that this was no longer his mother. In other words, for him, changing one part of the familiar mother configuration meant that the whole configuration had changed. Werner and Kaplan (1963) refer to this as a *pars pro toto phenomenon* and find that it is characteristic of small children as well as disordered people. The strip around the boy's mother's wrist was effective in allaying his fears because it provided a connection to the long-sleeved dresses and thus the familiar mother.

I'm going to get you!

"Threatening" to catch the child and tickle or bounce him or her is an excellent way to stimulate heightened awareness that both the child and you exist and that you will catch the child if he or she doesn't quickly run away from you. When the child runs away giggling and looks over a shoulder to see how close you are to catching up, the game is going well.

An important variation of the game is to make it reciprocal: Just before you catch the child, suddenly turn and start to run in the opposite direction. Pause from time to time, looking over your shoulder to see if the child is chasing you. Sometimes, another adult can help the child to understand that when you turn away the child is to chase you.

Even extremely limited children are responsive to the "Get you!" part of the game.

Peek-a-boo game

This is an excellent game for developing self–other awareness among many young children on the autism spectrum. After playing rough and tumble for a few minutes, interrupt the play by suddenly dropping a cloth over your face. When the child removes the cloth say, "Here is Mommy!" (etc.). Later, place the cloth over the child's face and ask, "Where is David?" When the child pulls the cloth off his face, tap him on his chest and say, "There is David!"

Still later you can begin to merge this game into hide and seek by disappearing behind a screen and then appearing unexpectedly at one or the other side of the screen.

Hide and seek

This is more advanced than the peek-a-boo game and is more difficult to establish. Usually a child will have little difficulty with the "seeking" part of the game, but will have more difficulty grasping the concept of "hiding." Often when a therapist is seeking the child and wondering out loud if the child is under the table, in the closet, etc., the child will then yell out to let the seeker know where he or she is.

In addition, the concept of hiding from the seeker is difficult for the child. Often, the child will conceal his or her head, ostrich-like, with feet and legs in plain view. This is all part of the child's not having a clear notion of the body and how his or her body looks to the seeker. The problem can be resolved by having another adult hide with the child and saying, "We have to be quiet so that Amie [or your mother] will not know where we are hiding." In this way, the child eventually grasps the concept.

Necklaces or ties

Another useful strategy for establishing self–other awareness is having the children take turns with the therapist in placing neckties or necklaces around each other's necks. In doing this the child must take into account the existence of the therapist and the precise location of his or her head.

A useful expansion is having the child place the necklaces around the heads of different designated people situated around the square. The therapist points at and names each person. The child must then walk to the designated person and place either necklace or tie around his or her head.

Removing tape from facial parts

Removing bits of masking tape from each other's faces is also a useful way of establishing more self–other awareness in the child. At first, the tape is placed on corresponding parts of the therapist and child. Subsequently, the child has to discover tape placed unexpectedly on both the child's and the therapist's body parts—an elbow, a knee, and so forth—and remove it.

Comparing images

Useful, also, is comparing images of the child with the adult when both are standing side by side in front of a full-length mirror. This provides the therapist with an opportunity to mimic the movements of the child while the child mimics the movement of the therapist.

I see you

This intervention is useful for children who have achieved some verbal capacity. It may be used in two ways:

1. During the morning orientation, each child is called up to the teacher who sings the hello song, including the name of the child, while tapping him or her on the chest, and also "sees" and reports something distinctive about the child—a new haircut, a new pair of shoes, or simply the color of the child's shirt. Just as the teacher "sees" different aspects of the child, the child is encouraged to "see" and report different aspects of the teacher.

2. Later, the intervention is expanded by pairing the child with each of the other children in the classroom—each facing the other. Then, each child takes a turn seeing and commenting on

something about the other. The net effect is to establish more awareness of each other in a very concrete manner as well as to establish a framework for conversation.

Having discussed various ways of enhancing body–other awareness, I will now, in the following, consider four ways of interacting with another.

FOUR WAYS OF INTERACTING WITH ANOTHER PERSON

Unless a child learns various ways of interacting with others—particularly other children—he or she is at a loss. Sometimes children with autism, wishing to play with and interact with other children, but not knowing how, will interact inappropriately by jumping on or hitting other children. Our children need to learn the "rules of the game" and to gradually learn to see things from the perspective of the other, if they are to "make it" with other children.

The four interaction skills the children need to learn in order to interact with each other are:

1. turn-taking

2. cooperating

3. competing

4. shifting to the other's perspective.

Turn-taking

A number of activities permit the teaching of turn-taking. The test as to whether or not the child is actually turn-taking is determined when, following an interruption of the activity, the child *waits* for the other to take his or her turn. If the child does not wait, he or she has not yet developed true turn-taking. One example of turn-taking that helps establish waiting for the other is the "tic toc" game.

The "tic toc" game

This game, usually played on the Elevated Square, is designed to involve the child in an interactive turn-taking experience with the therapist. The game requires a large box three and a half to four feet high that can be pushed back and forth between child and therapist (see Figure 6.3). The term "tic toc" refers to the rhythm established as the box first falls against the child's chest, *tic*, and then as the child pushes it away, *toc*. The therapist establishes the rhythm by pushing the box over so it lands on the child's hands. This induces the child to push the box away so that it tilts toward the therapist. With practice, the child soon enters into a continuous interaction with the therapist and, eventually, with another child.

Typically, the "tic toc" game alternates with other Elevated Square activities on the stations.

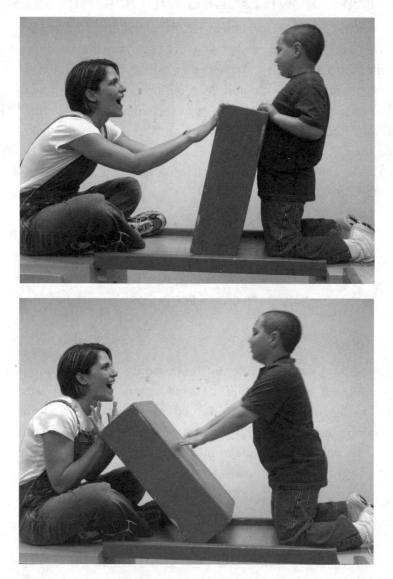

Figure 6.3 "Tic toc" to develop an interactive system. Photographed with permission from Crossroads School, Westfield, New Jersey

The "zip zap" game

An important distinction between "zip zap" and "tic toc" is that with "tic toc" therapist and child are close to each other as the pushed box lands first on the child and then on the therapist. In contrast, the "zip zap" game takes place with the child and the therapist or two children operating at a distance from each other. The "zip zap" game involves a toy which consists of two strings that pass through an oval-shaped plastic form. Holding handles that are attached to each end of two strings, each child can open his or her arms and send the plastic form zipping over to the opposite child, who can reciprocate and send the plastic form back simply by spreading wide his or her arms.

The beauty of the game is that one child cannot send the plastic form until the other child has received and returned it. The child *must wait* and in this way begins to understand the essence of turn-taking.

Once established, the principle of turn-taking should be expanded. Children can then take turns in dropping blocks into a metal can, sending cars down a ramp, and so forth. In all turn-taking, however, there should be periodic pauses to determine if the child understands that he or she must wait for the other child's turn to be completed before he or she has a turn.

Transforming "destructive" behavior into turn-taking

One parent of a special child contacted me for help because of the "destructive" tendencies of her 27-month-old autistic daughter, who was knocking over every tower of blocks the mother built for her. My advice to the mother was to build an array of block towers and then to join her daughter in knocking them over. Then, after she had built a second or third array of towers, she could negotiate with her daughter as to whose turn it was to knock over a tower. Such "joining" transforms acts viewed as "destructive" into playful interactions that—as they took turns knocking the towers down—could only further cement the bond between mother and daughter.

Cooperative interaction

The essence of cooperative interaction takes place when an adult and child (see Figure 6.4), or two or more children, must combine their efforts in order to achieve a particular outcome. For example, in the course of repairing the "messed-up classroom" (see Chapter 1), teachers turn over some rather heavy tables and desks. Righting this furniture requires two or more children to work cooperatively under the teacher's guidance. The same principle may be applied when there is a need to push a heavy table or desk into its proper place or to carry a heavy object from one place to another.

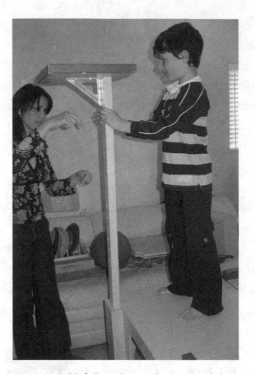

Figure 6.4 Dillan, an autistic child, follows his mother's signed direction to replace a station on the Elevated Square. Photographed with permission from Crossroads School, Westfield, New Jersey

Other examples of cooperative interaction include children holding hands to maintain their balance, or carrying a pole placed through the handle of a bucket loaded with blocks which enables two children—each grasping one end of the pole—to carry the bucket from one side of the room to another. They can then dump the blocks and go back for another load and so forth. Meantime, another child who is receiving the blocks can be using them to make a structure which requires many blocks.

Holding hands

Children can be taught to hold each other's hands (Figure 6.5) by having three of them walk up and then run down three inclined boards (one for each child). Each board is about six inches wide, and helps establish a need in each child to hold another child's hand to maintain balance.

Subsequently, the children are more able to hold hands when on trips as a class.

Interactive object-down sphere

The device shown in Figure 6.6 provides an opportunity for four children to participate in a highly coordinated manner. As the figure indicates, one child

Figure 6.5 Learning to hold hands to maintain balance

sends an item down the ramp (car, ball, rollerskate, etc.) which the child at the bottom of the ramp receives. This child hands that object to another child who sends it down the other ramp. After a time, roles are reversed so that the child who has been receiving objects now has the opportunity to send them down. With brisk pacing the children can interact with minimal adult support for between five and ten minutes.

A variation of the interactive object-down sphere adapted for two is shown in Figure 6.7.

Broken objects

Figure 6.8 shows how a specially designed broken table can be a means of encouraging interaction between two children who work together to repair the table.

The two-child scooter

Recently, I observed how two children on the spectrum became more aware of each other by trying to move a scooter (see Figure 6.9) on which both were sitting. The easiest set-up was when both children were seated side by side. Then, both could make the same crab-like or pushing-with-feet motion to move the scooter. It was more difficult for the children when they sat back to back. Then, the scooter would not move unless one child coordinated pushing with his or her feet with the other making a pulling motion with his or her feet. When two pairs of children are on their respective scooters, they can have races with each other.

Figure 6.6 Interactive object-down system for four children

Figure 6.7 Ben, an autistic boy, participating in an object-down system adapted for table-top

Figure 6.8 Two children repair a "broken" table

Figure 6.9 Scooters to help develop (a) cooperation and (b) competition. Photographed with permission from Crossroads School, Westfield, New Jersey.

Competing

The "competition cup" game is effective with special children who have some dawning awareness of the other person as an independent being. The goal for the competition cup game is to set up a situation in which the special child can compete first with the therapist and then with another child to gain a desired object under a cup. There are two phases involved in setting up the competition cup game: The first phase establishes a need for an item under a cup; the second involves competing for that item.

Needs can be established with any one of a variety of objects by setting up systems involving these objects; for example, having a jar with a slit in the top and repeatedly giving the child discs (washers, frozen orange juice tops, coins, etc.) that fit through the slit in the jar's top. (It helps to have a transparent glass jar so that the child can see the disc fall and hear it clink as it hits the bottom of the jar.) Soon you will find the child accepting the disc and putting it in the slit without any assistance. Once the disc-in-jar system is established in this way, you can interrupt it by starting to give the disc to the child but then suddenly changing your mind (interrupting the system) and placing it under the cup. Typically, the child will pick up or knock over the cup so he can get the disc, put it through the slit on top of the jar, and complete the system.

Another example of establishing a need is having the child repeatedly place a series of small pegs in a pegboard (this is good for developing pincer grasp) and then interrupting the system by taking the peg and placing it under the cup. Alternatively, you can set up a system by repeatedly handing the child small cars to go down a zig-zag ramp and then interrupting the system by showing the child the next car but, instead of handing it to him or her, placing it under the cup.

Allow the child to pick up the cup a few times to retrieve the object and complete the system, whether it be by putting the peg in the peg board, sending the car down the zigzag ramp, or putting the disc through the slit in the glass jar.

Once the child is demonstrating a need to get the object, he can learn to compete for it with another. The competition phase begins with the therapist (or parent) on one side holding her hands flat behind a line about a foot from the cup with the child on the other side, doing the same. The assistant says "Ready, set, go!" at which point the therapist rapidly lifts the cup with one hand and gets the object with the other before the child can do so. Then, ostentatiously, the therapist (or parent) taps her chest and proudly says, "Amie won!" Subsequently, when the child has won, the assistant helps him pat his chest and says, "Dillan won!" (see Figure 6.10).

If the special child is now "tuned in" to the challenge presented by his opponent, he will on the next and subsequent trials often move more swiftly to lift the cup before the adult can do so. (One child "solved" the problem of the competition by refusing to pick up the cup. Instead, he slid it over to himself and then—with the cup safely out of his competitor's reach—carefully lifted the cup so only he could get the object underneath.)

Advanced expansions

To further expand the competition, objects related to as many as three different systems may be used. This might be a car for the ramp, a peg for the peg board, a puzzle piece for a puzzle.

Once the child has mastered the basic competition format and is able to compete, additional concepts are added. These include concepts of "cheating" and "playing fair." The therapist "cheats" by picking up the cup before the assistant says "Go!" or by inching his or her hands over the line so they are closer to the cup than the child's hands. When this happens and the therapist is first to pick up the cup, the assistant points an accusing finger at the therapist and says, "No fair! You cheated! Your hands were closer to the cup than David's." Ultimately, of course, the intention is for the child to spot the cheating and to tell the therapist to play fair.

To further expand the competition, objects from as many as three different systems may be placed under the cup. Then, for example, if the child wins the car, he must search for the ramp to send it down; if he wins a peg, he must look for the pegboard, and so forth.

Hitting the coin

A slightly different format is used in the hitting the coin game. Here, the therapist and the child bounce a ball toward each other in an effort to hit a coin placed between them. The one who reaches five or ten hits first is the winner. Scores are written under each competitor's name. Periodically, the child is asked, "Who has more hits?" "Who is winning?" "Is it a tie?"

Here, in addition to the competition, children learn more about numbers as well as these rules of the game. Those who do so are better able to interact with typical children in various games.

Figure 6.10 Dillan, a six-year-old autistic boy, doing "competition cup" with his mother

Shifting to the other's perspective

Empathy depends on the ability of a person to see, visualize, or understand things from the other person's perspective. Children on the autism spectrum have great difficulty putting themselves in the position of the other. As Simon Baron-Cohen (1995) and Baron-Cohen, Tager-Flusberg and Cohen (2000) have stressed, autistic children's "mindblindness" has important implications for many facets of their functioning.

Among nonverbal or limited children we see this in their failure to hold a swinging door open so that it does not hit the person following them in the face. In high functioning or Asperger children, "mindblindness" accounts for their commenting on characteristics of people without regard to its potential to embarrass. For example, one Asperger child said to a woman friend of his mother's, "How come you have such a big nose?" It was also evident in another Asperger child's failure to note that his compulsive talking about airplanes was boring to his captive audience.

While I am in general agreement that "mindblindness" is an important aspect of autistic children's behavior, it is not the underlying or "core" issue. Clinical experience indicates that at the root of the autistic child's functioning is the difficulty with establishing a well-defined sense of the body/self. The remarkable account of his fragmented body experience by an autistic boy named Tito (Mukhopadhyay 2000) is consistent with this view. I suggest that only as Tito developed a more coherent sense of his own body could he attribute intentions to others. Lacking the "consciousness of body/self," the child has no basis for attributing a body/self or intentions to others. I propose that it is out of this body/self deficit that the phenomenon of "mindblindness" develops.

Before attempting to help a child achieve a shift in perspective that permits his or her sensing what another person's perception is like, it is desirable to assess how close the child is to achieving this capacity. Several tasks may be used for this purpose: One is Piaget's (1948, 1954) doll test. Two dolls are placed on a table in such a way that one doll is facing the back of the head of the doll in front. The child, facing the doll in front, is asked, "What does the doll at the the back see?"

If the child reports that the doll at the back, who is facing the back of the head of the doll in front, sees what she herself sees, then the child has failed to put herself in the position of the other.

To help correct this, the child is asked to walk around the table so that she can see what the doll at the back sees. This may have to be repeated on a number of occasions before the shift in perspective takes. Then, the child goes back to her original position and is again asked what the doll at the back sees. Can the child now overcome the impact of what she sees and draw on the prior experience of seeing the doll from the perspective of the doll at the back? If not, the child requires further work in this area.

Cards with different pictures on each side

Howlin, Baron-Cohen and Hadwin (1999) have used an elegant variant of the Piaget doll test by presenting the child with a card with different pictures on each side. For example, on one side of a card there is a picture of a dog; on the other side there is a picture of a tree. After the child has had a chance to see both pictures, the card is held up with the picture of the tree facing the child. The child is then asked, "What do *you* see?" Then the child is asked, "What do *I* [the therapist or teacher] see?"

Children who correctly report what the examiner sees demonstrate the ability to shift perspective and, in effect, place themselves in the position of the other. This task is less demanding than the Piaget doll test because it is easier to shift to a person's perspective than it is to shift to a doll's perspective.

Tic tac toe

A somewhat more advanced strategy to get at the same issue involves the "tic tac toe" game—otherwise known as noughts and crosses. The task, of course, is to see who can be first to get three circles or crosses in a row. To do this, of course, requires the child to shift to the perspective and intentions of the other. Often, even an autistic child with considerable verbal ability will get so caught up in lining up his or her own circles or crosses he or she completely "forgets" to block the path of the other. As a child learns to shift from his or her own involvement to what the competitor is doing, he or she will have more success in "blocking" the path of the other.

So, how can one train a child who seems to lack this quality? I suggest the following sequence.

Self–other differentiation

As I indicated earlier, unless the child has developed some awareness of himself or herself as separate from but related to another, there is no basis for him or her to shift perspective. In other words, the achievement of body/self–other differentiation is prerequisite for the ability to shift perspective. Without awareness of the other as a separate being, the child lacks the foundation for shifting perspective.

Identifying body parts on self and on the other

As indicated earlier, many autistic children can identify at least some of their body parts but cannot identify these parts on the person or persons opposite them. Helping the children to establish this correspondence with different people is an important precursor to experiencing others as separate from but related to them.

Mine vs. yours

Another early step toward perspective shifting is evident in the child who grasps the distinction between toys or things which are his or hers (my toys) and those which belong to someone else (your toys). Recognizing that the other "owns" toys suggests that the child is beginning to understand that the other feels about his or her special toys as the child does about his or her own toys. To help develop this capacity, parents should vigorously defend the ownership of toys and not push for premature sharing.

Turn-taking

To be able to "take turns" with another person is another early sign of developing awareness of the other's intentions. When the child learns to "wait" for the other to perform an alternating activity, the child is in effect recognizing the other person's existence and their role in the turn-taking activity.

Responding to the other's need

In the next chapter Kristina Chrétien describes in detail a technique which requires the child to notice what the other needs before a trade occurs in which the child gets what he or she needs. Let's say the child is working on a puzzle: all the puzzle pieces are next to the therapist on the other side of the table; meanwhile, the therapist is also working on a puzzle and the pieces the therapist needs are next to the child. First, the therapist and child trade puzzle pieces so that each gets from the other what he or she needs to continue the puzzle activity. Then the task is complicated by the therapist changing her task. The therapist may have, instead of a puzzle, a pegboard and needs pegs, or he or she may need a marble to send down a ramp. In order for the child to get what he or she needs, the child must notice what the therapist needs. Only when the child gives the therapist what the therapist needs can the trade be completed.

The net effect of this training is that the child has to examine and become aware of what the therapist is doing and meet the therapist's need for a particular object. When generalized, this helps teach the child how to meet the needs of others.

Responding affectively to the children

"That hurts!" To further establish an awareness of the other's feelings, teachers, therapists, and parents are urged to dramatically express themselves when the child—perhaps in an effort to make contact with them—strikes out. The teacher who forcefully says "It hurts when you do that!" gives children the opportunity to develop awareness of their own impact and to begin to sense what the other is feeling. The more vivid the teacher or therapist's response, the more likely that the child will assimilate it.

Training the child to shift from person to person

Since one facet in perspective shifting is detaching from one involvement to another, it is likely that training in shifting from person to person may help. A typical example of such training involves two people; one located to the left and one to the right of the child. Initially, the two people on either side of the child alternate saying "Here!" while giving the child a block to send down the slide. Subsequently, the blocks are offered in a rapid, unpredictable succession so that the child must swivel to the person offering the block. Through this intervention the child learns to shift rapidly from person to person and eventually *expects* to shift his or her orientation.

The therapist playing the game of tic tac toe helps the child playing with him or her to shift by telling the child "I am trying to get three in a row…" Eventually, such cues may not be necessary to have the child note the intentions of the adult and to block off the adult's effort to get three in a row.

Orienting the child to others in the class

A useful exercise in establishing more awareness of others is to have the children go through the following exercise.

Pick a child. Let's say his name is Danny. Then tell one child to put his chair to the right of Danny; another child to put her chair in front of Danny; another, to place her chair behind Danny's chair. Then, teach the "middle" concept by asking, who is in the middle? Repeat the exercise by having different children being the focal point for sitting to the left, right, in front of, and behind.

Once the children can do this, line them up two by two, then ask each child who is to the right or left of him or her, in front of and behind him or her, until they can do this from any combination of circumstances including standing in one line.

Staging situations to assess a child's understanding of a social situation

In our effort to determine how much of a social situation a child understands, teachers periodically stage a dramatic situation which requires a child's participation. One very effective sequence is when a teacher simulates falling down a set of stairs (carpeted). Then, the teacher pretends that she has hurt her ankle and asks the child with her to get help from a teacher in a downstairs classroom who has been apprised of the scheme.

In the dramatization to be described, the teacher whose help is sought is named Carol. The child involved is Zachary. Here is the sequence of events:

Teacher: (*crying out as she falls downstairs*) Oh!

Zachary—a six-year-old, limited verbal autistic boy—responds by falling down the stairs just as the teacher has.

Teacher: Zachary, I hurt my ankle (*groans*). Zachary, I need help. Zachary, get Carol!

Zachary listens impassively then hurries down the stairs presumably to get the teacher, Carol. Soon he returns with a small child whose name is Karen.

Teacher: (*groaning and holding her ankle*) Not Karen, Zachary, get Carol!

Finally, after Zachary again returns with another child, the groaning teacher says, "Carol, Zachary! Bring Carol!" And then she says with a pulling gesture, "Pull Carol!" Zachary arrives at the scene of the "accident" pulling teacher Carol by the hand.

Analysis of Zachary's response to this situation, suggests that he knew something was wrong—and so demonstrated a partial empathic reaction to the "injured" teacher's situation—after she fell/rolled down the stairs. His imitating her fall may have been a way of telling himself what had just happened. When the "injured" teacher told him to get Carol, he knew he was supposed to bring someone. However, the person he chose ("Karen") was a child. Here, he was probably influenced by the similarity between Carol, the name of the teacher, and Karen, the name of the child.

Clearly, what Zachary did not understand is that when someone is hurt you go for an adult and not a child. His eventual success in bringing teacher "Carol" seemed more due to the injured teacher's making the "pull" gesture as she said "Pull Carol" than any understanding of the total situation. Such staging dramatically highlights both a child's ability to understand and empathize with another, and the limits of this understanding.

In the next chapter, "Prelude to Communication," Kristina Chrétien describes interventions used to deepen the child's awareness of the other and which, in so doing, prepares the way for perspective shifting as well as functional communication.

SUMMARY

This chapter discussed a three-step procedure for establishing mother–child bonding. The steps include the mother physically engaging the child, cataloguing the child's various action–object systems, and teaching the mother how to insert herself within these action–object systems.

Beyond mother–child bonding, it is important to help children on the spectrum develop relationships with other children. For this to occur, the children require—in addition to self–other awareness—a range of interactive skills.

To develop self–other awareness the author introduces a range of interventions which include collision, "Grand Central Station," disrupting clothing or accessories, "I'm going to get you!" games, peek-a-boo, hide and seek, trading necklaces or neckties, and the "I see you!" game.

Turn-taking is established with the "tic toc" game, as well as the "zip zap" game, while cooperative interaction may be facilitated by two children lifting heavy objects in repairing the "messed up" classroom and by various devices such as the two-person scooter.

Competing is an important aspect of children's play and may be taught via the "competition cup" game which also permits the introduction of "cheating" and "playing fair" concepts.

Shifting to the other person's perspective may be facilitated by self–other differentiation, distinguishing between "mine" and "yours," teaching the children to respond to another person's needs, and responding affectively to the children. The chapter closed with an analysis of a staged, dramatic event to gain insight into a child's understanding of a social situation involving shift of perspective.

Chapter 7

Prelude to Communication

Kristina Chrétien

In this chapter, I will share with you some of the systems (activities) that I have found helpful when working with children with autism at the Language and Cognitive Development Center (LCDC). In the previous chapters, you have become familiar with two types of children on the autism spectrum: the ritual-captured child (closed system disorder), and the scattered child (system-forming disorder). Though no one child fits perfectly into either of these categories, these divisions are helpful when thinking about the different children and planning the interventions most likely to help them develop. As each child progresses, the differences between them tend to become less obvious. After a time, you may be surprised to find, for example, that your previously scattered child now responds best to interventions previously planned for the ritual-captured child.

SYSTEMS FOR THE RITUAL-CAPTURED CHILD

Children like Damon (described in Chapter 5) usually have developed a number of simple, repetitive action–object systems (rituals) by the time they are three years old. They show strong preference for specific objects and become intensely focused on them. They might also become fixated on certain repetitive actions—such as throwing objects. Other things which often seem to capture them are ceiling fans, running water (including toilet flushing), and swinging doors. *The Wheel of Fortune* is likely to be the favorite TV program of such children. Similarly, rolling objects such as balls and marbles are especially pleasing to them. They might, for example, put a marble on a ramp, watch it roll down, pick it up, and repeat that sequence over and over again.

Here, we see a nicely organized behavior that shows their interest in and partial understanding of cause and effect. The problem, of course, is that this kind of activity can go on for hours without any change. Abruptly remove the ramp just as the child is ready to place the marble on it (system interruption) and the child is likely to become very distressed—sometimes to the point of a catastrophic reaction. For such a child, it is as if the predictability of the little universe she had created and sustained had suddenly collapsed and thrown her into an unknown world.

Many of our ritual-captured children find comfort in lining up their favorite objects. Sometimes color markers are lined up in accord with a certain color sequence. At other times, blocks or cars may be examined for minute differences and arranged over and over, again in a way which takes these differences into account. Shape, size, and color are important attributes for a child like Damon who needs to create an ordered and consistent visual pattern. Sometimes alphabet and number puzzles with their unaltered sequences and cut-out insets, which precisely fit the letter or number shapes, become their favorites.

Before you start to work or play with a ritual-captured child like Damon, it is wise to follow the suggestions put forth in the chapter on "Getting Started with the Miller Method®." You need to observe what the child is doing while you remain passive. You observe what attracts his attention and engages him. Let us assume that our ritual-captured child is sitting on the floor, lining up his favorite toys, or removing and then systematically inserting letters into an alphabet puzzle. When engaged like this, the child appears oblivious to what is going on around him and does not notice or respond to parents' or teachers' attempts to gain his attention. What is the best way to proceed?

Before answering this question, I would like to share a basic principle of the Miller Method® (MM):

> When working with a ritual captured child's systems, begin with small expansions and—guided by the child's acceptance of these changes—gradually expand, vary, and complicate the nature and quality of the systems with which the child is engaged.

Kinds of expansions

As briefly described in Chapter 1, expansions include the introduction of people, location, object, and position changes[1] within the child's systems. Of these, the most important—given the nature of the child's encapsulation—is people. Once a child like Damon accepts a person into his previously solitary engagement with lining things up, the activity becomes interactive because it now involves the child and another person—a significant step forward for children with this disorder.

In addition to *person* there are *location* expansions. These consist of placing the object critical to the child maintaining the system at varying distances from the child. For example, if the child is engaged by marbles going down a zig-zag ramp, then a location expansion might consist of placing that marble at varying distances from the ramp.

Object expansions also play an important role. For example, we would like the child who has been engaged with marbles to accept a different object—cars—to demonstrate increasing flexibility by having cars go down the ramps previously reserved only for marbles.

Finally, there are *position* expansions. There is a tendency among children with ritual-captured styles to require that the objects handed them always come from the same orientation. By handing the child the objects from the left, the right, high, low, the child has to reach in different ways for the object she needs to maintain her systems. In doing so, her ritual becomes less rigid.

Children whose systems are expanded in this systematic manner more readily generalize the learning achieved in one setting to other settings. Now, let us get started by dealing first with the important issue of the child's awareness of people.

Increasing the child's awareness of you and others

We begin with Damon's letters of the alphabet system—not because we are interested at this time in teaching the alphabet, but because of the orderly nature of the different forms and how they fit their insets. The orderliness of the forms—each in their special inset—often captures children like Damon. However, the method described here to build people awareness applies to any system with which the child is engaged such as lining up cars, blocks, and so forth.

1   PLOP is an acronym for person, location, object, and position expansion first suggested by psychologist Dr. Louise Ross.

Give needed item to the child

Initially, you simply put the letters—one at a time—in the child's hand so that he can place them in their proper insets where he needs to put them. As long as the letters keep coming the child is content and may not give any indication that he has noticed you. Remember, the pacing of the activity is always important. You must adjust your pacing to the child's tempo. Some children need to visually inspect each letter before placing it in the proper insets in the sequence of letters. Other children are driven to complete the alphabet puzzle as quickly as possible.

Distance the item (location expansion)

Next, hold the letter (car, block, or other puzzle piece) a short distance from the child's hand. All he has to do is extend his hand slightly to get the object from your hand. Gradually increase the distance so that he has to reach toward you to get the needed object. In doing so, of course, he has to take your existence into account.

Provide resistance

Now, we want to increase the child's awareness of you still further. We do this as follows: As the child tries to take the object from your hand, exert some resistance so that the child has to pull the object from your hand. See if you can get a little "tug-of-war" going. But don't overdo it. If the child begins to get distressed, let him have a few objects without a struggle. Then, try to resist again. If this turns into a gentle teasing game between him and you, that is quite wonderful!

Including another person (person expansion)

Having gotten this far, we now want to use the child's investment in objects to help him include another person in the system (person expansion). This is accomplished by having the new person gently "tease" the child. Have the child's mother (or another person) playfully dangle the object in front of her face, a short distance from the child, saying, for example, "Here is H! Mommy has H. Get the H!" The child will most likely not understand what the mother is saying. But that doesn't matter at this point. What matters is that he starts to notice and attend to another person in order to get the item he needs to continue his system. The more people who relate to him via the object in a slightly different way—and whom he can accept within his ritual system—the more likely it is that he will become aware of you as distinct from other people.

Using the object to enhance person awareness

Now we want to deepen the child's contact with you and with other people by incorporating the various items he needs (letters, cars, blocks, etc.) to complete his ritual with simple games. Hold the letter next to your eyes. As the child looks at the letter, move it back and forth in front of your face so that as he takes in the object he also takes in features of your face. Talk to your child. "Here is Mommy. Mommy has P." After many repetitions the child will look toward you (and others who play this game with him) expectantly, while searching for the next letter.

Partially hiding the object on your body (position expansion)

Now, we work to further increase the child's awareness of you (and others) by placing the object somewhere on your body. Partially hide the letter in your shirt or pants pocket—at first letting a bit of it stick out so he can see it—then put it on your head, your shoulder, or stick it in your shoe. Vary the position of the letter *so that he has to scan you thoroughly* to find it. As the child looks toward you, point to the letter and say, "There it is! Come get it!" This activity not only helps the child become more aware of you as he scans you for his precious object, it also begins to help him follow your pointing...but more on that later.

Expand the child's "zone of intention"

Continue to increase the distance between you and the child (location expansion) so that he can begin to locate you—and his precious object— even at a distance from his body. Many children begin by only responding to things close to their bodies. Sometimes only things that are in direct physical contact or "collide" with them have any relevance. This means that anything out of their immediate "zone of intention" either does not exist or is irrelevant for them. However, by gradually increasing the distance between you and the child, the child learns to traverse increasing distances to gain from you the object needed to complete his ritualized activity. In this way, the child's zone of intention may be systematically expanded or stretched. When this expansion works, the child will walk or run across the room to get the object he needs from you.

Exploiting "maximal tension"

Incidentally, the best time to increase the distance between the child and you is at the point of "maximal tension" (Lewin 1935). This may occur when there are only a few objects (letters, cars, etc.) left that the child needs to complete his ritual (the tension builds as he sees that there are only one or two spaces to fill). However, if the attempt to establish a longer distance between him and you fails, move closer to the child so that you are within his zone of intention and he can get the object from you.

If these gradual expansions have worked, the child will walk to you and accept a short "tug-of-war" or some other playful interaction before he gets what he needs (letter, car, etc.) and walks/runs back to put it in the puzzle board or line up the car with the others. When this happens, you are now an important part of his ritual even when you are at a distance from him. Repeat this procedure as long as you can but remember to *change your location* in the room so that he has to scan the room to find you and then run to get the object needed to complete his ritual. If you are working with an alphabet puzzle, you can always count on 26 repetitions!

Vary your affective contact with the child

Try to make your contact with the child as exciting, pleasurable, and interesting as possible. Use hugs, tickles, restabilizing, and mutual face-touching to induce the child to become simultaneously aware of both you and the object he needs for his ritual. Introduce these activities before you give him the object he needs. This awareness of both you and the object is necessary before the child can roll a ball to you, hand you objects, or begin to take part in back-and-forth play with you or anyone else. It is also an important prerequisite for developing receptive language. However, before discussing receptive language, it is useful to share with you a means of establishing it—a means which was discussed in Chapter 5. But first let us summarize the various steps in developing person awareness using the child's object investment.

Summary: Increasing the child's awareness of people

- *Give needed item to the child.* The child's compulsion to complete the system with the item handed him (puzzle or alphabet piece, etc.) provides the means for building in the awareness of others as described.

- *Distance the item (location expansion).* As the child has to reach for the object he needs and which you are holding, he must begin to take your existence into account.

- *Provide resistance.* As you enter into a mini tug of war with the child around the object, his awareness of someone at the other end of the object increases.

- *Including another person (person expansion).* If you have different people holding the object he needs to complete his ritual system, the child will learn to distinguish one person from another and to go to the one who is holding the object he needs.

- *Using the object to enhance person awareness.* By moving the object he needs in front of the therapist's face, the child inadvertently takes in not only the object but also the features of the face behind the object.

- *Partially hiding the object on your body (position expansion).* By hiding or locating the object in different places on your body, he learns to scan you and to distinguish you from others.

- *Expand the child's "zone of intention."* The child learns to traverse increasing distances to gain from you the object needed to complete his ritual.

- *Exploiting "maximal tension."* If you move further away (while possessing the object he needs) at the point where he needs it most to complete his ritual, the child is more likely to recognize you at a distance.

- *Vary your affective contact with the child.* If you introduce playful interaction with the child (tickling, hugging, restabilizing, face-touching) before releasing the object to the child, the child will develop a relationship with you over and above his relationship with his precious object.

Teaching the child to hear and be guided by your requests

Before a special child can be guided by the spoken word she must first experience the spoken word as part of the action–object ritual with which she is engaged. The principle of inclusion accounts for how this occurs.

Essentially, the principle of inclusion (Miller and Eller-Miller 1989, 2000) states that when a spoken word is paired with an action–object system (ritual) the child begins to experience the word as an integral part of that ritual system. Then, when the word is presented by itself, the child has to bring into play the rest of the system.

For example, if, while the child is pushing a box (action–object system), she keeps hearing "Push…push!" soon she will experience the word *push* as part of the pushing-box system. Then, when the child hears the word "push" by itself, she will feel compelled to push something in order to complete the system.

In other words, the task for you, the parent, teacher, or therapist, is to make it possible for the child to incorporate within her ritual the sound of the human voice, her name, pointing, and the directive significance of a spoken word. If, as is often the case, the child does not respond to her name and no amount of calling gains her attention, you can use the same ritual activity described above to help her realize that the human voice is a useful signal that helps her maintain her ritualized activity. In the following sections I discuss the steps required to make this happen.

Get the child to turn toward your voice

Start by calling the child before you show him the letter (or car, etc.) that he needs to maintain his ritual. As soon as he looks toward you, pull out the letter or object. If he doesn't look at you at a distance, get so close that he cannot miss the sound being directed toward him. Again, when he comes to you, play with him for a short while before you relinquish the object he so urgently needs.

Call the child from different locations

While the child is busy inserting his letter or adding his car to the row of cars, move so that he has to turn toward the sound of your voice coming from a different part of the room. Don't be surprised if you find him looking toward the place where you were last seen instead of turning toward where your voice is coming from. Sometimes, when that method doesn't work, a mechanical sound (a bell, rattle, a squeak toy), used just before calling his name, is effective. After a time, revert only to calling without such support to find out if he can now respond only to his name.

Have different people call the child

Once the child responds when his mother calls him, he has to learn to respond to whoever calls him. To achieve this, two or more adults take turns calling him. Whoever calls the child shows him the object he needs as soon as he turns toward the caller. Again, each of you calls him from different directions. In this way, the child begins to respond, not only to his mother, but to anyone calling him from any direction. At this point, the child might or might not recognize his name, but the human voice has become part of his system, part of his reality.

Get the child to follow your pointing

Pointing, which is such a dominant behavior in the average toddler, and so important for defining the object, is strongly missing in our child. He does not point to tell us what he wants, to tell us what he sees, or to ask us what it is he sees. He neither points nor follows our pointing. How do we help the special child understand that pointing is a communicative gesture…to follow our pointing? As always, we expand on his rituals.

Let's assume that the child is inserting into his beloved alphabet puzzle letters which you are handing him one by one. He has gotten to "J" and is eager to get "K." You, now, as the child watches you, hide the K under one of two identical cups that are placed on the opposite ends of a small table. You have to hold the child back while you do this. If not, he will most likely try to snatch the letter out of your hand before you can put it under the cup. Remember, our ritual-bound child can become frantic in his need to complete the system. As soon as the letter is hidden, you point to and tap the cup containing the letter, saying "It's here!" Then, release the child, let him pick up the cup, retrieve the letter, and insert it in the puzzle board. Repeat the procedure with several more letters, alternating the cup under which you hide the letter. Swiftly place the letter under the cup so he must focus on your pointing as a cue to where the letter is located. After several repetitions of this, you hide the letter while the child is busy with the puzzle. You have to act fast. As soon as he looks up, you dramatically point to and tap the cup containing the letter. If the child consistently picks up the cup you point to and not the cup where he last found the letter, he is ready for further pointing expansions.

Increase possible locations of the needed object

Gradually increase the number of cups until you line up eight to ten identical cups. Again, hold the child back while you point to and tap the relevant cup. Next, make a row of different-colored cups. The reason for using different-colored cups is that we want to make sure it is the pointing that communicates where the object is, not the color distinction of the cups. Do not be surprised if the child reverts to searching for the object where he last found it. Our child relies on visual cues for information and these color markers are at first more compelling than our gestural and verbal directions. Eventually, the pointing wins out and we can continue the expansions.

Point to the relevant cup from a short distance (five inches). Use fewer cups and place them far enough apart so there is no ambiguity as to which cup you are pointing to.

Get the child to come to you for help

Until now, you have been close to the child, holding him back while you try to get him to focus on your pointing. If all this has worked, you can now place

yourself between the child and the cups. This can be done by placing the
puzzle board in the middle of the room and a cup on a chair or stool in each
corner of the room. As the child looks for the next letter, you gesture for him
to come to you (unlikely to work) or you catch him as he runs to pick up a cup.
Hold him, squeeze him, do reciprocal face-touching to make him aware of
you. As soon as he orients to you, point to the cup that hides his treasure.
Repeat this procedure as long as necessary. Remember to act fast and to be
precise. Eventually, the child will come to you and expect you to "tell" him, by
pointing, where to find the object. He comes to you for help and information
and understands the pointing as a communicative gesture.

Summary: Teaching the child to hear and be guided by your requests

- Get the child to turn toward your voice.
- Call the child from different locations.
- Have different people call the child.
- Get the child to follow your pointing.
- Increase possible locations of the needed object.
- Get the child to come to you for help.

Establishing the child's awareness of you as a source of information about the needed object

Toward the end of the first year, the average child will start to interact with
people around an object. The child hands you her empty bottle and expects it
back filled with milk, or she hands you her juice bottle and expects you to
open it and give it back to her. But she also hands you objects for no obvious
reason other than the novelty of watching the object pass back and forth
between herself and the other person. This hand-to-hand exchange is one of
the pre-language communication behaviors that is mostly absent in our
children.

Children with autism do not usually engage in reciprocal games. They do
not throw or roll a ball for the pleasure of seeing someone catch it and throw
it back. They do not spontaneously integrate person and object. Children like
Damon are intensely preoccupied with all sorts of objects, but, on their own,
they do not take turns, exchange, share, or play reciprocally with objects.
They often behave as if the adult trying to interact with them is an intruder.
To encourage interaction around an object, we, as always, expand on the
child's ritual.

Use a cup with a needed object to help child connect with you

As the child is lining up or in some way arranging his favorite objects (letters, cars, blocks, or what not), you drop into a cup the next object to be inserted in a puzzle or lined up and hand it to him. The child picks up the object from inside the cup, places it exactly where he wants it, and hands you back the empty cup. In the beginning, he does not understand that he has to return the cup to you. You can work on this hand-over-hand and help him place the empty cup in your hand. As soon as you get the cup, you put in the next object. In a somewhat mechanical fashion, he will give you the cup in order to get what is needed to complete his ritual. The cup becomes a shared object that passes between you.

Vary the way you put the object in the cup

Once this is accomplished, try to get his attention and have him focus on you and your actions. Dangle the object in front of your face before dropping it in the cup. Put in the "wrong" object and quickly correct yourself. Bang the object against the cup, throw it in the air, catch it, and drop it in the cup. Make it as vivid and playful as possible. You want the child to watch both you and the objects (cup and letter) and start to realize that your behavior affects him. Remember, he is highly motivated to finish his ritual and has to make sure that you do not mess it up. Stretch his limits, but avoid a meltdown.

Change the vehicle for transporting the needed object

Instead of a cup, you can use a wagon or a small toy truck to pass between you and the child. In this instance, the child is seated opposite you at a table. The table should be large enough so that the child cannot reach across and grab the desired object. You show the child the object before you slowly and dramatically place it in the wagon and send it to him. The child picks up the object and adds it to his puzzle or whatever system he has going. He is then helped to push the wagon back to you and the process is repeated until he has finished his ritual or you decide to introduce another ritual system.

It is amazing how difficult this task is for most of our children. It often takes many assisted trials before they spontaneously send the wagon back to the therapist or parent. As soon as the child intentionally sends the wagon back to you, you can expand further. Try to get the child to focus on you and what you do with the object. Again, the aim is to get him to realize that your actions at the other end of the table affect him. Use the magic of the object to hold his attention. Wrap the object in tissue paper or put it in a small box before you place it on the wagon and send it back to him. Use several boxes of different colors and hide the object in one of the boxes before you place them all in the wagon. Make certain the child sees what you are doing.

Often you will find that the child opens the box in which he last found the object rather than the box into which he saw you put the object. However, over time, the child will become more observant and aware of you and your actions. You have, in a way, tricked him into integrating you (the person) with his object interest. However, if all this has not worked and the child does not seem to understand why he has to hand you the cup or push the wagon, you need to simplify the procedure using food as a more beguiling object.

For the more limited child use food

With the child sitting opposite you, put some cereal, or a small amount of his favorite finger food, in an empty cup and hand it to him. The child picks up and eats the cereal and, with help, hands back the empty cup for more. You return it with another cereal. Continue this 15 to 20 times or as long as it takes for him to intentionally hand you the cup. Work fast. The pacing is important. If the child is allowed to "drift off," the connection is not made. Remember, give him only a morsel of food. No apricots or raisins that take forever to chew.

This procedure works just as well using the child's favorite drink. Pour a small amount (two or three teaspoons of his preferred liquid) into a cup and hand it to the child, who drinks it and hands back the empty cup. Instead of passing a cup back and forth with the desired food or drink, you can use a spoon. Try it with ice cream, pudding, or anything that is not easily eaten without a spoon. Once the child spontaneously hands you the cup or spoon, you can, as described earlier, use his ritual to integrate yourself (the person) with the object. After that, he is ready for more expansions.

Distance yourself from the child (location expansion)

Increase the distance between you and the child. First the child has to reach to place the cup in your hand, then he must walk a few steps to get to you, and finally he has to look for you to give you back the cup or spoon. This sounds so easy. It is not. If you, for example, put his desired object on a shelf and yourself a short distance from the shelf, he will likely run to the shelf and hold up the cup as if the object will magically leap from the shelf into his cup. The further you are from the object he needs, the more difficult it is for him to include you and understand your connection to the object.

Location expansion

In this case the increased distance between the child, the object, and the other person needs to be done very gradually. Once this expansion is accomplished, the child must do the same thing with other people, in different locations, and with different objects.

One of the most common mistakes that we make when working with autistic children is that we take generalization for granted. Our children *do not* automatically generalize—perhaps because they experience each object as locked into its context. To counter this, it is always wise to quickly go over all the expansions that demonstrate the existence of the object in different contexts.

After all this, we might logically expect to see spontaneous reciprocal play behavior, such as rolling a ball back and forth with another person. This tends not to happen. Our child learns to hand us objects for a specific purpose. There is at first no inherent delight—as there is for typical children— in simply watching or experiencing an object pass back and forth between him and someone else.

Summary: Establishing the child's awareness of you as a source of information about the needed object

- Use a cup with a needed object to help child connect with you.

- Vary the way you put the object in the cup.

- Change the vehicle for transporting the needed object.

- For the more limited child use food.

- Distance yourself from the child (location expansion).

Getting the child to trade objects

Up to now, we have described how—with the use of a cup or other vehicle—we can teach the child to come to us for a needed object. More challenging, however, is teaching a child to understand the concept of a "trade" where the child gives one object in exchange for another. To help the child exchange objects and to get something she needs while giving something to the other person, we again organize the interventions around the child's ritual.

Use two incomplete systems

Start by setting up, for example, two puzzles: one for the child, one for you. The child gets her favorite puzzle; you get the second best. Now, place the puzzle pieces belonging to your puzzle in front of the child and the puzzle pieces belonging to the child in front of you. The puzzle pieces the child needs should be clearly displayed, but out of reach, since you are seated at opposite ends of the table. The child is now helped to give you a puzzle piece as she gets one from you. Have the child place the puzzle piece in your hand just before you give her her piece. Once the first two pieces have been inserted, continue at a steady pace until both puzzles are completed. In the beginning this is carried out somewhat mechanically, but the child quickly learns that she does not get her puzzle piece before she has given you yours.

Expand with two other incomplete systems

You can now expand the child's behavior by exchanging other objects. These have to be objects she is interested in or fixated on. The trick is, as always, to use either objects that she needs for her ritual, such as lining up or stacking, or objects that are quickly disposed of, such as pegs dropped into a bottle. You do not want to give the child something that she is content just to hold on to and look at. The aim is to keep the exchange going.

Expand systems with new people

Once the child, without assistance, can exchange a variety of objects, you must make certain that these exchanges extend to other people. It always comes as a surprise, though it should not by now, that what the child has learned to do with one person she does not automatically transfer to another person.

Vary your incomplete systems

To increase the child's awareness of you and what you are doing, you might try to change your activity from time to time. As the child is absorbed with his puzzle, you place something new and unexpected in front of you. It is best to choose something with which the child is familiar. You might, for example, exchange the puzzle for a pegboard, a marble ramp, a few blocks, a piece of paper, or a different puzzle. You now need from the child a peg, a marble, a block, a marker, or a puzzle piece depending on what is in front of you. All the various objects are in a box in front of the child. Does the child notice what you are doing and what you need next? If not, you demonstratively play with your toy, trying to get her attention. You might, for example, drop a few marbles down the marble ramp, hold out your hand, and ask for another marble. As soon as the child hands you a marble, you give her her puzzle piece. She might need some hand-over-hand assistance for the first few exchanges. From then on, you unpredictably and randomly change your activity. The child can no longer just hand you an object. She has to look—if not at you—at least toward you and be cognizant of what you are doing and what you need. For each exchange, hold out your hand and gesture and verbalize "Give!" in an imperative and direct manner. Once she understands what is expected of her and spontaneously looks to find out what you need, you can relax the tempo and make it a less pressured and more natural exchange.

At this stage of development, it is the child's need to complete the ritual that drives her behavior and "seduces" her to attend to another person's action. As soon as the child has finished her ritual (puzzle in our example), she will most likely become oblivious of you and your request for another object and act as if you all of a sudden had disappeared. To activate her interest, you simply steal a few pieces from her completed puzzle and you are magically once again there and the exchange can continue.

Summary: Getting the child to trade objects

- Use two incomplete systems.

- Expand with two other incomplete systems.

- Expand systems with new people.

- Vary your incomplete systems.

Helping the autistic child move into a larger world

So far, we have seen how we can use the rituals to expand the child's behavior. Without these rituals—no matter how non-functional—the child might not exhibit any organized behavior. At the same time, the child is a slave to his rituals. He is compelled to complete his rituals and any sudden interruption in them can be quite traumatic. Many seemingly unprovoked tantrums are triggered by interruptions or sudden changes to the child's rituals. The child can only respond to an interruption if he has an expectation of what is supposed to happen next. At this stage, our autistic child has a limited construct of reality. Often his only predictable and secure reality is his rituals. We change his ritual and his whole world disintegrates. This means that one of our major tasks is to help make his world more predictable. We do this by helping him connect his past, present, and future actions. For this connection to happen, he must be able to interrupt and detach himself from his ritual and focus more on other aspects of his immediate surroundings.

At the LCDC we use elevated boards as a tool in our work with autistic children. For the ritual-bound child, we use these boards—particularly the Elevated Square—to help him interrupt his engagement in rituals without catastrophic reactions. We also use the Elevated Square to help him connect and integrate his actions into meaningful behavior, and to introduce him to new tasks and activities (systems).

Setting up a "jury-rigged" Elevated Square

While plans for the Elevated Square can be purchased from the Cognitive Designs website, www.cognitivedesigns.com, often the typical family has neither the space nor the resources to install an Elevated Square in their home. However, you can create your own square by arranging four picnic benches in a square configuration and placing planks across them to build up their height to the desired two to two and a half feet above the ground. Large C clamps can secure these added boards to the benches. At each corner of the square, place a small table adjusted to a height that allows the child to use it comfortably while he is standing on the bench. To do this you may have to build a small platform for each table to stand on.

We are now ready to introduce the ritual-bound child to our Elevated Square. Our goal is to help the child interrupt his preoccupation with rituals and to engage him in new and more functional activities.

Standing on the Elevated Square in front of one of the stations designated as Station 1, the child engages in one of his favorite rituals. He might line up blocks or dice or simply scoop up rice from a bucket and let it dribble down in front of his face. Whatever he is doing, it should be something that he easily gets engaged with and has difficulty interrupting. After a few minutes of this, you take his hands and firmly and quickly move him to the next table. At this Station 2, you have already prepared another activity. At the beginning of this exercise, you present the child with a similar activity. That is, if he has lined up blocks on Station 1, you let him line up cars, or anything else that is part of his lining-up rituals, on Station 2. Allow him to engage in this activity for a few seconds before you return him to Station 1. You then guide the child back and forth between the ritual at each station. Vary the time he is allowed to engage in each ritual. When he tolerates the interruptions and moves freely between the two rituals, you replace the activity on Station 2 with a less seductive activity. It could be an activity with which the child is somewhat familiar, but is not fixated on. It should not be a ritual similar to the one on Station 1. The aim is to have the child interrupt his ritual to do something different. The activity should be within or slightly outside his range of activities. Use objects and materials that he is likely to engage in. In the second activity, the child can, for example, throw blocks into a bucket of water (the bucket stands on the floor), bang on a drum, stack cans, scribble with a marker, send cars down a ramp, drop pegs into a plastic bottle, insert popsicle sticks into play dough, cut play dough with a plastic knife, spray water from a spray bottle onto an inflated balloon, throw balls into a bucket, or use a shape-board or nesting cups.

Again, you guide the child back and forth between the two activities. In the beginning, he might protest strenuously or throw himself down on the connector between stations. Be strong! If necessary, carry him to Station 2. Put his hand on the new activity and hurry him back to Station 1. After several rounds back and forth, the child seems to realize that his "world," the predictable ritual, does not disappear when he leaves it. He retains it even as he engages in something else. You will notice how he starts to look back at his favorite ritual as he is guided to the next activity and how he occasionally glances at it as he is busy with the other task. His line-up is there, he can return to it, he calms down. Once he is content to alternate between the two tasks, you set up a third activity on Station 3. You now guide the child, in a predictable sequence, between the three activities. The added activity might renew his distress. Work fast! Guide, or, if need be, carry him from one task (system) to another. When the child makes contact with the new toys or objects, just let him look at them, or observe you, as you, for a few seconds, play with them. Then hurry back to the reassuring ritual. After repeating the sequence several times, in the same order, the child is, once again, calmed by the predictable reappearance of his ritual. The child internalizes the sequence of the tasks and gains an awareness of his past, present, and future actions. You can now expect him to spontaneously interrupt his engagement in one activity and intentionally move on to the next. At this point, you should also change the order in which he engages in the tasks. If he can handle this, he is beginning to be aware that the things around him have an order that is separate from him. His world is starting to be predictable and less confusing.

Once the child has internalized the activities and the space they occupy, he starts to enjoy some, or all, of the new activities. For this enjoyment to happen, it is important that the new tasks are within the child's developmental reach and incorporate objects and materials likely to engage him.

Eventually, the child will, on his own, move around the Elevated Square going from one activity to the next. He will like some activities with objects more than others and might linger longer with them while skipping the less engaging ones. Whatever he does, he is no longer a slave to the ritual and can leave it to explore and play with other objects. At this stage, he might no longer need to start with the ritual and you can simply set up the activities you wish him to engage in. You can use the Elevated Square—or some elevated variation of it—to introduce new activities with objects. As a rule, only add one new action–object system at a time. By now you prepare for the "lesson" by introducing one new activity among a few familiar ones. Many short and repetitive contacts with a new activity works well for the ritual-bound child who tends to be resistant to change. There are also numerous objects or tasks that our child strenuously avoids. These can be "sneaked in" among more pleasurable tasks. Each contact with these undesired tasks is too short to cause real distress and, before he knows it, a soothing and familiar activity will reappear. The multisystem strategy makes it easier for the ritual-bound child to accept new objects and activities.

However, the child is not going to grow up on the Elevated Square. As soon as he feels comfortable with a task and can both play and interrupt his play, it is time to present the same task on the floor. He can now play with a few objects in a more typical and less driven fashion. Don't forget, though, that our ritual-bound child's tendency to get "stuck" will not magically disappear. He will, if allowed, simplify and change any task into a ritual and repeat it over and over, in exactly the same way. Before he becomes too fixated on his newly acquired task you must slowly expand and complicate it, or it will be lost as a functional activity.

Sometimes, a ritual-bound child is so intensely attached to a particular ritual with an object that any attempt to interrupt him with it seems impossible. You simply cannot move him from one activity to another no matter how skillfully and empathetically you try. A prolonged tantrum on an elevated structure is not recommended.

In general, our children are little acrobats who love to climb, but there is always the occasional child who reacts negatively to being elevated. In short, for a very small number of children on the autism spectrum, the Elevated Square (or other elevated structures) does not contribute to better functioning. For these, the following variation of the multisphere is often helpful.

As the child is busy with one of his rituals, you place yourself close to the child. You can stand next to him, or he might want to sit in your lap. Whatever he is doing, lining up blocks or inserting letters into his alphabet puzzle, you hand him the needed pieces one at a time. Keep an even pace. When he has, for example, lined up a few blocks and is eager for more, you hand him a different object. Whatever it is—a peg, a marble, a ball, a cup—it has to be something that he can easily and quickly dispose of. Suppose that instead of a block, you place a peg in his hand. Before he has time to be upset, you quickly help him drop the peg into a bottle or glass jar. The jar can have a lid with a cut-out circle in the middle—a hole just large enough for the peg to slip through. If your child is hypersensitive to sound, line the bottom of the jar with tissue paper. As soon as the peg is in the jar, you hand the child another four or five blocks before you surprise him with another peg. Again, help him quickly slip it through the hole and drop it in the jar before he has time to get upset. Now, continue the pattern of one peg for the bottle for every three or four blocks you give him for his lining up ritual.

When the child starts to spontaneously drop the peg into the jar as soon as you give it to him, you start giving him more pegs and fewer blocks. He is now content to alternate between blocks for lining up and pegs for dropping in the bottle. At this point you add another object, perhaps a small ball to throw or drop in a bucket. The bucket—like the jar—is within easy reach of the child. All he has to do is extend his arm and drop the ball.

Each time you introduce a new object that deviates from the pattern the child expects, you begin by giving him only one for every five or six of the familiar objects. If the child gets troubled by the intrusion of the new object and rejects it, you ease his distress by giving him only his familiar ritual object. Once he is calmed down and, for example, eagerly lining up his blocks, you again try to "sneak" in the ball. This procedure is almost always effective. As soon as he accepts the ball, you can proceed by randomly handing him blocks, pegs, and balls. Any sign of distress and you immediately go back to the blocks for lining up.

You then continue and add a new object as soon as the child, on his own, can put away all the previous ones. More than five to six object systems becomes cumbersome, as there is a limit to the number of containers you can place within the reach of the child. Apart from pegs and small balls, you can, for example, use small cars to send down a slide, rings to place on a pole, cups to stack or put on cup hooks, shapes to push in a shape box, puzzle pieces to place in different puzzle boards, or tissue paper to squeeze into the narrow neck of a bottle with water inside. Be inventive and use as many different objects as possible.

The child is now, while standing or sitting in one place, randomly getting five or six different objects. He knows what to do with each one of them. They are not all lined up…you use them differently. For our child it is the beginning of functional use of objects.

It is now time for location expansions. That is, you gradually increase the distance between the place where the child receives the object and the place where he acts on the object. A few inches at a time is all some children can tolerate, whereas others can handle more dramatic changes in location. As a rule, the more familiar the object is, the more distance the child can tolerate without losing track of what he wants to do with it.

If all has gone well, we can now expect the child to look at and recognize the object we placed in his hand, scan the room to see where it belongs, walk or run there, act on the object (drop it in its container), and come back to us for another object. The child, by now, is not only "weaned" from his ritual, but he shows some nice intentional behavior and is starting to play with a few objects in a functional manner. It looks great! But be reminded, there are seldom any giant leaps in his development. All new and unfamiliar objects initially have to be introduced as described. Stand close to the child's body, sneak it in while the child is busy with a favorite activity, and expand the distance once he knows what to do with the object. Luckily, this process goes faster and faster with time.

As the child's world expands and he starts to use a variety of different objects, introduce him to more "typical" toys. Continuing the same process, give him symbolic toys, such as small cars to "drive" down a slide, dolls to put in bed, spoons to feed the dolls, little animals to "walk" into a barn, frogs to "swim" in a bucket of water, and so on. This is, of course, not yet true symbolic play, but it gets the child to handle symbolic toys and to use them according to their representational features.

SYSTEMS FOR THE SCATTERED CHILD (SYSTEM-FORMING DISORDER)

We now go on to the scattered child on the autism spectrum. In doing so let's first reiterate that most children do not fit neatly into any of the categories. Most often what we find is a child with an emphasis on one kind of pattern but who nevertheless shows properties of the other pattern. It is, for example, not unusual for a scattered child—while showing primarily scattered behaviors—to sometimes shift to behavior suggestive of the ritual-captured child. That is, the child may run around the room oblivious of his surroundings but then, suddenly, stop and pick up an object, perhaps a spoon or a pen, and then become intensely involved with that object that he treats in a stereotypic fashion. He might twist it in his hands or simply hold it up to his face and look at it from the corner of his eyes. This may occupy him for some time while he seems at that time much more lost in his own world than scattered. Then again, he will pick up objects and drop them as soon as he turns his head, distracted by something else. Objects literally fall out of his hands, forgotten, as he turns toward a new object or event. For the scattered child, objects are not part of any system or ritual. They don't belong anywhere and they have no function or meaning.

The scattered child is often labeled hyperactive. He seeks movement and jumps, twirls, or simply runs around. On a playground structure where he gets haptic feedback (combining touch with proprioception), he can be surprisingly adaptive; a real little acrobat. He is a fast and agile climber but easily distracted and without any awareness of danger. He needs constant supervision and leaves us exhausted at the end of the day.

For our type of interventions, the important distinction between the closed system, ritual-captured child and the scattered child is the scattered child's lack of rituals (systems). He has no need to complete a ritual and we cannot seduce him with objects and in so doing become part of his ritual. There isn't any behavior we can expand on and make more functional. This, initially, makes him a more challenging child to work with.

Establishing an action–object system

Before we can do anything else, we must help the child develop a ritual or system, a simple two- or three-step activity that we can expand on and become part of. We choose activities that are similar to what the typical child engages in during her first two or three years of life: Dumping, filling, nesting, stacking, pushing, and pulling objects are all part of early play behavior. We also want to use objects that the child finds exciting. Many autistic children, including the scattered child, like to watch moving objects. They seek movement, both motorically and visually. Outside, they like to dribble sand, dirt, or leaves in front of their faces. Inside, they can, if allowed, spend hours in front of running water. For them, jumping in front of anything in motion, such as a moving picture on a TV screen, is pure bliss. Over the years, we have designed numerous systems for our children, but the most successful, by far, is the "pouring water" system.

Prepare the room

For the scattered child you want to avoid any unnecessary distraction. Keep the room as plain, empty, and quiet as possible. It might help to cover the windows with a shade or a cloth. Also, make sure that all toys and materials not in use are stored out of the child's sight.

Start the water-pouring system

To start the system, have on hand two large plastic buckets (trash cans will do fine) and fill 20 or more plastic bottles with water. (I collect and use empty soap-bubble bottles, which are just the right size for small hands.) Place the buckets next to each other and position the child in front of one of the buckets. Stand behind the child, who is now caught between you and the bucket. Keep the child as contained as possible. The bottles need to be within easy reach. Place one of the bottles in the child's hand and help her pour the water into the bucket. Then guide her hand to the second bucket and, if she doesn't drop the bottle into it, help her release her grip on the bottle by using the knuckle-pressing technique (see Figure 4.2) so that the bottle falls into the bucket with a satisfying clunk. If this sounds pedantic, it is because our scattered child (with system-forming disorder) needs very precise hand-over-hand assistance to complete a system. On her own, she might not hold the bottle, might not know how to pour, and, if she does, she might drop the bottle as soon as the water starts to pour. Then, again, she might cling to the bottle with surprising strength—almost as if it had become an extension of her hand. You have to physically model each step, each action part of the system.

As soon as the empty bottle drops into the bucket, swiftly place another one in the child's hand, guide her hand to the water bucket, and help her pour. Repeat this sequence as long as you can, or as long as the bottles of water last. Work fast and try to get into a rhythm of pour–drop–pour–drop. The child will likely squirm and wriggle and try to get away. No matter how loving and gentle you are, you are imposing your actions on the child and making her engage in an activity she cannot do on her own. The rapid repetition of the same actions is essential if she is going to integrate the several parts of the system. This cannot be done in a casual or haphazard way.

After a while, perhaps 20 bottles later, you will notice that the child is beginning to move with you. Withdraw your support for a few seconds and see if she continues the activity on her own. If she does, it will most likely not last long. She might do part of the system and, for example, continue to pour the water, but will fail to drop the empty bottle in the correct bucket. Instead, she allows the bottle to fall from her hand into the water and makes no attempt to retrieve it and continue the activity. On her own, she cannot re-establish the system. You must do it for her. Do not let her escape, but quickly place another bottle in her hand and continue to provide her with hand-over-hand guidance as needed. Most critical are the connecting steps. These are learning to drop the empty bottle in its designated container and reaching for another bottle. When the child starts to lead in anticipation of what should happen next, you can probably withhold your support altogether. When she continues on her own, she has internalized the sequence. She "owns" it and it has become part of her mental structure.

Once the child has formed a system, such as the "pouring water system," she might, if allowed, carry it out in the exact manner in which it was originally presented to her. The system easily becomes a ritual and will stay that way if we are not vigilant to help her expand and vary it. I remember one little boy who found the bottles before the buckets were in place and started to pour the water on the exact spot where the water bucket used to stand and then drop the empty bottles where the other bucket should have been. I cannot stress enough how important it is to systematically expand and vary a system once it is firmly established.

Expansions for the scattered child

The expansions are basically the same for the scattered child with system-forming disorder as they were for the ritual-captured child with closed system disorder. Instead of letters and numbers, you work with bottles (or whatever objects you used to establish the basic system). In general, the scattered child needs more hand-over-hand assistance and more repetitions both to form a new system and to incorporate new expansions. Each expansion usually requires more time and might not go as smoothly as it did for the closed system child.

Location expansion can be especially tricky for the scattered child. He has difficulty maintaining organization when he moves around and is easily distracted by extraneous stimuli. Often the location expansions have to be done on the Elevated Square to provide the structure he requires. No matter how much the scattered child eventually enjoys an activity, he is never as driven to maintain or finish it as the child with closed system disorder. The scattered child's systems never "pull" the child in the same way as does the system for the ritual-captured child. Interruptions usually do not result in tantrums and you need not worry about transitioning him from a favorite activity to another one. Instead, you worry about maintaining the child's engagement and how to get him to return to an activity once it has been interrupted.

Location expansion for the scattered child

When the sequence (picking up, pouring, and dropping) is solidly integrated and the child, on his own, turns to pick up the next bottle, gradually increase the distance so that he has to reach for the bottle. At this point the scattered child might not look around for the bottle or walk across the room to get it. His engagement is maintained only as long as he stays near the objects. His "zone of intention" is often limited to his arm's length. To increase the distance over which he can function, we structure the activity on the Elevated Square.

Location expansion on the Elevated Square

Place one bottle filled with water on Station 1. Place only one bottle at a time on the station. The other bottles are under the table (Station 1) within easy reach for the adult. Now, help the child pick up the bottle and guide him to Station 2 where he pours the water into the bucket which is standing on the floor directly below. With the empty bottle in his hand, guide the child to Station 3 where he drops the bottle into another bucket, which is also standing on the floor. He then returns to Station 1 and picks up another bottle filled with water. Repeat this sequence (picking up, pouring, dropping) until the child anticipates what is going to happen next and without help maintains his engagement while he walks from station to station. That is, until his "zone of intention" has increased. This increased zone may not happen the first few times you attempt it. It has to be repeated for a short time over several days or weeks before it "takes."

Structure the system on the floor

Remember, the Elevated Square is a tool that is used only as long as needed. As soon as the child has integrated the correct sequence of the water-pouring activity, independent of its location on the square, it is time to structure this same activity on the floor. Start by arranging the objects in more or less the same configuration as they originally occupied on the Elevated Square. Place the bottles, one at a time, on a small table or stool, the water bucket a few steps away, and the bucket for the empty bottles another few steps away. Then, gradually increase the distance between the stations on the floor to as far as the child can handle and still complete the system. Also make sure the arrangement of the bottle and the buckets vary so that the child has to constantly search for them. As always, the child must integrate the actions (picking up, pouring, dropping) regardless of the location of the objects. Eventually, the child will stay engaged as he walks from room to room or up and down a flight of stairs.

He might, for example, get a bottle of water in the kitchen and walk up the stairs to pour out the water in the upstairs bathroom. "Typical" behavior necessitates integration of our actions over space and time and awareness of our past and future actions. Before we get carried away and send the child on a bus across town to pick up bottles, we return to the playroom where the child has just learned to walk a few steps without "forgetting" what he is doing.

Increasing the child's awareness of you and others

Once the child enjoys the "water-pouring" activity and will walk a few steps to get the next bottle to continue the activity, it is time to increase her awareness of people. We now have a chance to become part of her system—to be included in her world. Follow the same procedure as described for the ritual-captured child. Instead of numbers and letters, simply use bottles of water, or whatever objects were used to form the child's first system. Have the child reach, come, and run to you to get the needed object (bottle). Play with her, tease her, and use any trick you can to get her attention.

Teach the child to hear and be guided by your requests

Again, use the same procedures described earlier. When getting the child to follow your pointing, you must use non-transparent bottles so that she cannot see which bottle contains water. Remember to start by using identical bottles before introducing bottles of different colors, shapes, and sizes. Our child relies heavily on visual cues for information and must learn to ignore the properties of objects (bottles) and to focus only on the guidance provided by the pointing.

Getting the child to interact with you around his needed object and to trade objects

The scattered child will probably respond best if, rather than having her hand you the empty bottle and waiting while you fill it up with water, you use a cup with food. The scattered child has little capacity to wait and, initially, needs the shared object (cup) to pass back and forth between her and the other person at a rapid speed.

You will also notice that the scattered child is not easily seduced into handing objects. The pull to continue the activity is simply not as strong as it is for the ritual-captured child. However, though performing the activity with her requires more repetitions and a faster pace, the scattered child will eventually come to you to get objects, will respond to her name, will follow pointing, and will share and trade objects.

Helping the scattered child expand his world

By now, our child has one meaningful play activity, but we certainly want her to do more than pour water—no matter how efficiently she does it. She has to develop a repertoire of play behavior where she uses toys and objects in a variety of ways. Each new behavior must also become interactive and include other people—both adults and children.

To increase the child's repertoire of meaningful behavior, we have to expand on her existing behavior. In our example, that is the "water-pouring" system that we helped her form. With the scattered child, it is important to remember that all new systems and expansions of systems must be introduced close to her body. The child sits or stands in one spot as she learns to manipulate and explore unfamiliar objects and integrate new actions within previously learned systems. Once she has mastered the new system or expansions, make certain she can maintain her engagement over distance. The location expansions work best when structured on the Elevated Square. Having worked on the Elevated Square and then on the ground, you can now alternate between working on the floor or at the table, and on the Elevated Square.

Further expansions of the water-pouring system

The child stands or sits in front of the two big buckets. You are right behind her. Next to the child is a table from which she picks up the bottles. By now, she likes the activity of picking up, pouring, and dropping, and carries it out with only a minimum of guidance.

Add one additional step at a time

First close the previously open bottle with an easy-to-open lid. The child picks up the bottle and, with hand-over-hand assistance, unscrews the lid—a new behavior—and drops it into a container. She then, on her own, pours the water, drops the empty bottle in the other bucket, and turns to pick up the next bottle. This sequence is then repeated for about five to six minutes. Work at an even, brisk pace and don't let the child escape. If the child demonstrates ability to integrate the new steps (unscrewing the lid and dropping it in the container), it is desirable to try it again later or the next day to make certain it is firmly established as part of the original system.

Now and then, a child will have difficulty with part of the system. For example, unscrewing the lid can be challenging both cognitively and motorically. For children with poor fine-motor skills or some difficulty starting an action (apraxia) this can be frustrating. In such a case, work separately on unscrewing the lid before incorporating it within the system.

Once the child has incorporated the new behavior within the system, continue with further expansions.

Pull a wagon

Place the bottle on a small wagon with a string attached. The child pulls the wagon, first with help, then by herself; picks up the bottle, unscrews the cap, drops the cap in a container, pours the water, and drops the empty bottle in the other bucket. Repeat the sequence until the child can do it on her own or until you run out of bottles.

Discriminate between different substances

Place an additional bucket for rice next to the water bucket, then place two bottles without caps on the wagon. One bottle is filled with water, the other with rice. The child pulls the wagon, picks up one of the bottles, and inspects it to determine what is inside. She is then guided to the correct bucket and pours water in the water bucket or rice in the rice bucket. She then drops the empty bottle in the empty-bottle bucket, picks up the remaining bottle, empties it in the correct bucket, and again pulls the wagon (loaded by the therapist with two more bottles) and deals with the new bottles in the same way. Repeat the sequence until the expansion is well integrated and the child spontaneously inspects the bottles to determine what is inside.

Add another substance

Place four buckets next to each other on the floor and three bottles filled with three different substances on the wagon. You can use beans or peas in the third bottle. The procedure is the same, with the exception that the child must now discriminate between three different substances and note into which bucket they must go. The empty fourth bucket adds to their challenge.

Extend the sequence

To develop the child's cognition, the sequence of required actions that the child must integrate becomes longer and longer. You can, for example, place two bottles with two different substances on the wagon. Close one or both of them with a cap. The extended sequence now goes as follows: The child pulls the string to bring the wagon to herself, picks up one bottle, unscrews the cap, drops the cap in the container for caps, notices what is inside the bottle, pours out that substance in its correct bucket, drops the bottle in the empty bottle container, and turns (after you have placed two more bottles on the wagon) to pull the wagon to get two more bottles. As always, the sequence is repeated (with narration) as long as possible or until the child has integrated the steps and can carry it out on her own. Once the child knows the sequence, she delights in the structure and predictability of the activity and often wants to continue even after all the bottles have been emptied. Luckily, the scattered child, in contrast to the ritual-captured child, can easily be diverted to the next task.

Distinguishing content from container

Up to now, the child has tended to fuse what was in the bottle with the bottle itself. In other words, the child tends to expect that water can only be poured from a bottle and not from a cup or other container. Instead of only bottles, now use cups, mugs, plastic glasses, etc. to hold the substances being poured. Also vary the substances that go into the different container so that, for example, rice is not always poured from the mug and so forth. When the container is empty, the child has to dispose of it in its correct location—mugs with mugs, cups with cups, and so forth. Now the complex task requires the child to be aware of and act on both the contained substance and the container. She is challenged, both cognitively and motorically, to adapt to small, but frequent changes in her surroundings. If you present the child with four different containers (cups, bottles, mugs, glasses) and three different substances (water, rice, beans), you have 12 different combinations, each of which must be dealt with in a slightly different manner. Always try to build in small, unpredictable changes within a well-established system whose basic structure remains constant. The child pulls, picks up, pours, and discards the empty containers. As always, repeat as long as needed, while remaining attentive to the child's state.

SUMMARY

In this chapter Kristina Chrétien shared the subtleties of treating "ritual-captured" (closed system) children as well as "scattered" (system-forming disordered) children. She stressed the importance of the principle of inclusion and of expanding the children's systems.

Kristina introduced creative ways of increasing the child's awareness of you and others by using, for example, the orderliness of alphabet forms that fit into their insets. She described how to go about expanding the child's "zone of intention" and how to exploit "maximal tension" to enhance the child's reactivity to the therapist.

She also described how to teach the child to hear and be guided by your requests as well as to establish the child's awareness of you as a source of information about the needed object.

In "Getting the child to trade objects"—an important precursor to communication—Kristina described the use of two incomplete puzzles and how the child offers the therapist the puzzle piece he or she needs in return for one that the child needs.

Commenting that the autistic child is "not going to grow up on the Elevated Square," she described in detail procedures for moving the child to the ground and to a larger world and how to wean the child from his or her rituals.

Discussing systems for the "scattered" child (system-forming disorder), Kristina stressed that this child "has no need to complete a ritual" so that there must be a great deal of repetition and use of very compelling, rapidly paced spheres (such as the water-pouring sphere) in order to form systems. She notes, also, that as the scattered child forms systems the expansions used are the same as those for the "ritual-captured" child.

Note from Arnold Miller

Kristina Chrétien is a master therapist with over 25 years' experience at the LCDC. Her skills and success with very challenging children are legendary. Much loved by parents, children, and staff, she is also known for her creative development of unique systems to engage the children. Now in semi-retirement—although periodically induced to participate in parent–child training at the LCDC—she graciously agreed to write this chapter so that others may benefit from her long experience and exceptional gifts.

Chapter 8

Becoming a Child Who Communicates

Father: ...the first word that had significance for him [Jack] was *bear* so we got him a pull toy with a bear in it and he pulled it at home just as he had at the center. He recognized it immediately and began to pull it around the room. It was his bear on wheels.

In the previous chapter Kristina Chrétien described how she treated two very different kinds of children, and how word-deaf autistic children begin to hear and be guided by spoken words (p.139). Pairing manual signs with spoken words both on the Elevated Square and on the ground was certainly a critical factor in this achievement. However, to communicate, the child must also be able to use signs and words to influence the behavior of others. Before sharing strategies that helped Damon and children like him to achieve reciprocal communication, it's useful to consider why manual signs are so important in this process.

WHY SO MUCH EMPHASIS ON USING MANUAL SIGNS?

There are a number of important reasons for emphasizing the use of signs with autistic children. The first reason is that spoken words are sounded one moment and are gone the next. This ephemeral quality makes it difficult for special children to "hold" words long enough to derive meanings from them. They literally do not know how to hear spoken words. All this changes, however, when spoken words are presented with manual signs that closely resemble their actions or object meanings. For example, it is not surprising to find that the manual sign for *eat* or *eating* (bringing hand to mouth) is more readily understood than the word *eat*, which lacks a visible link to eating. However, when the spoken word "eat" is paired with the eating sign, the special child has an opportunity to hear *and* see the combined form which relates to eating. Then, as the spoken word "eat" becomes fused with the eating sign—and both become part of the eating system—the child is able to invest the spoken word with the same *eat* meaning as is expressed by the eating sign.

The unique power of manual signs becomes clearer as we note that the understanding and use of gesture signs, such as reaching to be picked up, occurs earlier in development than does the understanding and use of spoken words. Studies (Acredolo and Goodwyn 1996; Goodwyn, Acredolo and Brown 2000) have shown that not only do typical infants aged as young as 8—12 months understand and communicate with gestural signs, but that those who are taught signs subsequently develop and maintain *more effective spoken language* than those who have not been taught signs. The documented ability of manual signs to contribute to spoken language is entirely consistent with our own research with children on the autism spectrum: This research (Miller and Miller 1973), since replicated by Konstantareas (1984, 1987) as well as by Konsantareas, Oxman and Webster (1977), demonstrated that nonverbal children who were previously unable to follow verbal directions could do so after they were simultaneously taught with both signs and spoken words. After training with signs and words, they were able to follow spoken directions even when spoken words were used alone.

But what about the frequently voiced concern that "the child will learn to depend on manual signs and therefore not learn to understand or use spoken words?" For almost all the hundreds of nonverbal special children with whom we have worked, manual signs paired with spoken language have resulted in the child understanding at least some spoken language—often for the first time. And, for some of these children, we find that the signs "pulled" spoken words and contributed to expressive spoken language. Then, as spoken language demonstrated its greater utility (since the child could not see or direct signs to people around corners), the use of spoken words became more frequent while the use of gesture signs gradually decreased. The other advantage of signs—and why it is important to use them—becomes apparent when a child tries but cannot retrieve a desired spoken word. Encouraged to use the appropriate manual sign, the child is often able to produce the spoken word which had previously been used with the sign.

Another important aspect of manual signs is their availability. The child always has his or her hands with him or her to communicate intentions. Further, the signs used are often iconic—in that they so closely resemble their referents, they are often easily understood by people who have not had exposure to sign language. In the next section we will describe the signs we introduce and the situations we construct to help make these signs—and the spoken words fused with them—a functional means of communicating.

THE INFLUENTIAL SIGN/WORD-MAKING CHILD

To begin to communicate, children who have learned to be guided by signs and words must learn how to use these same signs and words to guide the behavior of others. The more the child understands that his or her signs and words can influence others, the more defined the sign or word becomes as a precious and powerful tool. At schools using the Miller Method® (MM) we begin to develop these expressive abilities on the Elevated Square. To bring this about we need to make the therapist an integral part of the child's systems. Once that occurs, the therapist is able to trigger communication around the system that he or she now shares with the child. In the following I describe how this happens.

Inserting the therapist in the child's action–object systems

In previous chapters we described how the children form systems at each of the stations. These systems may involve pouring water over a water wheel, pushing blocks or bowling pins off a station into a metal can, sending cars down ramps, cutting clay into pieces, completing puzzles, and so forth. However, these systems *do not directly include the therapist*. The procedure which allows the therapist to become part of the child's system occurs as follows.

At first, the therapist simply narrates the system by saying "Jeremy *pours* water over the water wheel!" or "Jack *pushes* the blocks into the can!" The therapist vocally accents the verb part of the narration as she makes the appropriate pouring or pushing gesture with the spoken word.

When these action systems are well established, the therapist begins to expand them to include a turn-taking component. For example, "Jeremy pours… Lisa [therapist] pours!" or "Jack pushes… Lisa pushes!" and so forth. When the child consistently pauses for the therapist to take her turn, the procedure is again modified.

This time, just before the therapist takes her turn pouring or pushing, she pauses (interrupting the system). The child—needing to have the system continued—may either say the appropriate word or make the gesture (pouring or pushing gesture), to which the therapist immediately responds by performing the expected action while narrating her own action, "Lisa pours...[or pushes]."

A supplementary procedure involves the therapist abruptly "stealing" the bottle (interrupted system) just before the child is ready to pour or stopping the car from going down the zig-zag ramp just before the child is ready to send it down; or preventing the child from pushing the blocks by interposing herself in front of the blocks to be pushed. Confronted with such interrupted systems, children frequently will produce the gesture or word needed to have that system continued. When either compensatory gesture or word is produced, the therapist behaves as if the child was directing it to her and immediately completes the action.

The child uses "Come!" with a gesture to influence another

The reader will recall that during the initial work on the square, Damon learned to respond to his mother's and therapist's sign/word *come* at all parts of the square. Now, the challenge was to teach the child to make the *come* gesture and the word "Come!" to bring therapist or mother to him. Unlike the other signs, the sign for *come* exerts its influence over distance.

The general procedure used entailed the child sitting at one end of the square—usually on a box—with the therapist behind the child to help him form the beckoning *come* gesture. The mother, at the opposite end of the square which was opened by removing the short connector, was instructed to take one dramatic step each time the child—with assistance from the worker behind him—made the beckoning *come* gesture. As the child's mother came within three or four feet of the child, the therapist released the child's hands. After a number of trials, the child often suddenly grasps the relation between his or her hand movements and the mother coming closer and begins to make rapid *come* gestures—sometimes *saying* "Come! Come!"—and resulting in the mother running rapidly to her child to give a big hug. Subsequently, the *come* gesture was expanded to be used with therapist and others as well as at home with family.

In the case to be described, the child did not respond as expected, so other measures were taken:

Developing a functional *come* sign: A mini case study

A fairly common problem in trying to establish the *come* sign to bring someone closer concerns the autistic child who seems not to understand that he or she must make specific movements of the hands against the chest to bring someone closer.

Amy, a four-year-old, nonverbal child, had been able to achieve only the sign for *more*, which consisted of putting her finger tips together. She used this sign for everything and had, up to this time, been unable to achieve any other sign. Instead of the *come* sign she kept reproducing the *more* sign.

Amy had previously formed a strong water-pouring system. Consequently, after she had used a number of bottles to pour water in a bucket, the system was interrupted by the therapist taking the last bottle of water—and backing away from her—to get her to make the *come* sign. The therapist then planned to come to Amy with the bottle she needed to continue the water-pouring system. Her assistant worked behind Amy in hand-over-hand fashion to model the *come* sign.

In response to the bottle being held toward her, Amy again produced her standard *more* sign. When that failed to produce the desired effect on either her mother or her therapist, she began to try to use the hands of the assistant behind her who had been modeling her hands. Finding that even after a dozen trials she was still unable to use her hands, I interrupted the effort.

Hand awareness

Reasoning that Amy's failure to use her hands might stem from a lack of awareness of how her hands worked, I set up a situation in which she would have to use her hands. With Amy lying down, some weighted objects (telephone books) were placed one at a time on her chest. As soon as a book was placed, Amy pushed it off, first with the right hand then with the left hand. Sometimes, one hand was held so that she would have to use the opposite hand. After five minutes of this she was returned to the *come* situation.

Immediately after the therapist again held out the bottle of water, Amy moved her hands decisively toward her chest in a perfect beckoning gesture, with the clear expectation that this movement would bring the therapist (and the bottle) a step closer. Subsequently, this new *come* sign was used with different people and from different locations to the child's obvious delight and the delight of all watching as she succeeded in bringing people closer to her.

Amy seemed to have become more aware of her hands through the exercise of using them to push books off her chest. This new hand awareness allowed her to use her hands in a different way to make this new sign to bring people closer. Similar interventions should be used with other children when their lack of hand awareness interferes with their ability to generate new signs. However, as we shall see in the next section, lack of hand awareness is but one part of a general body awareness issue confronted by autistic children as they try to communicate.

THE BODY–OTHER CHALLENGE TO COMMUNICATION

Several observations by parents illustrate what I mean by the body–other challenge to communication.

The first example has a humorous quality because it shows the resourceful manner in which five-year-old Jack—an autistic boy who lacked a clear sense of himself in relation to another—was able on at least some occasions to work around that challenge:

> Jack very much wanted one of the chocolate chip cookies that his mother had just baked. While he had some words, he didn't know how to ask for something directly. He finally solved the problem by imitating his mother's voice asking him "Jack, do you want a cookie?" to which he answered in his own voice, "Yes!"

Apparently, it was much easier for Jack to replay the entire situation than to directly say, "I would like a cookie!"

Without an adequate sense of the distinction between the body/self and other or between body/self and object, children cannot directly initiate actions, signs, or words to communicate their intentions. Then, you get the kind of behavior that a mother described for her six-year-old autistic son, Eddie.

> Eddie's mother reported: "I finally got Eddie to make the signs for *get up* and *sit down*. Then, I tried to get him to use those signs to tell his sister to get up and sit down. The problem was that each time he made the sign for *get up*, he got up; every time he made the *sit down* sign, he sat down. He didn't have the foggiest idea that the signs were supposed to influence his sister who was sitting not four feet from him."

Perhaps Eddie's mother would be less frustrated if she understood that his behavior reflected an important stage in language development. Typical children from 14 to 20 months of age display a similar need to relate their new words to themselves before they are able to use these words to refer to others. For example, one 20-month-old girl (McNeil 1970) said "Walk!" as she got out of a cart to walk, "Away!" as she pushed an object away, and "Blow!" as she blew her nose. While typical children soon learn to relate their words not only to themselves but to others, special children like Eddie often get "stuck" at the earlier stage and need help to make this shift.

> In Eddie's case the effective intervention required him to make the *get up* sign while he remained seated and the *sit down* sign while he remained standing. In this way we taught him that the signs he made did not have to relate only to himself. We accomplished this by his mother or therapist physically holding him in his seat while helping him make the *get up* sign and then preventing him from sitting down while he was making the *sit down* sign. Then, since his *get up* sign while seated induced his sister to get up and, later, when he made the *sit down* sign, to sit down while he remained standing, he had repeated opportunity to notice that his hand gestures influenced her independent of whether he was standing or sitting.

As children like Eddie suddenly "get the idea" that their signs can influence someone's behavior, they sometimes get excited and try to make all members of the family get up and sit down. It is wise to go along with this new ability the first day or so—perhaps as a substitute for calisthenics—until the special child fully grasps the "magic" that his gestures brought about. Children who "break through" in this way often accumulate a whole range of action signs to communicate their needs and intentions.

It is exciting to watch a child grasp the notion that signs for *come* or *get up/sit down* can influence the behavior of another. But it is illusory to think that the "breakthrough" extends to the effective use of *all* language. As the next section indicates, it is more difficult for autistic children to refer to objects than it is to refer to actions.

Sign/words for actions vs. sign/words for objects

My decision to begin with sign/words for actions over those for objects was based on the fact that signs such as *come/go, eat, push, pull, pick up, drop, get up/sit down,* and so forth closely resemble their action referents. These signs relate in a 1:1 manner to their actions. This similarity makes it relatively easy for the children to respond to these sign/words and to use them effectively. Sign/words for objects are more difficult for the children. For example, even though there is a clear *cup* sign for cup (lifting an imaginary cup to the mouth as if to drink from it), that sign may not generalize readily to a cup hanging from a cup hook or placed upside down on a table. Similarly, the sign for *bird* (beak motion simulated with thumb and forefinger) must refer to a quick-moving, chirping entity that flaps its wings, pecks, digs for worms, or may come close and eat from one's hand. Unlike action signs, which clearly relate to a single action, the signs for objects attempt to refer to an object which has multiple properties or functions. Beyond this, there are all kinds of cups that are called cups and all kinds of birds that are called birds.

The "pull" of context

Still another aspect of the relation between the sign/word and its object is the child's experience of objects as "locked" into their familiar settings. For them, it is as if the object and its usual context are one entity. Place the object in a new setting and the object may suddenly not exist for them. Tito, the nonverbal autistic boy from India who learned to communicate his experience in writing (Mukhopadhyay 2000), described what it felt like to see his familiar toys in the new home his family had moved into:

> It was a terrible feeling to be in the new house. The toys looked so different and frightening that the boy [Tito always refers to himself in the third person] stopped playing with them. He could not find any association between things that changed places. (p.9)

This means that, in addition to the problem of relating to an object with several properties, there is also the problem of recognizing the object as an entity by itself no matter where it is located. These issues result in children having different levels of understanding with regard to the sign/word–object relation. Even when the child has some notion of the relation between a sign/word and its object one must determine the level at which the child understands and can maintain this relation.

Levels of sign/word guidance

An autistic child may have sufficient sign/word guidance to give a requested object when that object is in its familiar place in the room but not outside that room. More advanced is the child who—when the object is requested—can get an object from another room as long at that object is in its familiar place (milk in the refrigerator; shoes on the floor) but is at a loss when the requested object cannot be found in its expected place, such as when the shoes are on the table. Most advanced is the sign/word-guided child who can get a requested object from another room even when the object is not in its usual place.

Kol'tsova (cited by Luria 1981) documents changes in the word–object relation as a typical child develops from the age of six months to the latter part of his or her second year. In this study Kol'tsova would name an object in the child's presence so that the child typically turned his or her eyes in the direction of the designated object and stretched a hand toward it:

> In the early stages, the child acquired the object reference only if he or she was placed in a certain position (e.g., in a lying position), if the word was accompanied by a *specific pointing gesture* [my italics] and if the word was presented with a certain intonation… Hence, if a child of 6 or 7 months was lying down and heard his or her mother's voice naming an object, the child responded by turning its gaze toward the object. However, the child failed to respond if any of these conditions were changed (e.g., if the child was in a sitting position).
>
> During the next stage, the child's position (e.g., lying or sitting) was no longer important for retaining the object reference of the word, but the identity of the speaker, the intonation of the voice, and the gesture accompanying the utterance continued to have a decisive influence. If the word "cat" was pronounced by the mother, the child turned his or her gaze toward it. However, if the same word was uttered by the father, the child did not respond in the same way.
>
> At later stages, the identity of the speaker ceased to be an important factor in evoking a response to a word, but the child obtained the object reference only when the utterance was accompanied by a pointing gesture… It is only by the end of the child's 2nd year that the word is completely emancipated from these attendant conditions and acquires its stable object reference. (pp.46–47)

Sign/word-guided vs. context-guided children

If a child has developed a stable reference between a sign/word and its object—independent of the surrounding context—we refer to that child as "word-guided." If, on the other hand, a child's ability to refer to an object depends on a fixed context (as in the example above) we refer to the child as "context-guided." A context-guided child has not yet found a way to firmly "hold" the meaning of the sign/words heard. Consequently, when the child hears the request to give or bring an object, the reference of the word is rapidly overpowered by the various objects in their contexts that confront the child as he or she tries to comply with the request. In sharp contrast, the child who is sign/word-guided has internalized the object meaning of the sign/word and may mutter the word or self-sign while searching for and finding the requested object. Fortunately, Vygotsky (1962) developed an elegant but simple test to rapidly determine whether the child is context- or sign/word-guided.

The Vygotsky test

Examiner and child sit opposite each other across a table. On the table are two familiar objects, for example a toy car and a ball. The ball is close to the child; the toy car, placed directly behind the ball, is closer to the examiner. The examiner holds out a hand, taps it, and says, "Give car." If the child is sign/word-guided he or she *reaches past the ball*, picks up the toy car, and gives it to the examiner. Then, the position of the objects is reversed. This time the car is closer to the child while the ball is further away—closer to the examiner. The examiner this time asks for the ball. If the child gives the ball to the examiner and behaves in a similar fashion with other object pairs, the child is word-guided.

All too commonly, however, children on the spectrum cannot overcome the pull of the near object and repeatedly give the examiner the object closest to them—clearly demonstrating that they are context-guided. In other words, they have not internalized the word and its specific object meaning sufficiently to overcome the pull of the context provided by the nearer object.

Children who are context-guided would not be able to give a requested object when there is competition from other objects. They certainly would be unable to get a requested object from another room. If children are context-guided, it means that, even if they have some spoken words, these words cannot be very functional. However, such children may often be able to respond to signed actions concepts. We have often seen children able to use action sign/words such as *come* or *get up/sit down* but be quite unable to respond to or use sign/word concepts for common objects such as *cup* or *fork*.

These findings have direct implications for the development of expressive spoken language. For expressive spoken language to be possible in a way that permits reference to an object even when the object is not physically present, the child must understand that the sign/word relation to its object exists *independent of the object's context*. In other words, the sign/word *cup* refers to a cup whether the cup is hanging on a hook, or is lying on its side on the floor. The child's achievement of a stable sign/word object reference prepares the way for an important insight into the nature of words that literally transforms the child's reality and prepares the way for functional communication.

THE HELEN KELLER INSIGHT

Many readers will remember the dramatic moment in the movie *The Miracle Worker* when blind and deaf Helen Keller suddenly realized that the sign for water which her teacher rapidly finger-spelled in her outstretched hand referred to the water she felt spilling over her other hand. Suddenly, Helen realized that each of the previously nameless things around her had names. As she realized this, she excitedly held up her hand for her teacher, Ann Sullivan, to spell out the names of each thing around her that she touched. With each newly named thing that aspect of her world seemed to become more defined. Because she now knew that "each thing had its own name" (Stern and Stern 1928, p.191) she also understood that the names of things could act as surrogates for the things themselves. This insight, for the first time, enabled Helen to think about things in their absence and to communicate about them to others.

The typical child aged 15 to 20 months grasps this same insight that Helen had, and this is evident in his or her repeated pointing at objects and asking of parents "What dat?" As the child acquires the names of things, the child has, in effect, established inner templates organized around the names for these things. That template allows the child not only to find the requested object but also to relate similar objects to that template so that all bird-like things may be called "bird," all variously shaped cups may be called "cup," and so forth. When the child has inner templates for a number of such things, the child has a basis for the insight that "each thing has its name." With that, the child understands—as Helen did—that not only can the word guide his or her search for a particular object, but also that the word can allow him or her to refer to an entire class of objects that have the required properties. Building on this, children are able to develop noun–verb and verb–noun syntax to communicate about objects and events to others.

In the following, I will compare the development and outcomes of two non-verbal autistic boys who started treatment at the Language and Cognitive Development Center (LCDC) at about the same age (two and a half years). One of the boys (Frank) had a system-forming disorder; the other (Jack) had a closed system disorder. Both had master therapist Kristina Chrétien (see Chapter 7) to work with them and their parents. However, only Jack achieved the "naming insight." The following account will indicate the impact the presence or absence of this insight had on the development of their language and communication. We begin with Frank.

Frank

Report from Frank's hospital evaluation

Frank stood in the middle of the room staring ahead. He occasionally rolled his eyes and head backward and around (as if stretching his neck). Periodically, he slapped his hands, postured, and shook his head in self-stimulating fashion. He touched a few toys, batted at some large blocks, and then sat rocking a cradle repetitively for a long time without interruption. He was inattentive to his mother or the examiner. His affect was bland and his face expressionless… Although Frank was able to execute repetitive motor sequences—such as stereotypically throwing any small object that came to hand—he did not initiate or play in a goal-directed manner. His eye contact was hard to attain and sustain.

Frank, 5 months later, aged 31 months; from his Umwelt at the LCDC

Frank's difficulty relating to objects was apparent from a number of sources. He could not at first readily track or push the swinging ball to the examiner. He could not stack blocks or cups. He could not use a string or a rake to pull a toy closer. Where spatial relations were concerned he seemed not to understand that he had to climb over the anticipation board that separated him from his beckoning father in order to reach him; nor did he at first understand how to avoid the holes in the "Swiss cheese" board or to go down a slide and return to the steps so that he could slide down again.

However, with repetitive, spheric presentations of the suspended ball, "Swiss cheese" board, and step–slide tasks, Frank's performance began to improve. He began to put hands in front of his face to avoid being struck by the swinging ball and then to push it away from himself (but not toward another person). On the "Swiss cheese" board he began to step over and around holes and on the slide sphere task he began in the course of a dozen trials to turn toward the steps in anticipation of another slide.

Viewed in terms of his Umwelt, Frank behaved as if things were real only when he collided with something or when it was small enough to throw. He had little sense of his surroundings, could not follow directions, and could only indicate his needs by becoming frantic or tantrumming. It was, however, encouraging that, with repetition, he could begin to assimilate steps in the step–slide sequence.

Accordingly, the first set of interventions was designed to help Frank learn about objects and how common activities with objects were sequenced in service of particular goals.

Therapist's plan

Using the Elevated Square, Kristina planned a series of both integrative spheres and multispheres for Frank. Through integrative spheres she sought to teach Frank familiar sequences—filling and emptying pitchers of water, cleaning and setting the table, washing and drying dishes, or putting food on the shelves—that are naturally linked together in performing particular tasks. Through multispheres she sought to help Frank—who often got stuck on one activity—learn that he could leave that activity, go to another, and still return to the first activity.

First integrative sphere

Frank was required to pick up a pitcher at one station, fill it with water at a second station, and pour it into a bucket at a third station. After pouring the water at Station 3 he had to pass Station 4 to pick up a new empty pitcher at Station 1. His father, at Station 1, beckoned him and called "Come!" to help him make the turn at Station 4. The sequence was repeated four or five times.

RESPONSE

Frank seemed intrigued by the task but seemed not to have grasped the necessity of doing things in a certain order. For example, at times after picking up the pitcher at Station 1 he would be drawn to the more engaging water-pouring at Station 3 and would bypass Station 2 (putting water in the pitcher). He seemed genuinely surprised, when allowed to do this, that no water came out as he tilted the pitcher.

These and comparable results with other integrative spheres indicated that when Frank could not sustain an inner thought sequence he would become confused and falter, resort to stereotypic throwing, or shift to magical solutions. To improve Frank's sense of the object and the possible relation of one object to another, Kristina introduced a set of multisphere interventions.

The goal of multisphere interventions was to extend Frank's action vocabulary and, at the same time, enable him to detach from one activity to go to another and then return—behavior that is critical for exploring one's surroundings.

Multisphere

At first there were a number of failures of different multispheres in which Frank—after becoming involved with one activity—was unable to continue with a second unrelated activity. Finally—after a dozen sessions—a multisphere was set up in which Frank, for the first time, successfully shifted among three unrelated tasks: picking up a ball and dropping it down a tube, stacking rings on a pole for graduated rings, and picking up a cup and placing it in a cup nest.

Frank could now cope with the structured reality represented by the Elevated Square and the tasks that were introduced on the square. He could also now deal with the form and function of objects as well as their varied spatial relations on the Elevated Square—shifting from one task to another and back to the first—without becoming disoriented. Further, Kristina was increasingly able to guide some of Frank's behavior on the square with the signs and words that had accompanied his actions—although he was still not able to initiate any signs or words. Lacking, also, was any indication that Frank could transfer his new capacities to the ground.

The goal of the third set of activities was to help Frank generalize to the ground what he had learned on the Elevated Square.

Sign/word guidance on the ground

During the next 40 sessions Frank showed substantial ability to respond to and be guided by sign/words on the ground. The nature of his progress is suggested by the following sections.

Integrative sphere

Frank (now aged 36 months) learned to follow directions on the ground.

PROCEDURE

Frank was required to walk over the artificial hill to his father who was signing and saying "Come!" When he arrived and his father signed and said "Pick up!" he was to pick up a bottle of water. Following this, when Kristina on the other side of the hill signed and said "Come!", Frank was to turn around and bring the bottle to her. When Frank reached her, she signed and said "Pour!" and pointed to the bucket at her feet, requiring Frank to pour the water into it. This procedure was repeated five to six times.

As Frank succeeded in following these directions, the procedure was expanded so that when Frank came to him, his father directed him to pick up one of two objects: a bottle of water or a car. Then, directed by Kristina's signs and words, Frank was asked to respond either to "Pour!" by pouring the water in the bucket or—it he had picked up the car—to the sign and word "Down!" by sending the car down a ramp positioned next to the bucket (see Figure 8.1).

RESPONSE

Frank followed directions well in the first part of the task, climbing up the artificial hill and then rapidly going down the other side first to his father and then to Kristina. He had some difficulty with the expansion that required him to discriminate between two different objects and two different commands—showing his old disposition toward stereotypic throwing. However, with minimal physical support he was able about half the time to alternate between pouring and sending the car down.

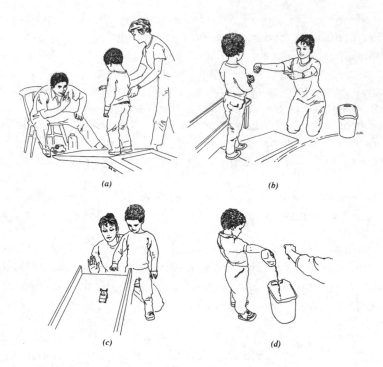

(a)   *(b)*

(c)   *(d)*

Figure 8.1 Frank choosing and using different objects after walking over the artificial hill

In a later integrative sphere Frank learned to wash, dry, and place dishes. With minimal difficulty, he would pick up either a dirty plate or cup at Station 1 (on the ground) and then walk to Station 2 where he picked up a brush, washed the dish or cup, and placed it on a towel. Then he moved to another location (Station 3) where he dried the cup or dish. Finally, he moved to Station 4 where he successfully stacked plates or put cups on hooks.

Spontaneous initiatives which began to appear during this period included Frank's ability to open a door so he could pull a wagon through. It also included limited tool use as he used a rake to pull a salt shaker he had been using toward him. However, he could do this only when the rake arm was directly behind the salt shaker.

Awareness of people
In the session to be described, Frank (now aged three years six months) started his own interactive game instead of following Kristina's plan. Kristina had planned to have Frank open a bottle with soapy water at station 1, walk to his father at Station 2 to get the bubble wand, and then walk to Kristina at station 3 where he was to put the wand in the bottle of water prior to bringing it to her mouth for blowing.

Frank, however, had other ideas. He came in unusually responsive to Kristina. He smiled when he saw her in the corridor, took her hand, and pulled her toward the room in which they worked. When she tried to involve him in the bubble task he had always enjoyed, he began, instead, to initiate simple, teasing/chasing games with her. At one point, becoming excited, he started throwing things and was reprimanded by his father and Kristina. At this, he began to cry bitterly. Later, as Kristina attempted to resume the session, Frank would repeatedly interrupt the activity by approaching Kristina and giggling. Then he would turn away while looking over his shoulder at her, waiting to be chased.

This was the first occasion at the LCDC in which Frank spontaneously— without prior structuring—initiated a game with Kristina. Clearly, his interest in her as a source of fun, coupled with a new sense that he could initiate activities, overrode her structuring his actions. With this new way of behaving, Frank showed promise, for the first time, of a whole spectrum of social development.

Social awareness coupled with increased response to signs and words was also evident in the course of contagious activities such as the "walk, jump, fall, get up, around a circle" sphere. This consisted of Kristina, Frank, and his father forming a circle and rhythmically but in a rapidly paced manner doing the circle sphere as Kristina chanted and signed various action-related terms (in the "walk, jump, fall, get up, around a circle" sphere). Over the course of five weeks Frank began to assimilate this sequence.

At first Frank showed no response to interruption after being led through the "walk, jump...around a circle" sphere. In the next session, however, after interruption, Frank jumped by himself and when his father did not immediately join the activity Frank pulled on his father to do so. Next session, Frank spontaneously started jumping as soon as they joined hands. The following session he not only jumped, he spontaneously fell down—indicating that he had now assimilated that part of the sphere as well.

During this period, Frank began to respond to the peek-a-boo game. In one session not only did he pull the scarf off the worker's head and his own head, he also spontaneously patted his head when he wanted the scarf put on his head so that he might be found. When found, he produced the sign for "Hi!" in conjunction with waving.

The goal of the fourth set of activities was to help Frank understand that his use of sign/words influenced the behavior of others.

The giving and getting sphere
Frank participated in a reciprocal give sphere in which, with a pile of objects in his lap, he faced Kristina. Each time she produced the *give* sign accompanied by the spoken word "Give!," he would give her one of the objects. Subsequently, when she reversed roles, Frank, for the first time, was able to produce the *give* sign to get objects from Kristina.

Later, Frank mastered an interactive object-down sphere in which his father required Frank to send a car down a ramp only when he signed and said "Down!" Subsequently, Frank used the *down* sign to get his father to send a car down the ramp.

Frank begins to produce signs, then sounds, then words

Frank's first signs were "natural" in that they derived directly from interrupted actions performed within spheres. A bit later, however, Frank began to reproduce conventional signs that the worker introduced within various minispheres. The first conventional sign appeared during the narrated and signed "walk, stop" sphere between the classroom and the therapy room. Frank, interrupted, produced the sign for *walk* (moving the hands in walking motion); he produced the *pour* sign when the worker poised a jar of juice over Frank's cup; he learned *open* and *bye-bye* signs. Most encouraging were indications that he was increasingly able to initiate spontaneous signs toward the worker as the following vignette shows:

Session 78. Frank, finding it difficult to leave the classroom, cried as the therapist led him to the therapy room. As soon as she sat down, Frank attempted physically to get her up from the chair. When that failed, he signed *Get up!*, went to the door, and spontaneously signed *Open!* at the door.

Frank's first imitated sounds came in context of a rhythmic sound–action sphere: The worker hit a drum with a stick first lightly and then more intensely, while saying in tempo, "Ba...Ba...," then, after an interruption to build up tension, "boom" or "bang" as she struck the drum sharply. In the course of half a dozen sessions, Frank for the first time said "Ba," then in a later session produced the "Ba" sound with the clear intent that the sequence continue. Finally, in Session 93, following interruption after "Ba...Ba..." he produced "Mang!" with the gesture for bang (the drum).

Frank's first spoken words "Get up!," "Pull!," and "Sit down!" occurred in the course of a contagious, alternating pulling (each other's hands) sequence accompanied by the command "Pull!" First the worker and then Frank was to sign and say "Sit down!" then "Get up!" In the course of several repetitions of this sphere, for the first time, signed and said "Get up!," "Pull!," and "Sit down!"

In the sessions that followed, spoken words sometimes emerged directly from a contagious sphere and sometimes from interruption of integrative spheres. Starting with Session 85, Frank began to use utterances with all his signs. *In no case did Frank achieve a spoken word unless he had previously been guided by it as a sign word and had learned to use the sign.* Frank's use of spoken words, however, was largely restricted to action reference. Not having grasped the name–object or Helen Keller insight into names, Frank could not verbally distinguish between one object or another. In spite of this, the following report involving his parents indicates that he found a way to use his action words to communicate his intentions:

Frank went into his parents' bedroom and signed and said, "Get up!" Startled, the parents got out of bed, at which point Frank signed and said "Walk!… Walk!… Walk!," looking at them over his shoulder as he moved toward the kitchen. With both parents following, Frank walked to the refrigerator and signed and said "Open!" Father opened the door and Frank pointed to the box of eggs and said "Break!" At that point, hearing a sizzling sound on the stove, they turned and saw that Frank had put butter in the frying pan and had turned on the stove. Now he waited for someone else to complete making breakfast.

At a more advanced stage (after the naming insight), Frank would have been able to stand in front of his parents and say, "Get up! I'm hungry. Make scrambled eggs for me!" Instead, he had to depend on his body actions to provide the missing syntax. Whether or not Frank will be able to cross the gap from action words to names of objects, and the syntax which follows, is uncertain. However, even with his limited language, Frank now lives in a larger, more predictable social world, in which he can share meanings and influence what happens in a way that was previously unavailable to him.

Jack

Jack's Umwelt assessment

Jack, a sturdy two-and-a-half-year-old nonverbal autistic boy, had great difficulty organizing himself and accepting the repetitive (spheric) activities offered him. He kept a plastic toy clutched in his hand throughout the session and would respond briefly to tasks, then either collapse into a screeching tantrum or cling to his mother. After pushing the suspended ball once or twice (although never reciprocally), he first clung to it but then abandoned it when it bumped into him. On the "Swiss cheese" board he first fell through a hole, then briefly walked around others to his mother, then collapsed into tantrums and refused to address the task further.

Jack's failure to turn spheres into systems was strikingly evident on big-body systems. Even after several experiences of going down the slide and being brought to the steps, he failed to connect the steps with the slide. Released, he tried to climb up the slide and ignored the steps.

Perhaps Jack's best achievement was pulling a string that brought a toy dog closer. When the examiner pulled the dog back, Jack responded several times by pulling the string to bring the toy dog closer. However, at no time did he indicate any awareness of the examiner pulling the string at the other end. His gaze was completely focused on the dog. He refused entirely to address the stacking cups and bowls task or the "croupier" task—turning away to burrow his head in his mother's shoulder.

In summarizing her findings, the examiner commented that "Jack seemed not to focus on anything away from his body although he was extraordinarily reactive to any changes directly affecting his body or the visual field near his body." His mother reported that even changing his clothes caused Jack great upset when she replaced one shirt with another.

Toward the end of the assessment, the examiner noted that she was at first unable to get him to take part in a sphere which had to do with dropping blocks down the slide:

I would take the block, gently put it on the slide, and push it down as he followed the motion with his eyes. Then I put the blocks near his hands before sending them down. Finally, he began to accept the blocks and send them down himself. I gave blocks to each parent so they could continue the process. He became noticeably calmer as he continued to take and send blocks down the slide—accepting his first sphere.

Below, Jack, then three years five months old, is the subject of an interview I conducted with his parents just before he began to understand the relation between words and their objects and move into the naming stage. Here, Mrs. H., Jack's mother, describes Jack after six months at the LCDC. I have just asked Mrs. H how she carried over the work of the LCDC to home. She answers by describing what she did and how he responded.

Jack's compulsion to categorize pictures and things

A.M.: How about the work at home? How would you decide what to do?

Mrs. H.: We…carried over to home [from the LCDC] the idea of him to use pictures to represent things. One way we did this was to put pictures on the walls of his room as you had done at LCDC instead of just in his hand. It worked for a few weeks and then he would take them down and make piles of them. I bought a bunch of animal calendars and would have a room full of frogs one day; the next day a room full of bears. The first time it lasted three or four days, and then he took them down and put them in piles. Piles that you couldn't disturb. And then I might put up a bear calendar round the room. This might last two days, and he would then take them down and put them in another pile.

He also began to make piles of other things at home. And that was new after Kristina [Jack's therapist] started with him. He would take everything out of the food closet after once seeing me take a can out of that closet. He would put everything from the food closet on the counter and protect that uneven pile of cans with his body. It became his and you couldn't touch it.

Three or four hours later, when he was into something else, I could start moving things back in. He did the same thing with the refrigerator—taking everything out—especially the jars. At first he would mix up what belonged in the food closet with what belonged in the refrigerator. But within a month and a half he was able to take everything out from both food closet and refrigerator in exactly the right spot. Refrigerator foods would go back in the refrigerator; canned foods would go back in the closet. He still has some of that quality. Even now, when he doesn't want something to change—like he's afraid I'm going to change something on the TV—he will literally push me away from it.

A.M.: So the connection between the way certain things go together—certain pictures with certain objects—that Kristina started working on with Jack at the center continued at home.

Mrs. H.: Yes. And the clothes… He would take all my clothes out of the closet and try to get me to wear everything at once—whether or not they fit. Then I discovered that I didn't have to put them on but just had to touch my body with the clothes… If I took a bath he would come after me with the sweater he needed me to put on. I'd say "No!" and he would go through a half-hour tantrum, screaming… Then he would go to his sister's clothes and do the same thing… But after a short time he wouldn't let me put his sister's clothes against my body; they had to be placed in contact with his sister's body. And this was frightening to her. I had to tell her it was a little game and not to worry.

Mr. H. (Jack's father): I remember the day he dragged my shirt downstairs.

Mrs. H.: He dragged it down in the middle of the night…his work shirt.

Mr. H.: He knew… He brought down my shirt for me. *He needed to connect each person's clothes with them just like he had to connect each picture with the right object.* [My italics.]

Mrs. H.: And this went on for a couple of months and now he no longer does it. Now, if he wants to go outside and he thinks I'm ready he will get me my jacket and his jacket…

Jack, apparently having reached the awareness that there are things out there, *felt compelled* to relate each thing to its proper place or owner. His urgent need to categorize, which Mrs. H. described at the beginning of the interview, is consistent with his closed system disorder but leads ultimately to the naming insight "that each thing has its name."

Changes in Jack's hearing

Mrs. H.: Another thing that happens to him now that didn't happen before he started the center is around his hearing. Before he started here, if I snapped my fingers in back of his head, he would turn toward the sound with a very unhappy look on his face. But if I were to bang my fist against a sheet-metal slide he probably wouldn't even blink his eyes. After he started at LCDC—as he became more aware of sounds—his hands would go up to his ears. Previous to coming here they would not go up to his ears except when he was screeching in a tantrum. It may be that sounds are more disturbing because he is opening up more and more. Before he came here—at age two—we felt that he was withdrawing into himself more and more.

Mr. H.: But as he started to open up, it seemed to me at any rate that the more he opened up, the more problems he had with sound sensitivity.

A.M.: As if he suddenly started to notice a whole universe of sounds.

Mr. H.: Yes, but Kristina told me to speak to him softly and to try to keep the object close to him… Yesterday, I, just out of curiosity, loudly yelled, "Jack!" And he turned around. Previously he would never respond to loud sounds. So I don't havfe to whisper his name any more.

Jack's first spoken word

Mrs. H.: Another thing Kristina did was to give special sounds that went with each animal—This is a cow it goes "Moo"—giving separate sounds to help identify each animal.

Mr. H.: We carried that over at home…the first word that had significance for him was *bear* so we got him a pull toy with a bear in it and he pulled it at home just as he had at the center. He recognized it immediately and began to pull it around the room. It was his bear on wheels. But he still wouldn't pull other similar toys around the house.

A.M.: Has his interest in objects continued?

Mrs. H.: Yes, but it hasn't increased. He has many more activities now. For example, now he likes to go upstairs with his picture book by himself. And he likes his quiet time so he sits down and reads his picture book by himself… He still has that [interest in pictures]… But after a few weeks he's used them up and he puts them under the rug. He just doesn't want to see them any more and I have to get him a new batch.

Mr. H.: Now, whenever you bring something new in the house he gets very, very excited. When we buy something for Ann [his sister] and not for him, he has to look at her object.

A.M.: What about naming things?

Mrs. H.: His vocabulary keeps increasing. With each week there may be two or three new words. It's not clear yet how consistent these words are. The day before yesterday somebody brought a cake and I put two plates on the table and I said "Here, cake!" and he walked right over to the table and said "Cake!" And that's the first time he said "cake." Our experience is that the words are not yet stable. One day he will have the word, and the next day he may not. But from a child who last September [age about two years eight months] had not one word, he now has 10 or 15 words and all the letters of the alphabet, he can recognize them by shape on the page…right through the whole alphabet.

Jack's new executive capacity

Mrs. H.: He can now also make a choice between two objects… Before we started at the LCDC if we presented him with a choice, he immediately started to tantrum. Now, given a choice between milk and juice, he will push away the one he doesn't want and take the other. The other day when I offered him toast, he looked at it and then walked over to the closet, got the cereal box, and brought it to the table.

Jack's changing social contact

Mr. H.: At first Jack very much enjoyed being a spectator. I would chase my little girl around the house and he thought that was the greatest. But I could not get him to join in…

Mrs. H.: In the past two days—where it has been very hot—I've taken him and his sister into the little wading pool in the backyard. And this is the first time he ever chased his sister around the backyard with the garden hose, trying to get her wet. He was doing to her the same thing she had done to him in the past. And he was enjoying himself. This was not to hurt her. This was actually the first time that he was the one who initiated the game. Also, he and his sister now hug a lot. She has taught him to hug. And he loves to hug her. Unfortunately, at the playground, he now goes to girls the same size as his sister and tries to hug them. And they don't know what is going on. But I look at it this way. He's a three-year-old boy. And he's certainly allowed to hug other children. And if the other children want to get freaked out, then it's their thing.

A.M.: Earlier, Mr. H., you commented that now you had a son. When did you begin to feel that way?

Mr. H.: When he came here [LCDC] six months ago, I had no relationship with my son whatsoever. None. No matter what I tried to do, I just did not exist for him. If I went into the back room where he was playing with an object and I started playing with that object—nothing. He wouldn't even turn away and go to some other object. He wouldn't even give me that. He would just stand there until I went away and then he would continue his play. It was like my presence was part of a dream for him. And if there was a block on the other side of my body that he needed, he would just step on me to get it as if I were stairs or something. I was nothing more than part of the sofa if I was sitting there. When I came home from work, if he was in the kitchen, there was never any response related to whether I had come or gone. I could've been hanging upside down. It wouldn't have made any difference. There was absolutely no contact whatsoever, no recognition, no anything.

Mrs. H.: And there was no name for you either.

Mr. H.: I really totally did not exist. And he would not allow me to snuggle up with him, give him a hug or pick him up… Only after we started at the LCDC did things start to change. We learned how to get eye contact by using the object at eye level with him while saying "Here [offering the object], Jack!" but most progress started to happen when you suggested that I be physical with him, bounce him up and down, do rough and tumble with him. That was very important. We found that he loved that and that it broke down the barriers.

And now he enjoys physical contact with his dad. He now likes to hug his dad…

Mrs. H.: To jump on and ride on your shoulders…

Mr. H.: And I notice now a lot of times if I'm lying down napping before I go to work, he will get up and snuggle next to me for a while. Now I feel—considering Jack's disability—that I have a very, very good relationship with him. I am very, very happy with it. There is no question in my mind that the rough and tumble—and the physical contact—was the turning point… Within three or four days [it] changed his entire attitude toward me. He started coming over and wanting to play with me while before [*laughs*] I just wasn't there.

Jack visits the LCDC

A number of years after the interview, Mrs. H. brought Jack, now a sturdy-looking, fully literate 13-year-old, who enjoys communicating on the internet, to visit the center. When we met again, his mother asked him if he remembered Dr. Miller. "Of course," Jack replied, "Dr. Miller with the white Sable, the black Taurus, yellow Volvo" (naming all the cars I drove during his five- or six-year stay at the LCDC). Clearly, the cars I had driven were, for him, an indelible part of the Dr. Miller system. While Jack's intellect is quite unfettered, it is likely that he—like many others who have emerged from autism—will continue to closely link people with their objects.

WHY JACK AND NOT FRANK?

When Jack's progress is compared with Frank's, one wonders why Jack achieved full language capability while Frank did not. After all, both started at the LCDC at about the same age and both had the same gifted therapist working with them. And both had a pre-existing relationship with at least one parent: Frank with his father and Jack with his mother… The answer seems to go back to the children's system functioning. Frank, a child with system-forming disorder, had—aside from his relationship with his father—only one action–object system, which consisted of throwing any small thing that came within reach of his hand. Jack, on the other hand, a child with closed system disorder who had great difficulty moving from one system to another, had a number of systems on which to build.

What assisted the development of both boys was the manner in which their parents carried through the program at home. Both Frank's father and Jack's mother learned how to take home concepts developed during therapy sessions at LCDC so that they could be generalized.

They learned, for example, that the best way to broaden their child's understanding of his surroundings was to first examine all the functional systems that existed in the home. Once these systems were identified it was an easy matter to include signs and words within these systems. For example, consider the everyday function of filling a glass with water at the sink. First, the child must pick up a glass with one hand, then he must place it and hold it under the faucet. Following this, he has to turn the faucet on so that water comes out. Finally, he must hold the glass under the faucet until the glass is filled and then turn off the faucet. He may then either bring the glass to the table or drink the water in the glass.

Look at the wealth of signs and words that can easily be included in this everyday action. *Pick up* glass. Glass *under* faucet. *Hold* glass *under* faucet. *Turn on* (with other hand) faucet. Water *in* glass. *Fill* glass with water. *Turn off* faucet. *Bring* (*carry*) glass to table. *Drink* water.

Note the italicized part of these sentences. These words are italicized because these verbal or prepositional terms should be emphasized first. This means that both sign and words should be used while helping the child perform this integrative system. The noun parts of the sentence can be taught later. Then, as the child both hears and learns to respond to these new signs, the parent elaborates the sign and word sentences by combining the verbal or prepositional term with the various nouns—adding *glass, faucet, water, table*. Now the parent could narrate with accompanying signs and spoken words all the parts of the integrative system that the child was performing as Frank or Jack went to the sink to fill a glass of water and bring it to the table.

It's interesting to note the different vehicles that led to the progress made by both boys. Frank's progress hinged exclusively on developing signs which eventually morphed into functional spoken words. In contrast, Jack's period of sign (gesture) dependence was relatively brief. After a brief period of using signs, he relied heavily on pictures in his progress toward the "naming insight" and eventual full language development. In our work we have seen both signs and pictures leading to this insight but, in general, those children who begin with few organized systems have a much longer journey toward language development than those who come to us with closed systems.

The next chapter, "Teaching the Child to Cope," considers the developmental needs of autistic spectrum children in a school setting.

SUMMARY

This chapter considered a number of challenges that children on the autism spectrum face in achieving communication. The first of these is the body–other confusion so common among autistic children. This shows itself in a tendency to relate the signs they learn to themselves and not to the other. Another challenge to communication concerns the distinction between sign/words for actions vs. sign/words for objects. Often, the children can respond to and use action sign/words more readily than object sign/words. Part of their difficulty with the latter lies in the fact that objects have multiple properties while actions have a single vector which signs closely mirror.

Another factor which makes reference to objects more difficult is the extent to which children "lock" them into their familiar contexts. Objects, out of their familiar contexts, may not be recognized. The Vygotsky test has been very useful in determining which children are sign/word-guided and which are context-guided. Sign/word-guided children—having internalized the sign/word—are able to ignore the "pull" of various contexts and are, therefore, able to find requested objects in a way that context-guided children cannot.

Following this, the Helen Keller insight was described in terms of the understanding that "each thing has a name." This insight enables children to use the word as a surrogate for the object. It is critical to the development of syntax and full language capability.

The chapter contrasted two nonverbal autistic children—Frank and Jack—both entering LCDC at the same age, and both treated by the same skilled therapist. One child, Frank, had a system-forming disorder; the other, Jack, had a closed system disorder. Frank, although he learned to respond to and use action sign/words, never achieved the Helen Keller insight, and thus had no means of referring symbolically to objects. In contrast, Jack, who did gain this insight, developed full language capability. The chapter closed with speculation that Jack's achievement was related to the fact that he began treatment with a variety of closed systems which could be expanded and developed into a compulsive need to categorize objects which in turn facilitated the naming insight. Frank, lacking systems, did not have this advantage.

Part III

EDUCATION

Chapter 9

Teaching the Child to Cope

As a small child I remember struggling to open a large, heavy, metal door at the entrance to my apartment building. For a time, I could only pull the door open a few inches—not enough to slip inside—before it would close. One day, after tugging at the door handle with all my strength, the door creaked open enough for me to enter… Long after I could open that door with ease, I continued to recall the pleasurable sense of competence that opening that heavy door had induced within me. (A.M.)

The sense of competence which typical children achieve in the first two or three years of life does not develop spontaneously among children on the autism spectrum. Lacking a clearly defined body/self concept—and the executive capacity this entails—the children are unable to explore and cope with their surroundings. In the following I discuss ways of helping the children develop a sturdy sense of their own being and how to help them meet the challenge of a confusing world.

BUILDING THE BODY/SELF CONCEPT

The body/self concept develops from ideas the child generates about what the body looks like to oneself and to others, and what it feels like; the attitude of the child and others toward his or her body; and what the body does or is able to do (Schilder 1950). The importance of being seen by others in establishing the sense of being is illustrated by the story of the typical three-year-old who was doing something naughty. Her teacher angrily said, "If you do that again, I just won't see you." To this, the little girl replied, "Oh please! If you don't see me I won't be there!"

A child who reacts in this way already has—although it is fragile—a sense of herself that hinges strongly on her being seen and accepted by significant people. In contrast, children on the autism spectrum lack this exquisite awareness of others and, therefore, are often impervious to whether they are seen or not. For them, as was true with Jack and his father (described in Chapter 8), direct physical contact was essential for establishing a relationship. Consequently, professionals and parents must draw on more basic, body-oriented means of helping the child become aware of his or her own existence until "being seen" or seeing others can become important.

Effective strategies include "rough and tumble" play, tickling, restabilizing, and reciprocal face-touching (see Figure 6.1). Used carefully, they also include teasing ("I'm going to get your nose!") or, with another, having a playful tug of war over the child's body ("I want that foot… I want that arm!") as well as unexpected interruptions to build body anticipation of what is going to happen next. These strategies enhance sensory awareness of the body through touch and, at the same time, contribute to body/self–other awareness. After some body/self awareness has developed, the "I see you" game described in Chapter 6, in which two children facing each other take turns reporting what they see when they look at each other, can be an important intervention.

Beyond this, we need to help the child develop a generalization about himself or herself as "a doer"—as someone who is able to do many things. Useful, in this regard, are tasks that require the child to do things like pushing, pulling, lifting, carrying relatively heavy objects from one place to another—or wearing weighted vests as well as wrist or ankle weights. Each time the child uses his or her body to cope with the resistance of objects—as in opening the heavy door described earlier—he or she experiences the body as an effective tool. Paraphrasing Tito (Mukhopadhyay 2000), the child can be viewed as saying, "I exist because I can push, pull, carry, throw, etc." By having the child demonstrate to himself or herself the capacity of the body to do things (body efficacy), we help establish a substantial body/self.

Narration

When the teacher or therapist tells the child what he or she is doing *while* he or she is doing it, the child has an opportunity, not only to develop receptive language, but to become more "self conscious" about his or her actions whether this be riding a bike, throwing a ball, climbing a tree, eating an apple, or carrying a heavy object.

The "can do!" board

Another way to accent the child's body experience and his or her competence is to establish a "can do!" bulletin board for the child. Each child in the class should have a "can do!" board with photographs of the child showing him or her performing different activities. These can include riding a tricycle or bicycle, carrying something, pushing, pulling, going down the slide, washing the blackboard, cleaning up a mess, and so forth. Periodically, the teacher should add new pictures to each child's board.

At different times, the teacher and the child look at the child's "can do!" board and together describe what the child is doing in the different pictures. Some teachers have added to the "can do!" board sequential pictures showing the child going through steps of an activity—going up steps, sitting down, going down a slide, or some similar multistep activity.

Parents should also have a "can do!" board at home indicating all the things the child does at home. From time to time, photos from the school "can do!" board should be brought home, while photos of the home "can do!" board should be brought to school. Whenever the child solves a particular problem or makes an academic advance a picture of it should be placed on the "can do!" board.

Will I ever be grown up?

All children—but particularly those on the spectrum—have difficulty grasping the fact that they are growing physically as well as in capability and that they will one day be fully grown adults. There are two good ways to help establish the fact that they are indeed growing. One is to place next to the "can do!" board a panel with marks to show the changing height of the child as he or she gets taller in the course of the year. When the teacher or parent marks the most recent growth he or she also calls attention to the child's previous height and how much the child has grown.

Another good way to establish this notion of "getting bigger" is through the use of picture histories of the child. Teachers or therapists can borrow from parents' photographs of the child as an infant, a toddler, a preschooler, and so forth, to communicate through the pictures that the child has grown and will continue to grow both physically and in his or her ability to do things.

Choices

The sense of self can be further enhanced by giving the child choices: For example, "Do you want to wear your red shirt or your blue one today?" Choice-making can easily be carried over into the classroom where the child is asked, for example, "Puzzle or pegboard?" Each time the child makes a true choice, the child adds to the self concept as one who has options. To avoid confusion, choices should be limited to two items at first.

Representing and accenting the body/self

Once the child achieves basic body awareness, it is helpful to have the child represent himself or herself and others in drawings. Teaching children to represent themselves and others helps the child to conceptualize himself or herself as a separate being in relation to others. To make progress with representation—and in the ability to shift to the other's perspective—the children need to first be able to discriminate body parts and distinguish them from those of another person. They must also have sufficient command of the marker to draw a circle and put dots in the circle, as well as draw vertical and horizontal lines.

Begin the process by determining whether the child can identify his or her body parts, and the corresponding body parts on another person. Say, "Show me your nose (mouth, ears, eyes, hair, etc.)." If the child can do this, then say, "Touch [teacher's] nose, mouth, ears, eyes, hair, etc." If the child has not established the accurate identification of body parts on his or herself and on the other, then work to help the child make these discriminations by emphasizing the functions of these various parts. For example, you *eat* with your mouth (pointing to child's mouth); you *see* with your eyes (briefly covering the child's eyes); you *hear* with your ears (briefly covering ears), and so forth. If, however, the child can discriminate body parts on his or herself and on the other, assess the child's drawing ability.

If the child cannot draw circles, dots, and vertical and horizontal lines, work with the child, first hand over hand, and then by having the child follow a model until he or she has established adequate control of the marker. Work on large surfaces initially—blackboard or butcher paper. (Chapter 10 describes a drawing program that systematically introduces different graphic forms.) If the child is still not developing adequate motor control, have him or her draw these forms in a clay pan where the resistance to the stylus provides more feedback and thus control of the stylus.

Once the child has reached this level, you then need a full-length mirror, a large sheet of paper, and a marker. Have the child draw a large circle to represent his or her head. Then have the child look in the mirror as you apply gentle pressure by cupping your hands around the child's head. Say, "This is David's head." Then point to the circle on the paper and say, "This is also David's head." Then, point to the child's hair in the mirror and, as you ruffle the child's hair, say, "This is David's hair." Now, point to the circle and ask the child to put hair on the circle representing the child's head. If the child draws hair on top of the circle, that is a good indication the child is relating the mirror image to the drawing. If not, refer back to the mirror, place the drawing alongside the mirror image, and show that the hair in the mirror image is on top. Then go back to the drawing and help the child place the hair on top of the circle.

Next, place a dot on the child's nose (or a bit of tape) and have the child look at the tape or dot on the nose in the mirror. (This helps orient the child to the nose's location in the mirror reflection.) Then, ask the child to add a nose to his or her face drawing. Continue in this way—back and forth between the mirror reflection, the parts of the child's face, and the drawing. Once the drawing has facial features, show the child in the mirror how a neck and torso look and how arms come out of the top of the torso and legs from the bottom. Squeeze the body parts to provide both visual as well as tactile feedback for the child.

Representing child with adult in drawings

In later sessions, stand next to the child so that both of you face the mirror. Indicate with gesture and pointing that your image is bigger than the child's. On another large sheet of paper see if the child can represent this distinction of you being bigger next to a smaller image of the child. This is more difficult and may take a number of sessions to achieve. If the child cannot do this, draw two circles: one should be higher on the page to represent you, the teacher (or parent); the other lower, to represent the child. Then, have the child complete both drawings using the mirror image as a guide. To help establish the relation between the child's self drawing and representation of the mother or therapist in the same drawing, it is useful at first to place a photograph of the adult's face in the circle for his or her head, then allow the child to draw the rest of the adult's body next to the drawing of the child's body.

FUNCTIONAL USE OF TOOLS AND OBJECTS

Teaching autistic and other special children how things work is another important way of building a child's sense of competence and strengthening the body/self concept. For example, some nonverbal autistic children cannot use a rake to bring an out-of-reach object closer. Others cannot use a doorknob to open a door or open a multi-turn jar. To use a doorknob the child must learn to both pull and turn since neither single action will open the door. Similarly, to open a multi-turn jar, a child must understand that the hand has to lift before each turn so that the lid will unscrew. Instead many children simply keep turning the lid back and forth and become frustrated when the jar will not open.

Many nonverbal or limited verbal children do not understand how an inclined plane works although they use its principle when they zip down a slide. At the Language and Cognitive Development Center (LCDC), the slide is detachable from its step supports. So we were able to observe one autistic boy's response—after he had gone up and slid down the slide numerous times—to the slide being placed flat on the ground next to the steps. We observed this child go up the steps as before then lower himself until he was seated on the slide lying flat on the ground. The child then remained there waiting for his body to move down the slide as it had done so many times before. Clearly, this child attributed his movement down the slide to the slide itself and not to the angle of the slide.

Such a child can learn about the role that angles play by first sitting on the slide while you lift one end of the board from the floor until he moves down it. (Obviously, this works best with children who are three or four years of age rather than 10 or 11.) Then, the person at the other end turns him around and does the same thing. This is followed by using objects—such as a large truck or car—which will not move until the board is lifted by you or by the child. Eventually, the child learns not only to interact with you in this way but something about the way that increasing the angle results in increasing the speed down the board of whatever objects are on the board. In Figure 9.1 a therapist is teaching Ben, an autistic boy, how the inclined plane works in a table-top interactive sequence.

Developing tool use

Tools may be thought of as extensions of the body. Using a stick to bring an out-of-reach ball or object closer occurs, according to Uzgiris and Hunt

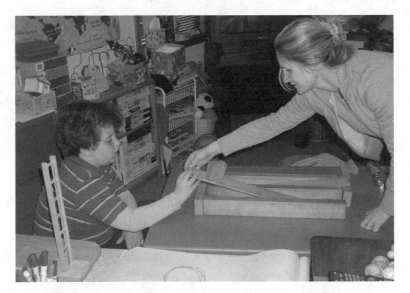

Figure 9.1 Ben, an autistic boy, being taught the inclined plane by his therapist

(1980), in typical development when the child is about ten months of age. Yet many autistic children ages three and older have still not achieved this basic skill. The children's powerful drive to grab the object with their hands seems to preclude awareness of any alternate means—such as tool use—for dealing with objects. In other words, for many children on the autism spectrum, tools are not part of their immediate realities. Our task, then, is to find a way to make tools and their varied functions relevant for the children.

Miller Method therapists and teachers go through a three-step process to make tools relevant. The first entails establishing an object system with small objects; the second is making the rake an integral part of this system; and the third is generalizing the new skill in using the rake to other people and other locations.

Establishing the system

The system is established, typically, by having the child place discs or dice within the slit or square hole in the lid of a glass bottle. Sometimes it is necessary to develop the system by working hand over hand with the child until the child takes it over. More often, the child develops a fascination with inserting the objects in the slit or square hole, watching the object drop, and hearing the satisfying clink it makes as it lands in the bottom of the glass jar.

Location expansion

Once the system is established, the therapist begins to place the disc or die at about a foot away from the bottle so that the child has to reach out to gain the object and complete the system by inserting it in the bottle. Gradually, the distance is expanded so that the child must reach far across the table to gain the object and complete the system. With the next expansion the disc or die is placed entirely out of the child's reach but with the arm of the rake around the object and the handle next to the child's hand.

Interposition of rake

In this situation, the child will—with little or no encouragement—grasp the handle of the rake and pull the rake until the desired object is within reach so that the system can be completed. Once the child achieves this, move the rake to the right then the left side of the object. Sometimes, the child requires a small cue to move the rake toward the object. When this is successful, place the rake in front of the object so that, in order to gain the object, the child must demonstrate knowledge of the rake's function by lifting it over the object and placing the rake head behind it.

Object expansions

After the child is successfully using the rake to retrieve out-of-reach discs and dice, the procedure is further expanded by introducing other objects such as small cars, animals, and so forth. In each case, the child must need the retrieved object to complete a system. With the cars, the need is to send the cars down a zig-zag track; with the animals, the need is to place the animals in a barn with other animals. Finally, it is desirable for the parent to provide similar opportunities for using the rake at home: to retrieve a ball that has gotten behind the refrigerator, or to bring down a needed object that has been hung on the wall or ceiling.

Steps in developing functional use of a rake

- *Establish a repetitive system* with small objects (blocks or discs in a bottle, pegs in a pegboard, etc.).

- *Do location expansion* with the small object so that the child must reach for it in order to complete the system.

- *Interpose a rake* with its arm around the small object (which is now out of the child's reach).

- Place the child's hand on the rake, and initiate small pulling motions until the child takes over. Usually that is all that is required for the child to start using the rake adaptively as a tool.

- Now do location expansions with the rake in relation to the object by placing the rake to the left, then the right, and then in front of the object. Adjust distances as necessary until the child can use the rake in all these positions. Finally have the child repeat the activity at home so that the function is fully generalized.

Learning how things work

Case study (Miller 2006, p.12)

Andy, an autistic five-year-old, limited-verbal child, made a dramatic shift from a child who groaned, cried and hung on his mother whenever demands were made of him, to a highly focused, competent child—with the help of two chairs and a table with removable legs. Andy's groaning and whining disappeared as he watched, wide-eyed, while we pulled the legs—one at a time—off the chairs. We then gave him a hammer and helped him hammer each chair leg back into its proper slot. When the legs were reinstalled we had him sit on the chair—now, for him, a very different chair—a chair that had legs which made it possible to sit on it. We did the same thing with the table. There was new learning with the table because the table legs had to be screwed into their sockets (see Figure 9.2)—like a light bulb—and not hammered into place.

Now we sought to exploit the table and chairs for interaction. When Andy wasn't looking, one of us removed one chair leg just before he sat on the

Figure 9.2 An autistic boy repairing a "broken" table

chair. Then, when he and the chair tumbled over, we expressed dismay, handed him a hammer and suggested that he fix the chair, which he promptly did. While he was fixing the chair one of us stealthily unscrewed one of the table legs. Then, when he began to scribble on the paper placed on the table, the table collapsed.

We again expressed wonderment at the unreliability of certain furniture, gave Andy the table leg which he—without complaint—screwed in. He then seated himself at the repaired table. Just then, his six-year-old sister—a co-conspirator—sat on her chair and with a dramatic cry of distress tumbled to the ground just as he had earlier. She then plaintively asked her brother—as she handed him the chair leg—if he would please fix her chair. He took the chair leg and very competently hammered it into place for his sister, who thanked him with a big hug for fixing her chair.

Through this whole table–chair episode, Andy did not cry or whine. He behaved very much like a little workman and seemed to take pride in his ability to fix the broken things. Judging from his behavior, we felt that his experience being able to repair the table and chairs not only created a new awareness of these objects but that his work with them created in him a new sense of competence.

Does this mean that we should have curriculum units on the working of rakes, doorknobs, multi-turn jars, inclined planes, broken tables and chairs, and how various hooks hold objects and door fasteners work? And should the curriculum also include how to push over a stool to get an out-of-reach object on a shelf? Yes, of course. Such units address the children in the "here and now" where they live. The ability of special children to cope outside the classroom depends on their ability to solve such problems and to behave in a resourceful, flexible manner. In Miller Method® (MM) programs, efforts are made to prepare the children to cope with these everyday tasks as well as with the disorder they must confront in everyday life.

Building structures

With a series of planks 18 inches long, 5.5 inches wide, and 1.5 inches thick, it is possible to build different kinds of towers as well as a tunnel. To build the tower, the adult first places two of the boards parallel to each other and then helps the child place the next two parallel but at right angles to the first (see Figure 9.3). This pattern is alternated until the child has a substantial structure on which he or she can stand to be as tall or taller than Mom or Dad—or tall enough to reach something from the ceiling (see Figure 9.4).

Figure 9.3 Dillan building a tower with the support of his therapist

Figure 9.4 Dillan standing on his tower to reach an object on the ceiling

Subsequently, these same boards are used to build an A-frame tunnel (see Figure 9.5). Once the tunnel is built the child rolls cars through to the adult on the other side. Various "catastrophes" happen to the tunnel (it collapses in the middle), preventing cars from going through. This necessitates the child repairing the tunnel in order to continue the activity. Another calamity that occurs is when a block in the middle of the tunnel obstructs passage of the cars, making it necessary for the child to use a stick to push the obstacle out of the way so that back and forth car traffic can resume. Having the child shift from building one kind of structure to building another kind (see Figure 9.6) increases the child's flexibility and helps develop a repertoire of ways of doing things.

COPING WITH THE ENVIRONMENT

Children on the autism spectrum are often "lost in space" because they lack the ability to "ground" themselves in their immediate realities. Consequently, they may not understand the layout of their house or apartment, or how to move from one room to another. In school, they may not understand, for example, the relation of the classroom to the entrance of the school building.

The Elevated Square, because of its predictability and circumscribed area, is an ideal vehicle for teaching the children how space is organized and how to manage detours in that space. Chapter 5 described the process in detail. The therapist helps the child to transfer spatial understanding

Figure 9.5 Ben, with his mother, using the A-frame tunnel he built

Figure 9.6 Ben, with therapist, learning to shift from one kind of tower construction to another (Dr. Miller, on the TV monitor in the background, is supervising via videoconferencing)

established on the Elevated Square to the ground, and to generalize it to the home and school. The therapist employs the same step-by-step procedures used on the square in other settings to help the children establish the notion of space.

"Messed up" rooms

Another means of helping the child understand spatial layout entails the unpredictable "messing up" of familiar settings (described in Chapter 1) so that the child feels the need to place things in their proper locations. In doing so, the child learns more about how the room is laid out.

Mapping the child's space

The query of a parent and my response to it indicate a child's problem with space and how this might be resolved at home:

> My little girl with special needs [26 months old] screams and tantrums when she has to leave the bathroom or kitchen to go to her room. What can I do to help her?

My response

For your daughter the different spaces in your home may seem disconnected from each other. That means that leaving the familiar space of bathroom and kitchen may be for her like "walking off the end of the earth."

You can do several things to help guide her to other spaces in your home. One effective strategy is to cut out footprints the size of her feet and lay them out from where she is to where she needs to go. Then have her simply walk on her footprints. You can also show her that she can venture from a familiar space for a few feet and then return to it. Then, support her as she expands the distance until she has made contact with another familiar space. Once she develops an "inner plan" for your home, the distress and tantrums at leaving one space for another should disappear.

Mapping the classroom

Just as the parent can help the child map familiar spaces at home, so may the teacher help the child map the classroom. In building a classroom map it is useful to have small photos of salient items in the room. Children can move the photos around on an outline representing the classroom and place them in the correct relative position to the real objects in the classroom. Then, in addition to repairing the "messed up" classroom, the teacher introduces "treasure hunts," where children have to locate items hidden in different parts of the classroom. The teacher can then determine how well different children can read the classroom map—with its symbols representing treasures at various locations—to guide them toward the hidden treasures.

Once the children have mastered the geography of the classroom, the same strategy can be used to extend their knowledge to the layout of the school. This can be done by having the child—first under supervision and then alone—carry messages from the classroom teacher to the principal's office, the nurse's station, speech and OT offices, and then bring back messages to the classroom teacher. Since there are several entrances to the school, have the child find his or her classroom as well as other sites in the school from either of these entrances.

It is a small step to take these principles and expand them to the school neighborhood and to where the different children live. Space takes on personal meaning when the children understand the relation of their homes to the school. In some MM schools, teachers have large maps of the area with circles showing where each of the children live and the route the bus takes to bring them to school.

To help the children "map" their immediate neighborhood, teachers take them on short walks. As they walk, teachers indicate "markers" along the way—perhaps a fence that the children can touch while walking or a small incline that they can run down, or a curbing that is brightly painted. These "markers" provide a "road map" for the children on the way to the neighborhood store. Some teachers take photographs of the different markers so that the children can refer to them when they return to their classrooms.

Even when you are pointing out the markers, it is important for the children to maintain orientation to the school from which they came by having them point toward the location of the school as well as to their destination. In this way they continue to remain "grounded" as they move from familiar to less familiar space.

Anticipating or recalling events

Many children on the autism spectrum seem to live so much in the moment that the next routine event—no matter how often it has been repeated—is upsetting to them. Those children with little or no language have no means of talking to themselves about what is coming next or what has just happened in the past. To help the children grasp the predictable sequence of events in the course of the day—and how, from time to time, the sequence changes—a template calendar is very useful (see Figure 9.7).

Figure 9.7 The template calendar

The template calendar helps mark the day's events for the child. It consists of a series of moveable three-dimensional replicas, somewhat larger than doll furniture, of the salient features of major activities common to each school day. The children see this miniature series of detachable replicas and soon learn that each section represents a particular activity that follows another in a certain order.

Before the children move, for example to the Sign and Spoken Language Program, the teacher shows them a small replica of the TV monitor on which they see this program; prior to lunch they see a replica of their table with stools. As the children progress in their understanding of time, the teacher may introduce more than one event at a time until the child understands the notion of a sequence of events (with tableaux closer to the left signifying those events that come first). Then, when there is a change in schedule, teachers can shift the tableaux according to the changed schedule, and in this way help the child master the changed sequence of events. With frequent reference to the tableau calendar, the children increasingly develop a clearer sense of how the day will unfold.

Somewhat more advanced children can benefit from picture calendars used both in school and at home. The drawings or photographs for each event should attempt to capture the most salient aspect of that event. Teachers should use these in the same way they use the tableau calendar.

Developing time concepts

In the course of the walks described earlier, teachers have opportunity to introduce time concepts. A teacher might say, for example, "*Soon*, not right now, but *soon* we will come to the store." By helping the children anticipate events the teacher combines notions of time and space with further exercise in the way that language can guide expectations.

Time concepts may be introduced in various ways: For example, to establish the concept of *tomorrow, yesterday*, and *today*, the teacher may have the children begin an engaging activity at the end of the day, interrupt it, and then tell the children that they can complete it when they come to school "tomorrow." Then, when they come in the next day, teachers can say, "*Yesterday*—before you went home—you started this. *Today*, you will be able to finish it." By interrupting the task the day before, the teacher deliberately builds a tension in the children to complete the task. This tension and the need to complete the task, when related to the time at which they can

complete the task, help the children achieve the time concepts of *tomorrow*, *yesterday*, and *today*.

Time concepts may also be introduced in the course of one of the children's favorite activities—baking cookies. Having children mix the dough for cookies and then place the cookies in the oven to eat later gives them a beginning notion of the passage of time. The children can also "watch" the food as it is baking and, in doing so, grasp concepts such as *later*, *wait, first this, then that*, and *now*. Narrating and predicting what will soon happen helps to keep the children engaged with the activity and to cope with the difficult delay between baking and eating.

In this context, I would like to suggest how best to teach the days of the weeks, the months of the year, and the seasons. Even though a child can reel off the names of the days of the week and the months of the year, they are quite meaningless unless the child anchors the passage of time in some personal and memorable manner. By marking each day with a special activity that is unique to that day, the children learn to distinguish one day from another. For example, let's say that Monday the children work with tools in the shop; Tuesday, the class is walking to the store; Wednesday the class is baking cookies, and so forth. Then, when the teacher asks what day it is and the child says "Monday," the child can also respond to the question, "And on Monday the class will…"

Teaching the months of the year is more difficult because they cover a longer time span. However, as a first step, cluster the months in terms of the seasons. Then, December, January, or February become the cold winter months when it snows and the children have to wear warm clothing; March, April, and May are spring months where it gets warmer: the children don't need heavy clothing and the grass is getting green and there are more birds; June, July, and August are summer months. It gets very hot and children go swimming and wear light clothing. September, October, and November are fall months where it starts to get colder, children need warmer clothes, and the leaves fall from the trees.

Note: In places where the seasons are not well defined—as in California or Florida—teachers might use the "seasonal" appearance of certain sports as a way of marking the months.

Finally, ritual events that occur with regularity, such as birthdays and holidays, help to give the child a beginning notion of what a year is and how events cycle. Each child's birthday—and the little party that accompanies it—helps the child not only to understand and share the ritual, but to

anticipate this event. Teachers circle on the calendar each child's birthday—with a picture of the child on that date. This allows the entire class to report whose birthday is coming next.

BREAKDOWN IN COPING BEHAVIOR

At times, in spite of the best efforts of professionals and parents, there is a breakdown in the child's coping behavior. This may express itself in tantrums, extreme passivity ("beached whale syndrome"), intense object preoccupation, or scattered, uncoordinated activity—all behaviors which interfere with learning.

In this section I will first discuss tantrums, as well as other kinds of breakdowns, and then consider ways of treating the children with these issues.

A tantrum or "meltdown" is one kind of breakdown in the child's organized functioning. Having said that, it is important to differentiate between two different kinds of tantrums: One, the "catastrophic" tantrum, results in chaotic behavior—screaming, thrashing around, arms flailing, legs kicking—in which the child seems completely out of contact with everyone; the other, which I refer to as a "social tantrum," also features a child who is screaming and thrashing around—even banging his or her head on the wall or hard floor—but who still exhibits an awareness of others and of the surroundings. The difference is that the first child is quite out of touch—and it takes time to bring him or her back into emotional contact with others. In contrast, as you watch the child with a "social tantrum," you will notice that in the midst of the tantrum he or she looks around—apparently checking people out to see how they are taking his or her display. The child may, for example, bang his or her head on the floor then glance at people as if to say, "How did you like that one? Would you like another? Take that!" followed by another banging of head on the ground.

With the "social tantrum" the first concern, of course, is with the safety of the child. Staff must first protect the child from hurting himself or herself. This may require restraining the child, placing padding in front of the child to reduce the impact of head-banging, or even having the child wear a helmet. In addition to these short-term efforts, we make the assumption that the child is seeking the teacher's involvement and, accordingly, we attempt to meet this need by periodically during the day finding occasion to interact with the child and to develop an ongoing relationship with him or her. These contacts are not associated with either "good" or "bad" behavior. They are

merely an ongoing expression of affection and interest in this child. With this combined program we find a gradual diminution of self-abuse among such children.

We view catastrophic tantrums as a failure in the child's ability to cope with people or things, or the sensory impact of his or her surroundings. We try to understand the meaning of the tantrum—since this varies from child to child. For one child it may come about because he or she cannot cope with the shift from one situation to another and needs help with this. For another, it may stem from a feeling of loss triggered by a teacher turning to another child or by the loss of an object. For still another, it can result, on the one hand, from insufficient sensory input when a child stays seated too long, or, on the other hand, from sensory overload induced by too much discordant sound in the classroom.

Whatever the source of the tantrum, we try to meet the need being expressed, to signal transitions from one activity to another more clearly, and to use repetitive (and often reassuring) rituals to help the child reorganize. If all else fails we hold the child while talking to him or her calmly about what is happening in the classroom, what will happen next, etc.

The following incident described by a parent illustrates one autistic child's response to the loss of an object:

Losing balloons

The tantrum in the department store yesterday occurred when seven-year-old Benny—a child on the autism spectrum—let go of two balloons he was holding and they went 20 feet up to the roof. He wanted those balloons. There were many others to be had the same color so I got him two more, but of course this did not do. He kept yelling "need help" which is his favorite chunk phrase these days, and freaked out, yelling and going after me as I tried to get him out of the store. It was bad, but I did everything I could think of. I stretched my arms up and said, "It's too high, can't get it," and gave him two more. Any ideas or suggestions that might be helpful in this kind of situation?

My response

Getting the two balloons of the same color and giving them to Benny was absolutely correct. However, for Benny, the problem seems to have been not the balloons *per se*, but the way they sailed away without him being able to do anything about it. (In our terms, the balloons floating away was an interrupted system for which Benny had no compensatory action that would allow him to retrieve the balloons.)

If that is correct, then recreating his original experience of "balloons floating away"—with the exception that this time Benny could pull on a long string attached to them and reel them in—could have made the difference. While hauling the new balloons in, Benny could overcome the feeling of loss of the first two balloons because the balloons with string attached would provide a corrective experience, and, in our terms, would re-establish the interrupted system.

Our method of coping with tantrums depends on the need the child is expressing and the kind of system disorder a child presents. For example, with a child characterized by a closed system disorder, the tantrum is usually triggered by new circumstances that are too disparate from the child's existing systems. With such a child, the introduction of rituals is often effective. One tantrumming closed system child responded very well to a crayon scribbling ritual in which the teacher placed the crayon in his hand and helped him make repetitive marks. Then, to bring him into emotional contact with her, she began to give him different colored crayons. Within two or three minutes the child became calm and could be brought back into the drawing program going on at the time in the classroom. With other closed system children, large-body rituals—rapidly going up, around, and down an elevated board structure a dozen times—often help them organize their functioning.

Tantrums among nonverbal children with system-forming disorders are typically more resistant because it is difficult to locate the sources of the tantrum and because the children have few systems to draw on. Consequently, such children may require a variety of interventions—compression, calm talking by the caregiver, and movement within a familiar setting.

In MM programs "time out" is not used to control inappropriate behavior. Neither may a child be deprived of food for previous unacceptable behavior. Our feeling about removal or time out is that it works against what we are trying to accomplish. If the task is to teach children how to make human contact and communicate with each other, it is difficult to see how the excluded child can learn to do this timed out in a separate room. If a child's tantrum cannot be quickly resolved, it is appropriate to have an aide take the child from the room and work with him or her without disrupting the entire program.

Tantrum utilization

The treatment strategies described here under the heading of "tantrum utilization" allow parents or professionals to use parts of a child's tantrum to help the child become organized. These strategies work best in a one-to-one situation between therapist and child or between parent and child. One utilization strategy—effective with children who have some receptive understanding—involves narrating the child's tantrum. Here, the therapist might say, "Daniel is very upset. He is kicking his feet, crying, screaming, and banging his fists on the ground… Now he is kicking, now screaming… Will he bang his fists now and then scream? No, he is kicking and then screaming. What will he do next? Oh yes, he is banging his fists," etc.

Often with this kind of narration, a child will pause in the tantrum activity to listen to what the therapist is saying. The child, too, becoming aware of his or her own behavior, becomes curious about what his or her body is doing. As this occurs, the intensity of the tantrum subsides and soon the therapist is able to say, "Daniel feels better now. A big hug and back to Karen's class."

Another kind of tantrum utilization involves the therapist taking a much more active role with the tantrum. Here, Bert, guided onto the Elevated Square, begins jumping, kicking, and screaming. As an assistant guides Bert to the therapist in the midst of his tantrum, the therapist, pointing to a block behind the child, firmly says, "Sit down!" When Bert sits down, the therapist says, "Get up!" This is repeated several times. Then, when Bert sits down still screaming and kicking, the therapist says, "No screaming…just kicking!" and then, with hand motions simulating kicking, says, "Kick, kick, kick!"

As Bert responds to the therapist's request that he kick, the quality of the kicking begins to change. Kicking behavior which was previously done without conscious awareness now comes under the constraint of language used by the therapist. At this point, the therapist may direct Bert to get up, and walk around the square (guided by the assistant). Bert's behavior is already much calmer and more directed. When he returns, the therapist again says, "Sit down!" "Get up!" As Bert again starts to scream, the therapist tells him to scream, touching the child's mouth to indicate where the scream comes from. Often a child will emit a small sound which the therapist encourages. Again, by having the child reproduce screaming behavior at the therapist's request, behavior which previously was emitted *without awareness* by the child is now responsive to the therapist's direction, and contributes to the child's conscious production of sounds. Tantrum abatement under these conditions is often very rapid.

Another way in which tantrum utilization may come into play is when a child who is brought to another station on the Elevated Square (or on the ground) finds the shift to the new system objectionable and protests with loud screams. At this point, the therapist (or a parent who has learned the technique) may say, "First Andrea scream, now Momma [or therapist] screams" (and repeats the child's scream). This turn-taking screaming behavior may be repeated several times until the therapist or parent says, "Andrea screams and then pushes the car down the ramp." Typically, after reciprocal screaming, the child complies with the request in an organized manner and, with repetition, does not find it necessary to scream.

This particular method of tantrum utilization is most effective with rather minor tantrums. Its effectiveness, I speculate, comes from the child feeling heard or received by the therapist or parent, who repeats the child's scream. Such interaction may also serve as a transition for the child who may then feel ready to follow the parent or therapist's direction.

Sometimes a child on the spectrum who has been progressing nicely over a period of months begins to tantrum at every change in the day's program. When this sudden shift in behavior occurs, it is desirable not only to treat the tantrum as described but also to explore with parents any possible changes which may have taken place at home. Concerned about one such child's sudden shift in behavior, I interviewed the mother:

A.M.: Johnny has been unusually irritable in school lately. Every change in the program seems to set him off. May I ask you a few questions about changes at home?

Mother: Yes, of course.

A.M.: Have there been any changes recently at home? Any relatives visiting? New children in the house?

Mother: No, everything is just as it always was.

A.M.: Has your schedule or your husband's schedule changed?

Mother: Now that you mention it, my husband has shifted from a day shift to a night shift. When he was on the day shift he would have regular rough-housing sessions with Johnny. With him on the night shift, that no longer happens. Do you think that his schedule change could be affecting Johnny?

A.M.: It is entirely possible. Perhaps we can work out a way for Johnny to have that rough-housing contact with your husband at a different part of the day. It might make all the difference in how he is at school.

Subsequently, Johnny's father resumed rough-housing contact with Johnny and the school tantrums diminished dramatically.

The "beached whale" syndrome

While not a tantrum, certain children—generally quite large and heavy—engage in a passive behavior, which has the effect of making it impossible for the teacher to continue working with them. This behavior consists of a large child flopping down on the floor, refusing to move, and passively resisting all efforts to be moved. Teachers, frustrated at their inability to physically move the child, called on me for cues as to how to deal with this behavior.

Having worked with a number of such children, I found that part of the motivation driving this behavior was often a wish for more nurturing from the teacher. Accordingly, I recommended that the teacher dealing with "a beached whale" not attempt to lift him (I have only seen this behavior with boys) but to breathe deeply and slowly to calm himself or herself, then to crouch down next to the child, talk to him quietly while gently rubbing his back for about five minutes, then slowly stand up and, *without saying a word*, simply hold out a hand. In almost every instance, a "beached whale" treated in this way will accept the teacher's proffered hand and allow himself to be led back to the group.

Sometimes, there is a tendency to dismiss this behavior and the child's need for nurturing by saying, "Oh, he just does that for attention!" To this I reply, "Yes, he needs attention in the same way that we need oxygen."

Holding or perseverating with objects

Often the children need to hold particular objects throughout the day. Alternatively, they may be repetitively involved with one or more objects such as flicking light switches on and off, opening and closing doors, or lining things up. Tantrums frequently occur when the children are required to give up an object or transition from one activity (system) to another.

Children may need to hold their "precious" objects because doing this provides them with comfort as well as a limited but predictable presence in their hand. Since the compulsive holding of objects seriously interferes with the use of the hands, treatment is organized around gently but systematically expanding the child's experience of hand-held objects.

Two methods are effective: One, *the trading method,* entails rapidly and repeatedly trading the child's object for another that is the same or similar.

For example, if the child is clutching a colored popsicle stick we gently remove the popsicle stick from one hand while simultaneously offering the child a popsicle stick replacement of a different color for the other hand. We repeat this rapid trading of objects while gradually increasing the time between taking and giving the sticks. The interval between trades is determined by what the child can accept. Subsequently, the trading method may be used with other long objects—such as crayons—to which the child may tend to cling. Trading a range of objects with the child not only helps wean the child from a compulsive holding of objects, it provides the child with opportunity to notice how one object differs from another.

The second or *balloon method* requires balloons of different colors which will provide an attractive substitute for whatever the child is holding. Inflate the balloon in front of the child, then offer it to him or her. Since holding the balloon requires both hands, the child will often drop the held object in order to hold the balloon. If necessary, remove the object the child is holding as you offer the balloon. Once the child has the balloon, allow it to deflate rapidly in his or her hands. (This usually delights the child.) Immediately, provide another balloon for deflating. Occasionally, allow the balloon to deflate in your hands while producing a sound as the neck of the balloon is constricted. Repeat daily for about ten minutes.

Treating perseverative activity

The children's tendency to compulsively persist with an activity may actively interfere with the child's ability to learn. Consequently it is important to find ways to reduce this tendency. Two interventions are effective with perseverative activity: One entails gradually expanding and elaborating the activity, the other, using a multisphere strategy which involves the child in several different but related activities. The following query by a parent and my response illustrate how certain perseverative activity may be expanded:

Obsessed with balls
My autistic son is obsessed with balls. When I take them away or hide them he cries inconsolably. My behavioral consultant recommends that I get rid of the balls. What would you suggest?

My response
First, let me say that our philosophy is—whenever possible—*not* to take things away from the children but to try to build on what they have. For your "ritual-captured" (closed-system) child, involvement with balls is an

important system. Repetitive play with them is at this time the very best that he can do with these intriguing objects.

So I would recommend trying the following. Get all kinds of balls—big ones, little ones; red, green, and yellow, soft, hard, heavy, light—then set up different locations so the little balls go in one place, the big ones in another place. Then—before your son gets bored with this sorting task—start pelting him with the light (nerf) balls to start a ball interaction (like a snowball fight), where you pelt him, he pelts you. Perhaps you get his father or another sibling to help him pelt you with the balls. Periodically duck behind some furniture so he can't see you, then suddenly reappear and pelt him again. If he ducks down wait until he pops up then get him again. See if he will try to get you as you move from one hiding place to another.

After a time (when you judge he's had enough excitement) tell him it's time to put the balls away. Then, sing the "Clean up!" song as you point to the different balls all over the room and guide him toward dropping them in their proper location. If, at that point, he wants to take a couple of balls with him as he prepares for bed, that's fine.

I'm sure that as you follow this line of thinking you'll find other productive ways of turning his "obsession" into important interactive play that will prepare him for playing with other children.

Expanding the activity means that one carefully intrudes within the child's activity. If lining up blocks is the perseverative activity, the therapist intrudes by slightly modifying the activity—perhaps carefully altering the position of the block. Negotiate changes in the child's system in accord with what the child can accept. Chapter 4 explains this strategy in detail.

Multisphere strategies often begin with a child's perseverative system—say, repetitively flushing the toilet—then interrupting that system and requiring the child (often protesting) to go to other water-related systems such as pouring water over a water wheel. Once the child engages the water wheel, this activity too is interrupted and the child is returned to his or her original system of flushing toilets. Then, introduce additional water-based activities. See Chapters 5 and 7 for more details on this procedure as well as its variations.

Scattered and disconnected behavior

Scattered children turn toward any stimulating event, without becoming involved with any of them. Often, for example, when presented with puzzles, children with system-forming disorder show a disconnect between their eyes and hands—their eyes looking one way while their hands fumble with the puzzle.

Scattered behavior implies that the child has not been able to integrate, sequence, or motor plan various steps of an activity in order to form an integrative activity (system). To help the child organize his or her behavior, it is important to introduce the activity *rapidly paced, repetitively,* and with a *salient outcome.*

For example, children who have eye–hand disconnect with regard to picking up and dropping an object require the therapist to work hand over hand repetitively with the child, helping the child drop the object into a sharply resounding metal pan, as described in Chapter 4. The repetitive nature and rapid pace of the activity provide the child with many opportunities to integrate eye with hand action while the salient outcome adds to the child's sense of causing something to happen. From time to time the therapist may find it necessary to orient the child's head and eyes toward what his or her hands are doing. This is best performed first on the Elevated Square and then on the ground.

Toileting

Many of the children come to school unable to toilet themselves—an issue of much concern for parents, many of whom have younger children in addition to their disordered child. Complicating the issue is the fact that many nonverbal children have only limited awareness of their bodies. If a child does not react to pain when he or she falls over, for example, the probability is that the child will not be sensitive to pressures from the bladder or colon indicating a need to urinate or defecate. The lack of such inner cues makes toilet training difficult for such children, particularly in the light of the complexity of toileting as an integrative system.

Toileting involves recognizing and interpreting an inner signal, approaching the toilet, lowering or unzipping pants, sitting down, urinating or defecating, wiping, getting off the toilet, adjusting or picking up pants, flushing the toilet, washing and drying hands, and returning to the classroom or family activity—a total of 11 components.

The teacher or parent begins to help the child establish the toileting system by first carefully evaluating the child's status with regard to forming the toileting system. It is desirable to know, for example, how many parts of the toileting system the child has mastered. The child may at first take in only the more salient, flushing-water part. If the child cannot carry through other portions of the system, the parent or teacher assists the child hand-over-hand until the child can do so.

At school and at home help the child complete the toileting system by flushing the toilet, adjusting clothing, and washing and drying hands. In developing this system it is important that the child perform each step in the proper sequence. At first, do not require the child to sit on the toilet for more than a moment or two before getting up, picking up his or her pants, and flushing the toilet.

Test the formation of the system by interrupting it at key points such as after the pants are lowered while the child is still standing or just before flushing the toilet. If, following an interruption, the child needs to sit down after lowering the pants or to flush after getting up and picking up the pants, then the system is forming.

Once the system is forming, the child may sit longer on the toilet but not so long that the rest of the system is lost. Sitting on the toilet should never become the basis for a power struggle between parent and child. At school it is helpful also for the child to notice the performance of a child on an adjacent toilet. As the child completes parts of the system, the worker expresses pleasure with a pat or a hug *whether or not the child has urinated or defecated*. As the system gets stronger, it will increasingly require that the child complete the system by defecating or urinating.

Parents have reported success in teaching toileting with the following additions to the preceding account. In addition to setting up a regular schedule for toileting after meals and before bedtime, some parents have found that gently pressing the bladder encourages the child to urinate. Others report that running water from the sink faucet while the child is sitting on the toilet stimulates urination. Still others find that quiet musical accompaniments set the right tone (Debussy rather than Berlioz). Boys have learned to urinate while standing up by modeling their fathers as they urinate. Squirting water between the child's legs or dropping bits of clay to provide more sensory support is helpful for some children.

One autistic child performed the entire system including sitting on the toilet while defecating. The problem, however, was that she refused to remove her diaper while doing so. The issue was resolved by allowing her to wear the diaper but cutting out a hole so that the feces would drop directly into the toilet. Eventually, the hole in the diaper became larger until only a strip around her waist remained. Soon she relinquished the need for that strip and used the toilet appropriately.

In order to help the most disordered children achieve and generalize toileting systems, the children are given several opportunities to practice toileting systems in the course of the day. Teachers and parents need to coordinate efforts forming the toileting system so that both carry through the same procedures. This will also hasten generalization so that the child does not toilet himself or herself only at school and not at home, or vice versa. Toileting systems seem to develop most rapidly when teachers and parents share procedures and progress with each other. With patience, calmness—and some fortitude—parents and teachers working together will succeed.

The next chapter will discuss relevant teaching.

SUMMARY

Building the autistic child's body/self concept—and the sense of "thereness" that emerges with this construction—is critical for the ability to explore, make sense of, and cope with the world around him or her. Effective strategies for helping the child build a stable body/self include rough-and-tumble play and experiencing himself or herself as "a doer" with the help of a "can do!" board both in school and at home that details the child's functioning in both places.

Helping the child represent himself or herself is helpful. For those children who do not know how to draw, teachers use the LCDC's drawing program to systematically guide the children from lines to scribbles and, eventually, to representations of the self, others, and objects.

Part of coping requires functional use of objects, whether this involves using a rake to bring an out-of-reach object closer, turning and pulling a knob to open a door, opening a multi-turn jar, and understanding how an inclined plane works. In this chapter, a detailed outline described how children can be taught to use a rake or to understand the workings of the inclined plane.

A case study described a four-year-old autistic child who developed a more competent stance after learning how to "fix" broken tables or chairs for himself and his sister. The chapter also provided descriptions of how children engage in building projects which require regular "fixing" as various "catastrophes" occur.

How space is organized and how detours may be managed is systematically taught first on the square and then on the ground. The children learn to conceptualize the space they live in through teachers helping the children map their classrooms and engage in "treasure hunts" which test their ability to read the map.

Children are then taught how the school is laid out and how to cope with the space outside the school by first developing a "road map" with "markers" that help guide the child from one place to another.

With the help of a template calendar children learn how their school day is organized. Time concepts also entail understanding the distinction between yesterday, today, and tomorrow, and how to mark the events of the year through birthdays and other special events.

Breakdowns in coping behavior (tantrums, "beached whale" syndrome, holding or perseverating with objects) were discussed with ways of treating them. Finally, the chapter described a systems approach to toileting which stresses the importance of teachers and parents carrying through the same systematic procedures.

Chapter 10

Teaching to Children's Reality[1]

When I asked a colleague if a particular autistic boy understood what he was reading, he impatiently replied, "Arn, if it walks like a duck and quacks like a duck, it's a duck!" However, when I showed him how nicely my battery-powered duck walked and quacked, he became unusually quiet.

A SAD STORY

Some years ago—working as consultants—my wife and I were asked to observe the "independent functioning" of a class of eight developmentally delayed children ranging in age from 8 to 12. All the children were seated around a large table. Each had a large reference book and a notebook in which they were carefully writing. Periodically, one or the other would reach for and open the large reference book, move an index finger down the page, stop at a certain point, and then carefully write in the notebook. The mood was quiet and serious—as in a library—and the children seemed hard at work gaining information from a reference book for their reports.

Curious about what they were working on, we sat down next to several children and watched closely. Soon it became clear that their "independent functioning" consisted of learning to open the dictionary, pick a word at random, and carefully copy it—letter by letter—into their notebooks until they had filled the page with copied words. That was it. No report and no use of the words copied: just an impressively staged illusion.

---

1   Material in this chapter is taken from the *Sign and Spoken Language Program* (1970/1989), copyright © Arnold Miller 1989; and from *Symbol Accentuation: A New Approach to Reading* (1968/1989), copyright © Arnold Miller 1989. Used with permission.

Let's be clear. There is nothing wrong with the perceptual task of copying words letter by letter into a notebook. It might even have helped the children's form perception. However, setting the stage so that the children *looked like* they were doing something much more advanced than copying was disturbing. Such manipulation of the children would not be tolerated by teachers today. And yet, without a careful test of the relevance of a lesson, children may appear to be learning something relevant when they are not.

Examples of irrelevant teaching include teaching a class of limited-verbal autistic children how the planets revolve around the sun when the children don't understand the relation of their classroom to the building's entrance. Or teaching the months of the year when the children have not yet grasped the notion of yesterday, today, or tomorrow. Or trying to teach adding and subtracting and expecting that the worksheet exercises which the children dutifully complete will somehow generalize into making change of a dollar or understanding how numbers relate to measuring things. Or teaching reading without determining how well the children understand what they "read."

Sometimes this kind of teaching is justified under the notion of "exposure." The notion here is that if the child is exposed to some of these concepts they might somehow "take root." However, unless teachers provide the children with a way of relating these concepts to the children's direct experience, such "exposure" teaching is of questionable value. We propose an alternative: Relevant teaching that takes into account the realities of the children.

TEACHING FOR RELEVANCE

Teaching for relevance depends on three things:

1. knowledge of the children's developmental and learning needs

2. knowledge of how to present materials to address these needs

3. adopting an "I'm from Missouri" stance in which the teacher assumes that the children *do not* understand what is being taught until they clearly demonstrate that they do.

Often, the way material is presented can make the difference between a child "getting it" and simply echoing what has been said. In this chapter I introduce ways of teaching that are consistent with the children's developmental needs. The goal of relevant teaching is not only to teach a particular set of concepts, but to do it in a way that contributes to the children's sense of competence.

I will first discuss ways of helping the children move into symbolic functioning. Following this, I will provide an overview of the Sign and Spoken Language and the Symbol Accentuation Reading Programs. I will also indicate how arithmetic concepts and the concept of time duration can be taught to children on the autism spectrum.

HOW CAN ONE HELP THE CHILDREN DEVELOP SYMBOLIC FUNCTIONING?

As we view the steps toward symbolic functioning from action–object to gesture or picture, to spoken and printed words, to symbolic play, the increasing abstractness of these symbolic forms are obstacles to the children's progress which must be overcome. Our strategy is to help the child experience the more abstract forms in direct relation to his or her more immediate experience. In this chapter I describe a number of ways of achieving this goal. One way is to use object replicas.

Using object replicas

In the preceding chapter I described the use of the template calendar to help the children forecast what events are scheduled next in the course of the day. The template calendar is—to the extent it forecasts for the children what is to happen next—an early form of symbolic reference. Object replicas like those used with the template calendar may also be used by the children to help them spontaneously represent their experience. This is done with the help of an exact replica of the Elevated Square that can fit on one of the workstations of the full-size Elevated Square.

> John, a four-year-old autistic boy with limited-verbal ability, had never symbolized any of his actions. To help him achieve this, the therapist first guided John through a series of actions involving the large square. These actions consisted first of righting a set of steps (which had been turned on its side) so that he could climb on the square. Following this John walked around the square until he got to the slide and then slid down. He repeated this sequence a number of times until it became a well-established system that he performed with little support. Then, John's therapist guided him to an exact replica of the square (on one of the square's work stations). This replica was set up to mirror the system John had been performing: the stairs were turned on their side and a small boy doll figure (to represent John) was placed next to the steps.

Spontaneously—and to the delight of those watching—John immediately picked up the doll and had it fix the steps. He then took the boy doll figure, bounced it up the steps, sat it down next to the replica slide, and then made the doll slide down.

While some children, like John, immediately grasp the relation between the large square and the small replica and perform as John did, others require a few trials before they "get it." The replica of the square with small doll figure can be used to help the child represent a range of activities that are first performed by the child on the full-scale square. The general principle guiding all such representation is that *the child first establish a system involving a vivid sequence of actions in the real world* and then *immediately* use the doll figure to reproduce these actions. For example, if the child has been bouncing on the physio ball, the next step would be having a doll figure next to a much smaller ball so that the child can bounce the doll figure on the small ball. This first step toward imaginative play can, with guidance, lead the child to more complex and spontaneous symbolic play.

Transforming perseverative action into symbolic play

Earlier we discussed how perseverative activity—such as lining up blocks—may be gradually transformed into interactive play. The key strategy is to negotiate the therapist's acceptance within the child's action–object system. Once the child tolerates and then accepts the therapist's slight adjustments of the child's systems, it is then possible for interactive symbolic play within the child's expanded system to develop. Then, instead of merely lining up blocks next to each other, the child gradually learns to participate in interactive play with cars going in both directions along the "roads," and going up and down ramps (see Figure 4.1). Soon the child begins to spontaneously initiate symbolic activity on which the therapist can readily build.

From object to picture

While many of the children have no difficulty in giving or pointing to a designated object—a cup, hat, ball, car, etc.—a certain number of children on the spectrum cannot identify picture representations of objects. For these children, the shift from three to two dimensions is too big a leap for them. To make this shift possible, we find that a 3D/2D strategy is helpful. This consists of mounting a salient portion of the object on one side of a card with an exact, two-dimensional replica of that object on the other side. The picture image is designed to line up with the object in such a way that when the card is flipped the child projects upon the picture the three-dimensional properties of the object (see Figure 10.1). This can best be accomplished, for example, by first encouraging the child to reach for the handle of the cup on the object side of the card but, before he or she touches the handle, flipping over the card so that the child directs his or her action toward the picture handle of the cup. Teachers can readily make these 3D/2D cards by following the format described. After children learn to invest in pictures through this method, they seem to find it easier to find meaning in other clearly drawn and colored pictures of objects.

THE SIGN AND SPOKEN LANGUAGE PROGRAM

Use of manual signs adapted from American Sign Language (ASL) and paired with spoken words is an important strategy in Miller Method® (MM) programs for developing communicative capacity. Signs are often readily grasped because they resemble the events they represent. The Sign and Spoken Language Program (SSLP) extends the work described in Chapter 4 ("Getting Started with the Miller Method®") and Chapter 5, on the Elevated Square. This program presents the manual signs in a way that takes into account the challenges that children on the autism spectrum confront in trying to understand and use language. In doing so, it advances the children's

Figure 10.1 Cards showing 3D/2D set up for transfer of meaning from object to picture: (a) objects (dog, cup, hat); (b) part objects/part picture; (c) pictures

understanding and use of symbolic forms. Before describing these strategies, I will first indicate the scope of the program.

Either a CD-ROM or videotape presents the program so that a number of children can view it at the same time. There are four categories of signs in the program: Category 1 presents action signs; Category 2, food-related signs; Category 3, objects/events; and Category 4, two-sign–two-word combinations (see Table 10.1).

Table 10.1 Concepts—in four categories—introduced in the Sign and Spoken Language Program (on videotape and CD-ROM)

Category 1 Action	Category 2 Food related	Category 3 Objects/events	Category 4 Two sign/two word	
walk	chair	boy	apple	eat apple
run	table	man	orange	eat orange
jump	eat	sleep	cookie	break cookie
fall	glass	awake		eat cookie
come	pour	wash		more cookie
go	drink	comb	chair	my chair
stop	knife	toothbrush		big chair
get up	fork	hat		little chair
sit down	spoon	sweep		chair falls
open	plate	house	fork	big fork
close	cookie	tree		little fork
pick up	bread	cat	spoon	big spoon
drop	egg	car		little spoon
push	salt	boat	falls	hat falls
pull	ketchup	ball		glass falls
break	roll	bird		orange falls
up	pie			apple falls
down			table	table falls
				pick up table
				table up/down
			egg	pick up egg
				drop egg
			cat	cat in (bag)
				cat out (bag)
				cat jumps
				cat eats

Features of the SSLP

An important rationale for using manual sign language is that it serves as a "bridge" between the spoken word and its referent. However, even with manual signs, a variety of distracting stimuli in everyday life may divert the disordered child from the intended relation between sign and referent. Having the children seated in front of a television or computer monitor with the teacher and aides seated *behind* them to keep them focused on the training material is one important step (see Figure 10.2) in reducing distraction.

Another means of reducing distraction is careful editing which perceptually marries or interweaves the sign with its object or event meaning. In developing the SSLP, I have taken the liberty of modifying some of the conventional ASL signs so that they are more dynamic and thus more readily grasped by the children. An example is *run*, for which we use the rapid patting of one hand with the other as the hands swing in an arc from left to right. This relates to the act of running through editing that merges the rapid patting with the same rhythm of people running. Similarly, the manual sign for *pour* (the hand simulates pouring) interweaves the gesture with the actual act of pouring from a glass (see Figure 10.3).

Interwoven and command sequences for *break* are shown in Figure 10.4. The purpose of the interwoven sequence is to blend the spoken word and the sign with its action referent. The purpose of the command sequence is to indicate how a person may use the sign/word to cause another to break something.

The same strategy is used with such manual signs as *eat, drink, fork, knife,* and *spoon.* These signs simulate everyday functions or use of objects in ways that intimately relate a sign, its meaning, and the conventional spoken word which always accompanies the sequence. With repetition, the watching children begin to experience the manual sign, and the spoken word paired with it, as part of and directly related to the referent action or object.

From the child's perspective

Because children initially experience the manual signs from their own perspective as if they were making the signs, the training sequences first presents the manual signs and their referents as they would appear to the child producing the sign. Only after this does the training sequence present the sign from other perspectives—including how the sign would look when presented by someone directly facing the child. For example, when the

Figure 10.2 Children sign and say "eat" with the Sign and Spoken Language Program

Figure 10.3 The animated interweaving of pouring with the sign for *pour*

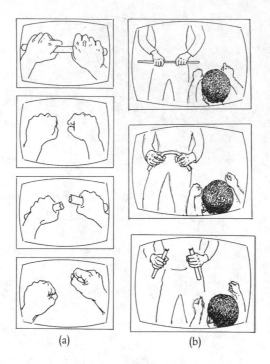

(a)   (b)

Figure 10.4 The term *break* in (a) interwoven and (b) command sequences

concept *come* first appears on the screen, the sign (beckoning arms and fingers) is interwoven with a child coming directly toward the signing viewer. Later presentations of the concept gradually shift from the subjective to the objective viewpoint. The child then has opportunity to learn that the relation between sign/word and referent is independent of perspective; that is, two people at right angles to the viewer may communicate certain meanings to each other independent of their orientation to the viewer.

The training sequences are designed not only to establish certain relations between sign, word, and event but—through the excitement they generate—to elicit a contagious response to these relations among the children. The training tape achieves this by combining images with vivid sound effects and brisk pacing, and by creating a sense of urgency through different voices uttering the words fused with the signs. For example, as the children hear "Stop! Stop!" and see the manual sign for *stop* (the edge of one hand strikes the palm of another), in rapid succession the *stop* sign appears in front of bike riders, a car, and so forth, coupled with the shriek of brakes and the skidding of tires. Such effects enhance the ability of the children to take in the significance of sign and word in life-simulated situations.

Generalizing sign/words from training sequences

Only when the child can understand the sign/word meanings—first learned in the SSLP—in a variety of settings does the child fully "own" these concepts. In other words, the child must learn that the meaning of the concept *jump* goes beyond the particular child jumping off a ladder seen in the SSLP. The child must learn that the concept may refer to a child jumping off a table, to a classmate jumping down the hall on a pogo stick, and so forth.

Before crediting a child with true receptive understanding of a concept, we must see clear evidence that the sign/word guides the child's actions even when detached from its familiar perceptual and contextual cues. For example, the child must understand that the sign/word *drop* refers to the sudden release of an object independent of the kind of object being released, who is dropping the object, and where it is being dropped.

Communication: A two-way process

Before children can communicate with adults or with each other, they must be able to receive and send messages. To develop the child's ability to be both guided by sign/word sequences and to use the sign/word to guide or influence the behavior of others, the child participates with each concept on the SSLP as it goes though two sequences: An *interweaving* to blend sign with action or object, and a *command* sequence. As the child makes the sign (with help) while watching the sign interweave with its referent, he or she begins to experience both the sign and the word accompanying it as related to their object or event. More precisely, the child begins to experience his or her hand gestures as invested with the meaning of the referent. Then, during the command sequence—also from the child's perspective—the child has opportunity to observe the effect of the sign on another person portrayed in the SSLP. Subsequent sequences show the sign being used effectively at right angles to the observing child and, eventually, directly opposite the child in the face-to-face form that takes place in everyday communication.

The intent with these sequences is to help the child understand that the sign/word retains its significance no matter what orientation it has with regard to the child. Once the child experiences both interwoven and command sequences for a particular concept on the SSLP, the teacher turns the child away from the monitor so that the child can begin to learn that the intentions conveyed in the SSLP are effective not only in the program but with adults and children in the real world.

For further information on the SSLP the reader is referred to Miller and Eller-Miller (1989) and to www.cognitivedesigns.com.

EXPLOITING NATURAL EVENTS FOR SYMBOLIC AND COMMUNICATION GAINS

The systematic use of natural events to develop symbolic function, and sequencing, as well as language, first developed after a hurricane that uprooted many large trees near the Language and Cognitive Development Center (LCDC). Observing the children's awe at the gaping holes left in the ground—and noting in particular how fascinated they were with one mammoth tree that had, as it fell, largely flattened an automobile— we decided to turn it into a causal sequence with the following steps accompanied by pictures, signs, and words.

> **A Tree Falls**
> Wind pushes.
> Wind pushes tree.
> Tree falls.
> Tree falls on car.
> Car breaks.

The advantage of such sequences is that they begin with the child's engagement with a real-life event. Capturing the causal sequence step by step with signs and words and acting out the sequence with the models of a tree and car provide the children with important language practice. In re-enactments one child (assisted by the teacher) was narrator, while another child responded by making the tree fall on the car. Then the children exchanged roles. Such role play provides a natural transition to the use of picture sequences that the teacher can draw in sequenced cartoon drawings, showing how the various events unfolded.

Other dramatic "live" events—blowing up a balloon that pops, an accident, a shopping trip—can be developed in similar fashion. As the children work with these live situations their maintained interest helps them develop expanded sign and spoken language vocabularies.

THE COGNITIVE-DEVELOPMENTAL ART PROGRAM

Based on the work of Kellogg (1970), and her belief that scribbling offers a way to discern more clearly children's developing vision and mental processes, we have been using scribbling spheres as a way of encouraging the development of symbolic functioning. It seemed likely that a cognitive-developmental art program (C-D AP) could help disordered children develop a transition to representational drawing. In proceeding, *we assumed that scribbles were to graphic symbols what babbling was to spoken words.* Just as meaningful language emerged from babbling, so meaningful drawings could emerge from scribbling.

Spheric (repetitive) activities were developed around the various scribbles that Kellogg had identified as part of the normal progression toward representational drawing. Younger and nonverbal children whose drawings are in the basic scribble stage are introduced to graphic interventions drawn from Kellogg's list of scribbles (dot, line, curved line, and so forth) as shown in Figure 10.5. After establishing these scribbles with marker, crayon, or finger paint, teachers introduced different media such as clay, paint, and collage to generalize the scribble. With all media, however, the emphasis is on helping the children convert a teacher-introduced scribbling sphere into a system that they can continue without support. To establish this, the teacher interrupts a child's graphic scribbling so that the child needs to continue the scribbling system and, as he or she does so, begins to "own" and invest in the scribbles.

Range of scribbles

Each week the teacher introduces new scribbles. For example, Week 1 might introduce the children to the "line." The process used could be drawing lines on paper (Figure 10.6) with markers, crayons, or pencil, using line strips of paper pasted in collages or lines, or using painted lines on paper. The teacher introduces a particular scribble working hand over hand with the child while saying, "Line, line, line…"—or using a straight edge for support— until the child takes over the activity.

The interruption used to bring about intentional scribbling on the child's part might consist of the teacher suddenly releasing control of the child's hand to see if the child will continue on his or her own.

Combining scribble spheres

If each introduced scribble is considered a minisphere, then combining different scribbles produces a multisphere in that each scribble is arbitrarily related to another. In helping children achieve scribble combinations—lines going through circles, dots inside circles—each scribble is best interrupted at

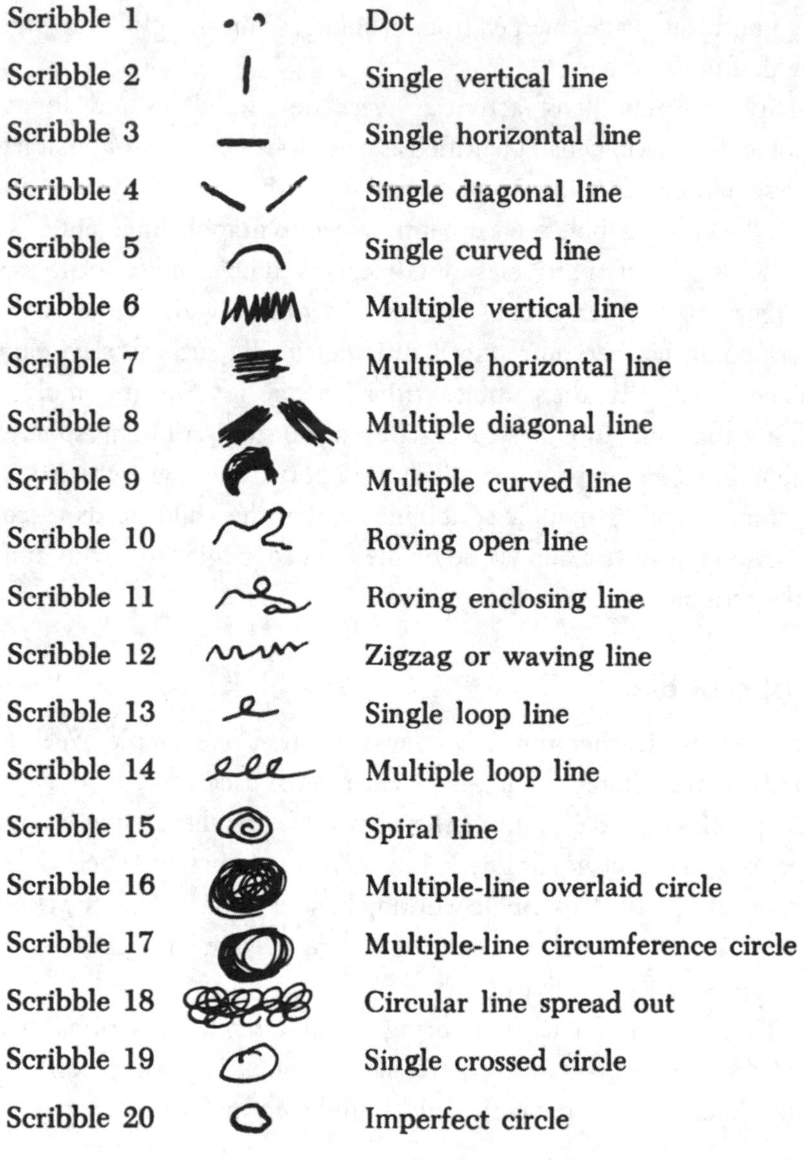

Scribble 1		Dot
Scribble 2		Single vertical line
Scribble 3		Single horizontal line
Scribble 4		Single diagonal line
Scribble 5		Single curved line
Scribble 6		Multiple vertical line
Scribble 7		Multiple horizontal line
Scribble 8		Multiple diagonal line
Scribble 9		Multiple curved line
Scribble 10		Roving open line
Scribble 11		Roving enclosing line
Scribble 12		Zigzag or waving line
Scribble 13		Single loop line
Scribble 14		Multiple loop line
Scribble 15		Spiral line
Scribble 16		Multiple-line overlaid circle
Scribble 17		Multiple-line circumference circle
Scribble 18		Circular line spread out
Scribble 19		Single crossed circle
Scribble 20		Imperfect circle

Figure 10.5 Scribbles used in LCDC's Cognitive-Developmental Art Program (C-D AP). Adapted from Kellogg (1970)

Figure 10.6 Dillan, an autistic boy, learning to draw a single horizontal line with the help of his mother and a straight edge

the point of maximal tension and the child introduced to an entirely different scribble. Once the child becomes engaged by the new scribble sphere, that sphere, too, is interrupted and the child brought back to the first scribble where the process is repeated.

After a number of cycles involving interruption to each of the two scribble spheres, the child begins to demonstrate, by glancing at the second sphere while still engaged by the first, a sense of relation between the two spheres. This combinatory process is assisted by the first scribble remaining in view while the child performs the second scribble.

Representational drawing

Just as it is impossible to predict precisely when a child will cross the gap from actions to names (as in the Helen Keller insight described in Chapter 8), so there is no way of knowing when the child will shift from even the most elaborate complex of lines, dots, and circles into the first representational drawing. One child spontaneously achieved representation when, in the course of drawing curved lines, he remarked that he was drawing "peeing." Apparently, the curved lines reminded him of that familiar trajectory. An Israeli three-year-old autistic boy being taught with the MM produced his first drawings of a human figure (Figure 10.7) in the context of drawing scribbles. His father's report of the drawings follows.

> Amit used to do a lot of scribbling before the drawing (actually it was a way for him to become calm and relaxed when people visited us or when he felt uncomfortable). His scribbling started with simple lines/dots with different colors and later progressed to concrete shapes (i.e. circle, square, rectangle, etc.).

Teachers can sometimes prod the process by suggesting and even accenting the combined scribbles. For example, if a child has produced circles and line combinations, the teacher might suggest that the circle is the head—just like the child's head—and the lines are legs and then put in dots for the eyes. If this engages the child, the teacher might then ask where the mouth or hair should go. If the child accepts the notion that graphic marks can represent the person's hair, fully developed representational drawings will quickly follow.

THE SYMBOL ACCENTUATION READING PROGRAM

The Symbol Accentuation (SA) Reading Program was developed in an effort to teach very limited, developmentally delayed children (with IQs in the 30 to 45 range) how to read. The advantage of working with such a population is that one can quickly discover the obstacles to finding meaning in printed words. However, before discussing these obstacles, we will describe two

Figure 10.7 Created by Amit, a three-year-old autistic Israeli boy, among his first representational drawings

kinds of reading. One, sight reading, sometimes called the "whole word" or configuration reading, requires the child to recognize a printed word by its shape or configuration. Here, the child is dealing with the printed word as if it were a picture. Obviously, with this kind of picture-like reading, the child must commit to memory the shape of many word forms. The great disadvantage of this form of sight reading is that the child has no way of discovering the meaning of unfamiliar printed word forms.

The second form of reading is based on an understanding of the letter–sound relation and how spoken words may be created by sounding out and blending the sounds that the letters represent. In this way, the child is able to find meaning in the printed word because it is part of his or her speaking vocabulary. As I will show, children on the autism spectrum confront very significant obstacles in developing this form of reading.

Because there seemed to be fewer obstacles to reading by sight, we began our efforts with this approach. It soon became apparent that the major obstacle preventing the children from achieving sight or configuration reading was that printed words (unlike pictures) do not look like what they represent. The problem was compounded by the fact that, for these children, spoken words were fused with their objects. In other words, when they heard the word "cat" they expected to see something cat-like. Finding that the printed word did not fit the template for *cat* that they had in mind, many seemed unable to accept such a form as meaning *cat*.

To help the children bridge the gap between the form they expected and the arbitrary form they found, we began a series of experiments—described in the next chapter—to provide a transition between a picture-like word and the conventional printed word. At first we began with flash cards; we then replicated the study using a stroboscopic projector that introduced movement in some of the words, in that the word *up* moved upwards and *down* moved downwards (see Figure 11.1b in the next chapter).

Following this, we developed animated sequences that began with the picture and rapidly morphed into the printed word (see Figure 10.8). These experiments indicated the value of this procedure for developmentally delayed and young typical children who were otherwise unable to find meaning in printed words.

To further strengthen the meaning of these printed forms we had the children produce actions or gestures directly related to the word's meaning. For example, as Figure 10.9 shows, gestures for *bird, cup, dog, mop,* and *falls* accompanied the animated presentation as the words morphed into their conventional forms.

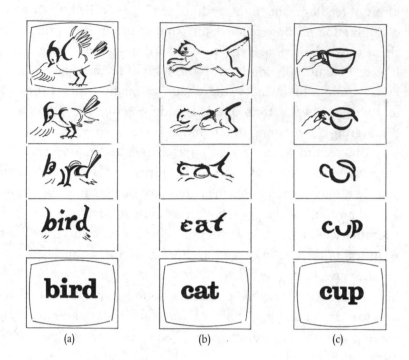

Figure 10.8 Animated transformation on videotape or CD-ROM of (a) bird, (b) cat, and (c) cup into their respective printed words

To help the children generalize the words they saw on the screen to the same forms presented in the classroom and elsewhere, we designed flash cards that drew on the animated sequences. Figure 10.10 shows a few of these flash card sequences while Figure 10.11 shows how teachers used them after the children had seen the animated sequences.

When a child could not identify the word in its conventional form, teachers would provide a quick glimpse of the word in its accentuated form, then return to the conventional word. If this was ineffective, the children were given the gesture that they had used in learning the word. Using these techniques, the children would rapidly acquire the printed word in its conventional form.

Subsequently, we taught the children to read simple sentences based on the words they recognized. To demonstrate their understanding of what they read, they acted out the meanings. For example, if they read *table falls*, they had to cause a large or small table to fall.

Noting that the children had difficulty transferring meaning from large printed words to their smaller forms, we showed the children that while the

Figure 10.9 Children simulate animated sequences: (a) the flying motion before and after the animated bird transforms into bird; (b) cup-lifting motion; (c) begging-dog motion; (d) mopping motion; (e) hand-falling motion

size of the word changed, the form and meaning remained constant. After the children could sight read 51 words (see Table 10.2) in large as well as in small type and using these words could act out meanings of simple three- to four-word sentences with appropriate actions, we sought to develop the children's understanding of sounding out and blending sounds into a word they knew.

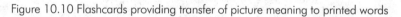

Figure 10.10 Flashcards providing transfer of picture meaning to printed words

Figure 10.11 Two points in the progression from picture to printed word

Table 10.2 Phase 1: Words taught by transforming pictures into printed words

Lesson	Words
1	bird, cat, cup, gun
2	table, dog, falls, mop
3	hat, nose, cold, pat
4	I, see, the, rat, jump
5	stop, girl, hot, walk, boy
6	lady, man, he, she, and
7	eat, come, candy, car, hand
8	up, down, far, tree, go
9	big, little, we, sit, near, foot
10	sink, toilet, window, door, bed, shower, sleep, awake

Phonemic awareness training

To provide a transition to phonetic reading we trained the children to "hear" the 51 familiar words they had learned to sight read when they were divided into two parts. This was first done auditorily, i.e., asking them, for example, "What is 'c...at'?" and then by showing the divided words on the screen. After each word had been divided and reassembled, the children would see a picture referent of the word so that in the course of dividing and reassembling the word, they would not lose its meaning. Following this training in phonemic awareness (Phase 2 in the SA program), we began to systematically introduce phonics.

Teaching phonics

This proved far more difficult: First the children had to learn the sounds that each letter represented, then to blend those sounds from left to right into a sound form, and then relate that sound form to a familiar spoken word to derive the word's meaning. Finally, they had to assign the meaning to that printed form so that they would not have to sound out the same word each time they encountered it. We attempted in every way possible to pare down the process to its absolute essentials.

Noting that the names of the letters were often very different from the sounds the letters represented, we eliminated one source of confusion by not teaching the alphabet and having the children designate the letters only by their sounds. To make these sounds more readily available to the children we developed letter-sound accentuation in which the children could see the mouth movements that gave birth to particular sounds. Figure 10.12 shows how this was done for *m, f,* and *b.* Research, which will be described in Chapter 11, supported this approach for children who had been able to sight read but had not been able to discover word meanings by sounding out words.

To solve the problem of sequencing from left to right, we developed animated sequences (see Figure 10.13) that literally "pulled" the child visually from left to right by virtue of the order in which these mouth-to-letter transformations appeared on the screen. Finally, to help the child realize that the sound forms created in this way were meaningful, a picture of the relevant action or object briefly appeared on the screen.

Another feature introduced to help the children grasp this new way of deriving meaning from printed words was to exclude all irregularities from the lessons. Our view was that once the children had solved the process of decoding with regular forms, they would be better able to tolerate the irregularities of our language.

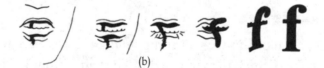

(a)

(b)

(c)

Figure 10.12 Transforming articulatory movements into letters: (a) *m;* (b) *f;* (c) *b*

Figure 10.13 Sequence for *boot* showing how letter-sound accentuation helps the child sound out the word

The first five phonics lessons helped the children understand that different consonants could blend with the same vowel and create different words. A story, "Sam and the Boys" (see Appendix C), helped the children grasp this notion as they produced sound forms such as *shoo, moo, boo, foo, oof,* and others, as their adventures on the road unfolded.

Once the children can sound out simple words like *shoo, moo, foo, oof, boo, boot, loop, root, roof,* and so forth, we introduce, one at a time, the short vowels. To help the children discriminate one vowel from another, we used two strategies: First, we relate a unique animated action for each vowel. For example, the *a* sound was related to the elongated mouth posture needed to utter it (see Figure 10.14). Second, the children were taught to feel with the tips of their fingers the way their mouth shapes changed as they uttered the different sounds. This hand-to-mouth strategy turned out to be invaluable as the children learned to turn the heard word into its written form. The range of words taught with these strategies is shown in Table 10.3.

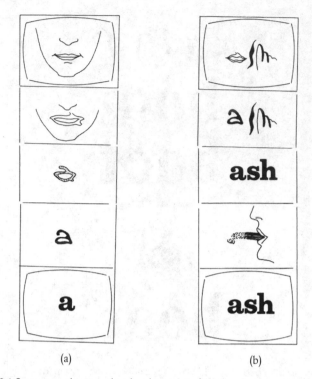

(a)   (b)

Figure 10.14 Sequence showing the development of (a) the short a sound and (b) the word *ash*

Teaching writing with reading

The SA Program brings about student control of written language by teaching phonetic writing in direct relation to phonetic reading. Children do this, initially, in coordination with the phonetic sequences as they appear on the screen. For example, as the *sh* of the word *shoo* develops on the screen, students refer to the screen, say "sh," and then write the letters. They do the same as the *oo* follows the *sh*.

Then the teacher requires the children to place a finger first under their *sh* and then their *oo* and sound out and blend the word *shoo*. Following this the teacher refers them to the screen where they see the word *shoo* immediately followed by a hand shooing flies, so they can establish the meaning of the word they have just sounded out. This repeated process helps students establish a direct relation between conventional printed letters and the letters that they (the children) produce. In addition, it firmly establishes the left to right sequence so critical for reading and writing.

Once children master this process of sounding and copying words and checking with the meanings portrayed on the screen, the teacher dictates

Table 10.3 Phase 3: Letter-sound relations blended into words

Lesson	Letter-sound blends
16	sh, oo ,c, b, f, m
17	shoo, moo, foo, oof, coo, boo, boom
18	t, h, r, p, l
19	toot, shoot, boot, hoot, roof, roo, root
20	poof, poor, loop, pool, loom, tool, fool, cool
21	s, see, sink, sinks, boot, boots, room, rooms, boom, booms, roof, roofs, root, roots, cup, cups, bed, beds
22	a, ash, sash, fat, hat, pan, lap, tap, can, fan, sad, bad, dam, pal, mad, jam, bat
23	i, sit, lip, pit, hip, hit, bit, dish, fish, fin, lit, rip, pin, sip, tip, ship, rim
24	e, pep, pet, net, hem, men, hen, shed, bed, step, wet, j, jet, v, vest, beg, leg
25	o, shot, top, pot, hop, mop, hot, g, dog, pop, sob, pod, cot, dot, rob, lot
26	u, up, cup, rub, nut, bus, sun, mud, gun, shut, jug, gush, dug, tug, hug, rug
27	boom, bed, bell, bib, bit, bud, bun, bus, bad, bag, bat, coop, cat, cog, cot, cub, cut, cab, can, cap, cash, cast, dog, doll, dot, den, dim, dish, dug, dam, dash
28	fast, fill, fin, food, fish, fist, fan, fat, fell, fog, fun, gush, gum, hoop, hoot, ham, hat, hen, hill, hit, hip, hop, hug, hush, hut, jam, jet, jib, jig, jug, ket
29	loop, last, lap, leg, lid, lip, lit, lot, mad, mat, map, men, met, mob, mop, mud, mug, net, nip, nut, poor, pal, pan, pat, peg, pen, pep, pest, pet, pill, pin, pit, pod, pop, pot
30	room, rag, ram, rash, rat, rest, rim, rip, rob, rug, run, rut, shoot, sad, sap, sag, sash, stag, shell, step, sip, ship, stoop, stub, tool, tag, tip, tub, van, vet, w, we, web, wet, win

these words *without* any support from the screen. Students must translate the heard word into its written form. The teacher frequently assists this transfer by helping the child place the finger tips of his or her free hand lightly over the child's mouth while slowly uttering the word. The mouth movements acting on the finger tips enable many students to isolate and establish the order in which the sounds emerge. As soon as a student has isolated the first sound heard in a word, the teacher urges the child to immediately write the appropriate letter for that sound on the left hand side of the page. The process is repeated as the child isolates subsequent sounds until the entire word is written.

After the child has written a number of such words, the teacher may request that he or she find one of the words just written, then another, and so forth. Children searching for the words they have written achieve several important things: They learn that they must form letters carefully or they will be unable to recognize them, and they learn that they must always begin sounding out and writing the words from left to right or they will be unable to derive the meaning. But, equally important, they learn that they can write words, return to them later, and still find meaning in their own writing.

These procedures—letter-by-letter copying and sounding out of words with the training sequences, translating spoken (heard) words into written words (dictation), and forced recognizing and reading of their own writing—resolve most of the left-to-right confusions so common among children. Beyond this, they begin to provide children with the understanding and skills needed to use written as naturally as spoken language.

Three phases

The SA Program, as it finally evolved from experiments and clinical work with the children, is divided into three phases. Each phase coordinates animated sequences on the CD-ROM (or videotaped sequences) with flash cards and/or workbook materials.

- Phase 1: Establishing sight reading—Ten introductory lessons. Children learn by becoming actively involved with animated sequences on the CD-ROM. Following this, they work with accentuated flash cards and workbook materials related to the animated word sequences previously presented on the computer or television screen.

- Phase 2: Phonemic awareness training provides a transition to phonetic reading. The next five lessons prepare children for phonetic reading and writing by sensitizing them to the sound components within the words they have already learned. Here, phonemic awareness is established by dividing the words into two parts and having the children attempt to combine the divided word first without and then with divided words appearing on the screen.

- Phase 3: Phonetic reading and writing—During the final 15 lessons students first learn to deal with words in which consonants combine with the strong vowel *oo*, and then to read and write words in which consonants combine with the short vowels *a*, *e*, *i*, *o*, and *u*.

The next chapter discusses controlled studies with SA as well as applications of the SA Reading Program with autistic, learning disabled, disadvantaged, and deaf children. For further information on the SA Program—including workbook materials—see Miller and Eller-Miller (1989) or visit the Cognitive Designs, Inc. website, www.cognitivedesigns.com.

DEVELOPING ADDITION AND SUBTRACTION CONCEPTS

Basic concepts of *more*, *less*, and *the same* are in play in many areas of life. They are used with regard to quantity (including money), measuring of objects, height, weight, and duration. Here, I provide ways of relating these concepts to quantity and to height to provide a foundation for teaching addition and subtraction. It will become clear that all these concepts can be taught to special children through their direct body and perceptual experience.

Class demonstration of quantity

Give each child a clear plastic bottle filled to varying degrees with marbles. (Have the top securely closed so they don't become more involved with the marbles than with the concept.) Assuming there are six children in the class, let the bottles be filled approximately as follows: Bottles A and B filled 100 percent to the top with marbles; Bottles C and D filled 50 percent with marbles; Bottles E and F filled 15 percent with marbles.

Once each child has a bottle, the teacher asks, "Which two children have bottles with *more* marbles than anybody else?" When these two are successfully located, the teacher asks, "Which two children have bottles with fewer marbles than anybody?" Then, "Is there anybody whose bottle of marbles is the same as somebody else's?"

After the children have successfully identified the various bottles by comparing them with the other children's bottles so that they are correctly identifying the bottles as "more than…," "less than…," and "the same as…," the next step is to place the C and D bottles (half full) in the center of the table and ask, "What must we do so that all the bottles have the same amount of marbles as these two bottles?" Then point to Bottles A and B (filled to the top with marbles) and put those bottles next to the E and F bottles which have the fewest marbles. Demonstrate and have the children indicate that one must *take away* marbles from the filled A and B bottles and *add* them to the E and F bottles until all the bottles are the same for everybody. When the class has responded correctly, allow two children to add marbles until everybody agrees that all are the same level as the half filled C and D bottles.

Repeat this procedure with pegs, blocks, candies, etc. until it is firmly established that the concepts apply to all objects. Ask parents to have their child perform the same operations with bottles at home. The task should be further generalized by spreading out *different* quantities of blocks or cars on the table and then having the children perform these same operations to make all the spread out quantities the same.

Applying the concepts to height

Line up all six children against the blackboard or another surface that can take marks. Place a mark to indicate how tall each child is. Then ask, "Who is the tallest child in the class?" Then, when the children have correctly related the mark on the board to a particular child, ask, "Who is the smallest child? Are there any children who are the same height?" Continue this way until the marks are correctly related to each child and the concepts of the *same* height or *more* or *less* tall are established.

Then, bring out three dozen slabs of wood—each one inch thick and about eight inches wide—broad enough for a child to stand on. Following this, have the tallest child stand next to the shortest and again indicate the difference in height between the two children. Put down one slab of wood and have the shortest child stand on it and say, "I added one piece of wood to make Andrew as tall as Mark. Is that enough? Should I add more?" When the class agrees that you need to add more, do so and have them tell you when the shortest child is as tall as the tallest child. Then ask, "Can we make Andrew taller than Mark? What must we do?" When class tells you to make him taller, add more slabs until this happens. Finally, to make him just as tall as Mark ask, "What should we do?" When the class tells you to take away some slabs, ask them how many you should take away.

The next part of the session consists of each of the children standing on a certain number of slabs which are added to until all of them are the same height as the tallest child. Place a mark on the board showing that each child is now the same height as the others. Finally, call attention to the slabs each child required to become the height of the tallest child who required no slabs. Ask how many slabs the next tallest child required until it becomes clear to each child that the shortest child needed a larger number of slabs than the others, and so forth.

Following this, develop worksheets which show how many slabs high each child is. (Measure the height of each child and convert the inches into slabs.) Then, have each child tell you how many slabs high he or she is. Draw an outline figure on the worksheet. Next to the outline draw a stack of slabs corresponding to the height of the outline figure. On the other side of the outline figure draw another, taller figure. Once that is established, have each child count how many slabs had to be added to his or her pile of slabs before he or she was the same height as the tallest child. (If necessary, have the children count the actual number of slabs they stood on earlier to make them as tall as the tallest child.)

From this format construct addition and subtraction problems directly related to the different numbers of slabs required for someone to be the same height, taller, or shorter than the tallest person. Addition and subtraction problems may then be applied to the marble demonstration described earlier as well as to spread out quantities of different objects in front of the children.

Note: The procedure with boards is very appropriate for one-on-one treatment. For example, tell the child, "We are going to make you as tall as your mommy or daddy." Then, let the child see and hear how you *add* boards until he or she reaches the required height of first the mother and then the father. It is useful to have a large mirror available so that the child can see when he or she is the same height as Mom or Dad. Then, have the child count the number of boards he or she needed to reach Mom's height and then Dad's height. When the child reaches Dad's height, you might ask, "What shall we do with the boards to make you the same height as Mom?" If the child doesn't "get it," show how "taking away" (subtracting) boards brings him or her to Mom's height.

DEVELOPING TIME CONCEPTS

All concepts—including that of "time"—begin with the body and gradually move through a series of developmental steps to "telling time" from an analog clock. In this section I will describe how children on the autism spectrum may be taught the concept of *duration* and relate it to the movement of second and minute hands on an analog clock.

Duration

The notion of duration can easily be taught through body experience, as follows.

Holding weights with arm fully extended

The children hold a one-pound weight with their arms fully extended while their teacher counts in one-second intervals, starting with one. Subsequently, the children compare the numbers to determine who has the largest number and therefore was able to hold an arm out longest.

The second trial involves a clock with a large sweep second hand. The children hold out their arms with the one-pound weight and watch the sweep second hand move. As each child's hand drops to the table, the child (or the teacher) writes down the number the teacher was saying just when his or her hand dropped. The teacher then asks each child what the number was when he or she dropped his or her hand. The teacher then explains that the larger the number, the longer the child held his or her hand up; the smaller the number, the sooner the child dropped his or her hand.

The teacher then shows each child where the second hand was on the clock when his or her hand dropped to the table. The teacher now relates the numbers to seconds on the clock and shows the children how larger numbers meant that the hand moved further around the face of the clock and that smaller numbers—fewer seconds—meant it traveled a shorter distance around the face of the clock.

Note: To keep the exercise within one 60-second circuit it may be necessary to have larger children hold a two-pound weight with their arms fully extended.

Competing with self and/or others

Children are then asked if they can beat their record by holding their arm out longer than the first time while the teacher counts off seconds. Children compare their first effort with the second to answer the question "Which was longer, the first or second time?" The teacher might also have the children compete with others around the table to see who can hold their arm extended with the weight longest.

Duration of a task

Following the exercise with seconds, the teacher helps the children relate the duration of a task to the passing of minutes. On a large clock where the minute intervals can be readily seen, the teacher counts off five one-minute intervals and marks that five-minute interval in red. The teacher then explains that the long hand on the clock is soon going to move past one red mark and—after a while—will reach the other red mark and that this hand on the clock moves slower than the second hand did. Then, the teacher has the children count as he or she points to each of the five one-minute spaces. The children note that five minutes will have passed when the long hand reaches the second red mark. The teacher tells the class that he or she will be busy so one of the children will have to tell her when five minutes have passed.

Using this strategy, the teacher can teach different durations during the school day going beyond 5, to 10, 15, and, eventually, 60 minutes.

Events of the day

Following the training in duration, help the children relate events of the day to the passage of time. This can be done with the help of a series of pictures depicting key events in the child's school day. The pictures should be of a size that will permit at least four of them to be placed on the face of the clock. The positions of the clock hands—their configuration—may be taught prior to the children's grasping the internal relation between seconds, minutes, and hours of the day.

The last chapter presents research and applications of the MM.

SUMMARY

This chapter emphasized the need to "teach for relevance." This requires knowledge of the children's developmental and learning needs and how to address these needs, and requires the children to demonstrate their understanding of what is being taught. To move the children into symbolic play, the chapter described the use of object replicas which precisely mirror their real objects. Children first perform an activity with the real object such as the Elevated Square and are then given the opportunity, immediately afterwards, to replicate that activity with a doll on a square replica.

The chapter also described a method for transforming perseverative activity into interactive, symbolic play and to help children make transitions from objects to pictures using 3D/2D strategies.

Subsequently, the chapter presented the SSLP and the SA Reading Program. Child-friendly aspects of both programs are evident in the SSLP's presenting signs interwoven with their referents, and presenting the material first from the child's perspective and then objectively, and by its beginning with action signs that closely resemble their objects. The need to generalize sign/words from training to a real world setting is emphasized as is the need for developing two-way communication.

Child-friendly aspects of the SA Program include its animated morphing of objects into printed words, and its sensitizing children to the sounds of words, and then morphing mouth movements into letters which the children sound out in sequence to elicit meaning. Children are taught writing in context of reading.

The chapter also described a drawing program which guides children from scribbles to representation of people and objects. The last part of the chapter dealt with helping the children achieve arithmetic concepts of addition and subtraction through direct perceptual and body experience. Similarly, the concept of time "duration" is related to the number of seconds which pass as the children hold a weighted object in their hands with fully extended arms.

Part IV

RESEARCH

Chapter 11

Research and Applications of the Miller Method®

A range of studies over the last 45 years are relevant to the development and application of the Miller Method® (MM). The earliest was my doctoral dissertation (Miller 1959, 1963). Other studies concerned the Symbol Accentuation Reading Program (Miller 1968; Miller and Miller 1968, 1971) and the effect of sign language and elevation on children with autism (Miller and Miller 1973). Additional studies examined the effect of the MM with specific populations (Cook 1997, 1998; Warr-Leeper, Henry and Lomas 1997). The most recent research was a two-year study of the effect of the MM on 71 children on the autism spectrum as documented by parents who filled out the Miller Diagnostic Survey on their children at one- and two-year intervals (Miller 2006).

In addition to the above listed studies a number of informal field studies assessed the Symbol Accentuation Reading Program with different populations. All studies and applications are briefly summarized.

DISSERTATION AND PUBLICATION

One might say that research on the MM began with my doctoral dissertation (Miller 1959, 1963), entitled "An experimental study of the effect of sensorimotor activity on the maintenance of the verbal meaning of action words." This study demonstrated for the first time that the performance of certain actions had a decisive effect on word meaning.

To study the effect of action on word meaning I used the "lapse of meaning" phenomenon which occurs when any word is repeated rapidly. If a

word is repeated at a rate of approximately three times per second for six to
seven seconds, people report that it turns into meaningless jargon.

I sought to determine if the rate of loss of meaning could be altered if
subjects performed certain actions in sync with certain uttered words. In the
major part of the study I had 16 subjects (typical college students) rapidly
repeat the words "push" and then "pull" while actively pushing or pulling a
spring-loaded drawer.

The results showed that when repeatedly saying "push" while synchro-
nously *pushing* the spring-loaded drawer, or "pull" while *pulling* the drawer
(concordant condition), that the spoken words maintained meaning
significantly longer (resisting dissolution) than in a discordant condition
where the word "push" was paired with a *pulling* action or the word "pull" was
paired with a *pushing* action. However, some subjects in the discordant
condition were able to overcome the more rapid loss of meaning in that
condition by interpreting the action that is conventionally thought of as
pulling (while they were saying "push") not as pulling, but as a *pushing toward
themselves*

These findings suggested the manner in which early actions interacted
with spoken words and how—when the spoken word was losing its
meaning— a person might draw on the available action meanings in much
the same way that an aphasic person, at first unable to retrieve the term
"scissors," could do so after simulating cutting something with scissors (Head
1926).

Subsequent work with the Sign and Spoken Language Program (SSLP),
as well as the Symbol Accentuation (SA) Reading Program, drew on insights
developed from this dissertation.

SYMBOL ACCENTUATION (SA) RESEARCH

Sponsored by the US Department of Education, my wife and I conducted a
series of studies with both developmentally delayed and typical children on
the effect of accentuation of words and letters. This research ultimately led to
the SA Reading Program. In the following sections, I summarize controlled
experimental studies followed by various applications of the SA Reading
Program.

Controlled studies

Several controlled experimental studies on SA were published (Miller and
Miller 1968, 1971). In the first experiment (Miller and Miller 1968) the

efficacy of an "accentuation" approach was compared with a conventional method of merely naming the conventional printed words. The presentation of words under the "accentuated" condition relied on flash cards on which hybrid word–picture forms had been carefully created on one side, with the conventional forms of the words on the other side. The accentuated word forms were constructed so that *walk* had letters which appeared to be walking, the word *wood* was made of wood, etc. First we showed each of ten severely developmentally delayed people (mean age 15, mean IQ 45) the hybrid word–picture forms, then we flipped the cards over to show the words in their conventional forms (see Figure 11.1a).

Lists of words were alternated so that both lists—nine words in each— were shown an equal number of times. Since each child was his or her own control, it was possible to examine the number of trials required before each child could recognize the word in its conventional form.

Accentuated words were learned with significantly fewer trials than were those words presented in conventional form. Further, when placed within sentences in their conventional forms, the accentuated words could be identified as well as those taught only in conventional forms.

A second experiment (described in the same article) was performed to test the reliability of the initial findings with a larger group (N=38) of developmentally delayed people whose mean age was 17 and mean IQ was 50. In this study a stroboscopic projector was used which enabled the accentuated and conventional presentations of the words to be projected on a screen in front of the subjects. In projecting words for the accentuated condition a slide with the word in its accentuated form was placed in one projector and a slide with the word in its conventional form in the other. This procedure resulted in the illusion of motion when the words were projected on the same space and alternated at a rate of 2.7 times per second. Then, the word *walk* appeared to walk, *jump* to jump, etc. This lively effect did not occur with the conventional presentation, during which both slide projectors projected the word on the same space in its conventional form. Figure 11.1b shows the words used in the stroboscopic experiment.

Substantially the same results were found as in the first study. The difference favoring rate of learning of accentuated over conventionally presented words was significant at less than the .001 level. As in the previous study, words learned with accentuation could be identified as well as those presented only in their conventional forms.

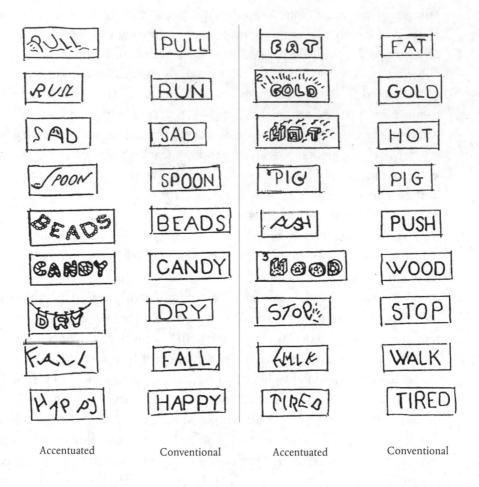

Figure 11.1a Lists of accentuated and conventional words from two experiments. Miller and Miller (1968)

The results of both experiments supported the hypothesis that accentuation works. Children learn to read accentuated words far more rapidly than words presented in conventional forms. The critical factor seemed to be the transition from pictured object to conventional word which accentuated conditions provided but which conventional presentations did not.

However, to clarify the source of accentuation's effectiveness, I conducted a study (Miller 1968) contrasting two groups of normal preschool age children (three- to four-year-olds, vs. five- to six-year-olds) using a different procedure. Later (Miller and Miller 1971) this same procedure was used with 40 developmentally delayed children.

The new procedure in these studies entailed contrasting an *accentuated* condition in which picture forms merged into printed words with a *separated*

Accentuated	Conventional	Accentuated	Conventional
	walk		Candy
	boat		jump
	wood		Cold
	cup		funny
	Come		Gold
	play		up
	down		Run, run
	look		dry
	work		see
	hot		Go, go

Figure 11.1b Lists of accentuated and conventional words used in stroboscope experiment. Miller and Miller (1968)

condition in which there was no merger between picture and printed word (see Figure 11.2). The two conditions differed only in the relation of the pictured object to the printed word. During accentuated sequences motion picture animation was used to project a moving object which rapidly tranformed into the appropriate printed word. For example, a nose in the course of being sniffed would transform into the printed word *nose*. In contrast, the separated sequence would present the identical sniffing nose above and separated from the printed word.

With each group the measure was based on the number of words which could be successfully identified at the end of four presentations under either

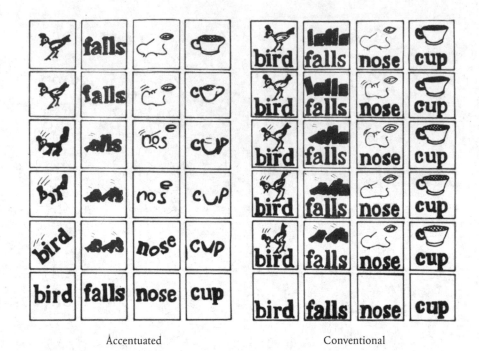

Accentuated   Conventional

Figure 11.2 Comparison of accentuated and conventional ("look say") presentations of printed words. Miller and Miller (1971)

accentuated or separated conditions. In studying the effect of accentuation with the typical three- to four- vs. five- to six-year-olds we sought to examine the relation between accentuation and typical development.

Results for the three studies indicated that while typical three- and four-year-old children as well as developmentally delayed children did significantly better on accentuated than separated presentations, there was no significant difference between conditions for typical five- and six-year-olds.

These studies indicate that by five or six years of age, typical children no longer require symbol accentuation procedures for printed words. Apparently, having grasped the symbolic function of printed words, they can deliberately establish relations between words and their referents without the relation being enacted for them by accentuation.

This raised the question as to whether typical five- or six-year-olds who no longer required accentuation for printed words might benefit from accentuation with regard to letter–sound relations. Accordingly, another study was conducted (Miller 1968) to clarify this issue.

In this study, the accentuated condition for each of five letters (*b, f, s, t, o*) consisted of a mouth appearing on the screen and going through lip and tongue movements required to utter one of the sounds symbolized by these letters. As these mouth movements progressed on the screen, they transformed into the appropriate letter. For the separated condition, the mouth went through the same movements but did not transform into the letter. Instead, the letters remained next to but separate from the mouth movements (see Figure 11.3).

The results of this study with typical five- and six-year-olds were consistent with the hypothesized effect of accentuation in that significantly more letter–sound relations were learned under accentuated than separated conditions. This evidence indicates that accentuation is important for teaching letter–sound relations even after it is no longer required for word–object relations. It indicates, also, that the word–object relation is, developmentally, more readily grasped than that between letters and sounds.

The finding that accentuation is related to typical development and is effective prior to children grasping the symbolic relation between word and object or letter to sound is important. It implies that the accentuation procedure would be effective for all children—including those on the autism

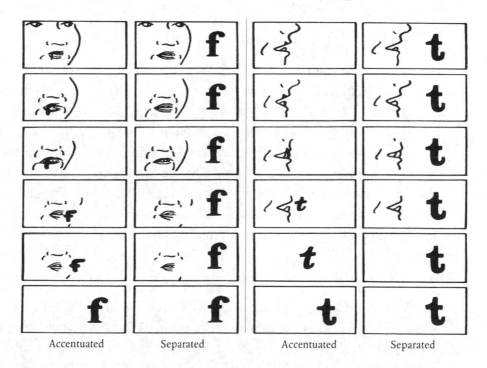

| Accentuated | Separated | Accentuated | Separated |

Figure 11.3 Accentuated versus separated presentations of *f* and *t*. Miller (1968)

spectrum—who had not been able to grasp the relation between words and their objects or letters and their sounds. The varied field applications described below sought to test this notion.

FIELD APPLICATIONS OF SYMBOL ACCENTUATION

The first field application of the SA Reading Program was conducted at Wrentham State School in Massachusetts (Marko 1968) with a population of trainable developmentally delayed residents who had not previously been able to learn how to read. The program was applied over a period of 18 months with 70 developmentally delayed residents with a mean chronological age (CA) of 21 years, mean Stanford-Binet mental age (MA) of four years eight months, and mean IQ of 38. These developmentally delayed residents learned to sight-read a mean of 28 words in a range of verb–noun and noun–verb sentences, in both large and small type size. Twenty of the seventy were able, with the help of letter–sound accentuation (Phase 3 of the SA Program), to sound out and decode the meaning of words with different consonant– vowel–consonant combinations.

This field application validated the results of the experimental studies previously described.

Disadvantaged preschool children

A doctoral dissertation involving a field application of SA was conducted by Messier (1970) with five-year-old economically disadvantaged children enrolled in Head Start Programs in Brockton, Massachusetts. Using control and experimental groups (20 children in each), Messier found that children taught with the SA Program achieved significantly higher gains on Metropolitan Readiness and Peabody Picture Vocabulary Tests than those children exposed to conventional readiness preparation for the first grade. He felt that preschool-age children were able to learn to read with SA because it was geared to their development level of functioning.

Autistic and schizophrenic children

A field application of SA with severely disordered children (E.E. Miller 1970) was conducted at the League School of Boston with ten children (mean CA eight years seven months). Eight of the ten children had been unable to achieve any measurable skill in reading and writing at the time the program was initiated. After ten months of SA training, seven of the eight had made substantial gains in reading and writing and had improved their Metropolitan Readiness Test scores a mean of 23.6 percentile points (from 5.2 to 28.8) and their Peabody Picture Vocabulary Test scores a mean of 20 points (moving from a mean IQ of 55 to 75). Important factors in the SA Program in stimulating development with these children were the habit of directed attention and increased contact with others which this program fostered.

Learning disabled children

An informal report from the Reading Department of the Wellesley Public Schools (A. Miller 1970) in Massachusetts indicated that SA had been an effective teaching strategy with ten learning-disabled children assigned to a learning center in one of the public schools for a one-hour session per day during a ten-month period. All ten first- and second-grade children assigned to this group scored substantial gains in their ability to read and write with comprehension as measured by the Stanford Achievement Test Primary 1 Battery.

REPORT ON THE SYMBOL ACCENTUATION READING PROGRAM BY THE REGIONAL SPECIAL EDUCATION INSTRUCTIONAL MATERIALS CENTER, STATE UNIVERSITY COLLEGE AT BUFFALO, NEW YORK

This federally funded instructional materials center introduced SA with three different groups of children. The Special Education Instructional Materials Center (SEIMC) report (Brown 1971) stated:

> Since it was not feasible to evaluate SA with all possible populations with which it might prove relevant, the Buffalo SEIMC limited its field evaluation of SA to Educable Mentally Retarded (EMR) children who had not been able to achieve first grade reading ability, to "High Risk" first grade children, and to a deaf population. (p.5)

The educable mentally retarded

This SEIMC-sponsored class of ten students (four girls, six boys) had a mean CA of ten years one month, mean Stanford-Binet MA of five years eight months, and a mean IQ of 69. Unsuccessful attempts to teach these children to read had been made for three years prior to their exposure to SA instruction. The children were taught with SA for ten months and evaluated on acquisition of sight-reading and phonics, as well as on Metropolitan Readiness and Peabody Picture Vocabulary Tests. Pre- and post-testing indicated substantial gains for nine out of the ten children, both on sight-reading and phonics tests—on average a 53 percent increase in sight-reading and a 45 percent gain in phonics.

Significant gains were also evident on the Metropolitan Readiness Tests (mean gain of 11.8 percentile points) and on the Peabody (mean gain of ten months in mental age and 5.6 points in IQ). The SEIMC report stated: "The Symbol Accentuation Program was effective in helping most of the students in the acquisition of basic reading and writing skills and improved listening skills" (p.8).

"High risk" first-grade children

This second SEIMC-sponsored class was termed a "high risk" first grade because the 12 children in it had spent two years in kindergarten, had low readiness scores, or were considered poorly motivated. The mean chronological age of the class (six years nine months) was closer to the norm for children beginning second grade than first grade. The teacher reported that by the end of the ten-month program, all of the children were well into second-grade-level reading materials. The SEIMC report continued:

> The Symbol Accentuation Program seems to have had some of its most dramatic effects on this "high risk" group. All 12 children showed gains in their abilities to sight-read words, sound letters, and translate the sounds they heard into the correct written letters. These results, coupled with the teacher's comments, support the view that most motivational problems which existed at the start of the program were eliminated. (p.12)

Deaf children

Two complete SA Programs were made available to St. Mary's School for the Deaf in Buffalo, New York, with the open-ended instruction to use the materials in any way that might seem useful with deaf children at different ages. Subsequently, four teachers used the materials in highly individual ways with their children. The SEIMC report stated:

> Teachers of deaf children were quite excited about the SA Program's ability to induce progress among children they could not previously move. The

teachers reported that the program's impact was impressive and that it had sufficient flexibility for individual use and/or in small groups. (p.15)

The SEIMC report closed with the following statement:

It has been claimed that the SA Program helps children who cannot read and write to do so. Previous SA studies have shown this to be the case under very controlled conditions. The present study has found nothing incompatible with that claim or with the findings of the previous studies. The results of instruction using the Symbol Accentuation Program, therefore, are entirely consistent with the claims that exist. Equally important are indications that the program's impact goes beyond effective reading and writing instruction; some of the subjects also acquired new confidence in their ability to learn and demonstrated this via increased academic competence. (p.17)

ELEVATED BOARDS AND SIGN LANGUAGE WITH 19 NONVERBAL AUTISTIC CHILDREN

The 19 nonverbal autistic subjects who participated in cognitive-developmental training (Miller and Miller 1973) represented a population of the most severely disordered and unresponsive children from four therapeutic centers. All had little or no ability to understand or use spoken words when they began the program. The median chronological age of the 12 boys and 7 girls was 11 years.

Training over a median of 13 months included regular sessions on elevated structures. On these structures, children would, for example, bring requested objects from one end of the elevated structure to the worker waiting at the other end. Once the child, in response to a signed and spoken request, could bring an object to one person, he or she was taught to bring the same object to another person, and so forth. Then, relative positions were reversed so that the child could learn that his or her response to signs was completely independent of his or her starting position. As soon as these and similar cognitive tasks could be performed on the elevated structures, the child was trained to perform them on the ground, in different rooms or outside.

In addition to regular work on the elevated structures, children had opportunities to view carefully prepared training films designed to accent the relations between many signs and the objects or events to which they related. (This was an early version of the current SSLP described in Chapter 10.)

The results in Table 11.1 indicate that, after a median of 13 months of training, all the children could respond appropriately, first, to signs paired with spoken words, and, later, to spoken words without signs. The longer children participated in the program, the better they did. The median number of receptive signs achieved was 27, while that of receptively understood spoken words was 26. The children were somewhat less able to understand and respond appropriately to two-sign paired with two-word combinations (e.g., pick up fork, bring hat, etc.) since only 12 of the 19 could respond correctly to these combinations.

Table 11.1 Achievement of signs and spoken words by 19 nonverbal autistic children

Name	Signs paired with spoken words		Spoken words without signs		Two-sign + two-word combinations			
					Recep.		Express.	
	Receptive	Expressive	Receptive	Expressive	yes	no	yes	no
Residential school children								
Mona	44	12	40	1	x			x
Hank	27	6	28	0	x			x
Nina	39	19	39	0	x		x	
Tom	24	6	25	0	x			x
Carl	7	3	9	0		x		
Marge	11	4	12	0		x		x
Teresa	27	4	26	3	x			x
Kirk	33	12	29	0	x			x
Barry	6	1	17	0		x		x
Sidney	13	7	14	2		x		x
Neal	22	2	23	0	x			x
Elliot	15	7	21	0		x		x
Bella	28	11	31	0	x			x
Day school children								
Karen	36	10	40	3		x	x	
Tod	40	12	40	0		x		x
Don	20	8	20	0	x			x
Larry	37	25	40	0	x	x		x
Philip	50	50	50	50	x		x	
Nancy	40	25	45	7	x			x

However, since none of the children could respond to or use signs when they began the program and all could respond and use some signs when retested, it was apparent that even severely disordered nonverbal autistic children could benefit from this approach. The procedure of pairing signs and spoken words both on the elevated structures and in other relevant situations seems to have facilitated the transfer of meaning to spoken words so that nonverbal autistic children could—after training with spoken words and signs—understand spoken words *even without the signs*. The results also suggested that training with signs may, at least for some, stimulate the development of expressive spoken language.

These results were subsequently confirmed by studies by Konstantareas *et al.* (1977) and a follow-up study by Konstantareas (1984).

The book *From Ritual to Repertoire* (Miller and Eller-Miller 1989) includes a number of case studies documenting the positive impact of the MM with children on the autism spectrum.

Cook (1997, 1998) did her doctoral dissertation on the application of the MM with several preschool children with autism or pervasive developmental disorder. Subsequently, she published a case study on the MM documenting significant progress with a child who had severe pervasive developmental disorder.

Warr-Leeper *et al.* (1997) reported on the positive effect of the MM in developing communication with five severely disordered and deaf children with pervasive developmental or communication disorders.

SOCIAL GAINS AMONG TYPICAL INFANTS

Ross and Kay (1980) conducted a study—using a procedure involving the systematic use of interruption—with 16 typical infants 12 months of age. Ross and Kay's study supports the present view as to the efficacy of interrupted systems in developing referential function. They reported as follows:

> The infants spent an average of 12 minutes playing with one of two adults (one male, one female) who were strangers at the beginning of the study. Typical games included playing peekaboo, passing a ball back and forth, and alternately throwing blocks in a tub. The adults did not interrupt the game until the pattern of turn-taking intrinsic to each game had been established. [In our terms this would be when the infants had established a minisystem.] Interruptions lasted for 10 seconds during which the adults maintained

relaxed facial expressions, seldom spoke, and watched the infants; during interruptions adults refrained from any game-relevant acts.

They found that during the interruptions, the infants were more likely to use referential gestures (gestures that could draw the adult's attention to the toy, such as looking alternatively at the adult and toy, pointing, reaching, and giving) than during the games. Infants were also more likely to partially or fully retake their own turns, or compensate in some way for the adults' turn-taking failure during interruptions, than they were during the games. Compensations included acts that were normally part of the adult's turns, such as lifting and dropping a blanket in a game of peekaboo, or behavior that would facilitate the adult's actions, such as placing a tub in the adult's hands when the adult's role included holding the tub out to the infant. The infants watched the game toys and the adults' hand as they manipulated the toys more during games than interruptions: they watch the adults' faces more during interruptions than games. Finally, the infants showed more positive affect during the games than during the interruptions. These differences were all statistically significant. (p.22)

These results with typical infants support the present formulation of systems theory: That interrupted systems result in compensatory behavior to maintain them. Further, these compensatory behaviors rapidly assume a referential function as the infant becomes aware of them and of his or her ability to initiate them in an interpersonal context.

LARGE SCALE MILLER METHOD STUDY

Recently, a large study—using the Miller Diagnostic Survey (MDS)—with parents of 71 children on the autism spectrum (Miller, Shore and Rankin 2006) documented gains of children from four schools using MM programs. Parents filled out the MDS's 107 questions covering children's functioning in body organization (gross and fine motor), problem solving, receptive and expressive communication, and symbolic functioning. The MDS was filled out by parents both before and after their children were in an MM program for one and two years.

Results indicated that the children on the spectrum had made significant gains in all major areas including both receptive and expressive communication. Correlations between gains in body organization and communication, as well as symbolic functioning, support the view that work with the body is an important component of successful work with children on the autism spectrum. This study also supported the clinical finding that children with closed system disorders responded to treatment more readily than those with system-forming disorders.

SUMMARY

This chapter presented research and applications of the cognitive-developmental systems approach now commonly referred to as the Miller Method®. The results consistently supported the efficacy of this approach with a variety of populations, but notably with children on the autism spectrum.

My doctoral dissertation demonstrated the manner in which directed action contributed to the meaning of spoken words. This, in turn, led to the study of manual sign language and its application with severely disordered children on the autism spectrum. Findings from this study clearly documented that signs which resembled their referents—and which were paired with spoken words—transferred meaning to these spoken words. Evidence for this transfer of meaning was implicit in the finding that, after training, severely disordered autistic people could, for the first time, be guided by spoken words.

Addressing the problem of early reading—particularly with populations having difficulty finding meaning in printed words (developmentally delayed or autistic children)—a series of controlled studies and applications of symbol accentuation were conducted. These studies and applications clearly supported the value of accentuation both in establishing sight reading as well as the phonetic relation between letters and sounds.

The chapter closed with a report of a large study in which parents responded to a questionnaire (MDS) both before and after the school year. The survey revealed that parents of four schools using the MM (including the SSLP and the SA Program) reported significant gains in a wide range of areas including body organization, communication, and symbolic functioning.

Appendix A

Theory Summary and Glossary

DEVELOPMENTAL STAGES

There are three stages in cognitive-developmental *systems* theory: The Sign Stage (from 0 to 18 months of age), Symbolic-Sign Stage (18 months to five years of age), and the Symbol Stage (five years +).

Sign Stage refers to the period during which the child's behavior is more or less dominated by the stimulus properties of objects and events. Toward the latter part of this stage—as the body–world relation becomes more differentiated—the child becomes progressively more able to deliberately initiate action and utterances.

Symbolic-Sign Stage. This stage is launched as the child becomes able to symbolize or represent the body as a coherent entity with arms, legs, hands, feet, a certain sex, and a particular name. It is also characterized by the achievement of naming—in this book this is referred to as the Helen Keller insight—which enables the child to designate objects independent of their contexts and to use their names as surrogates of their objects. In spite of this achievement, the child is still not completely liberated, as evidenced in the need for ritualized ways of doing things and by the requirement that words as names continue to be fused to their referents.

Symbol Stage. As the child achieves symbol stage functioning in one domain after another, liberation from the "pull" of objects and events becomes complete. The child can now demonstrate knowledge of the arbitrary relation between words and their referents and that one can establish new relations between symbolic forms and objects or events by fiat. This stage permits categorization and subcategorization of objects and events, reciprocal relations, the ability to shift perspectives, reversible thought, and "practice action" in thought instead of actual trial and error. This stage also makes possible phonetic reading and writing, arithmetic and algebra.

Note: These three stages are discussed in depth in Miller and Eller-Miller (1989).

Umwelt. A term coined by Jacob von Uexküll (1957), zoologist, which literally means "world around one." As we use it in the Umwelt assessment procedure it refers to our effort to understand the world around the child as it exists for the child. As the child develops through the three stages, the Umwelt changes—the child experiencing the same objective world differently.

Lateral and Vertical Development

The stages described above are evident in both lateral and vertical development. "Lateral development" refers to coping with objects and events in the "here and now." It includes the ability to make detours around obstacles to go from one place to the other (understanding spatial relations), the ability to problem solve (using a stool to get an out-of-reach object on a shelf), and the ability to use tools.

In contrast, "vertical development"—or distance from reality—refers to the progressive ability to *represent* the "here and now" via symbols. The transition from object to picture of object, to sign or spoken word to written word to represent the object, to the use of algebraic symbols—each progressively more remote from the object—reflects vertical development.

Ultimately, successful development requires the integration of lateral (the "here and now") and vertical development (representations of the "here and now") so that the child not only can solve problems in the immediate environment but can communicate with himself or herself and others about the experience. Often, to help a disordered child achieve lateral and vertical development as well as their integration, carefully designed transitions are required.

STEPS IN THE FORMATION OF SYSTEMS

Orienting. The disposition of a child is to "turn toward" the most salient source of stimuli, and this is known as "orienting." Sometimes orienting is induced by a sudden change in the level of stimulation, i.e., the child may orient toward you when you shift from a normal to a whispered voice.

Engagement. Once *oriented* by a salient event a child *may* become engaged by it, e.g., a child orients toward a moving ball then picks up the ball (becomes engaged with it).

Note: Engagement with the object is not, by itself, sufficient to establish a system. Only when the child is repetitively engaged with the object to do something—for example, picking it up and dropping it, bouncing it—can one refer to that action–object relation as a "system."

Compensatory reaction. Once a child is repetitively *engaged* (system formed) any interruption of the *system* will trigger a "compensatory reaction"—a tendency to keep the system intact. For example, if someone takes the child's ball he or she may try to get the ball back or, if this is not possible, make a gesture as if playing with the ball, say "ball," etc. The systematic use of interruptions is a major means of eliciting gestural signs or words from the child. When the teacher, therapist, or parent responds to those gestural signs or words *as if* they were intentional the child rapidly learns to use them to communicate.

SYSTEM PROPERTIES

Children's systems differ from each other in terms of their *rigidity*, their *complexity*, and their *distance from reality*. "System rigidity" refers to how urgent the child's need is to maintain a system unchanged; "system complexity" refers to whether the system is simple—in which case it is designated a minisystem—or more complex—in which case it is referred to as an integrative system. "Distance from reality" refers to the extent to which children substitute symbols for direct physical contact with a person, object, or event. It is also referred to as "vertical functioning," in contrast to "lateral functioning" which is concerned with the "here and now."

DIFFERENT KINDS OF SYSTEM DISORDERS

Closed system disorder. A child profoundly and repetitively *engaged* with an object (action–object *system*) who cannot permit people to become part of his or her action–object systems demonstrates a closed system disorder. We refer to it as a "disorder" because such behavior actively interferes with coping.

There are two types of closed system disorder: Type A (involvement with one or two action–object systems) and Type B (involvement with multiple action–object systems).

System-forming disorder. A child who has great difficulty forming *systems* because he or she is constantly driven by various stimuli in the environment, *or* because poor coordination interferes with the ability to *engage* with objects or events, demonstrates a system-forming disorder.

There are two types of system-forming disorder: Type A (related to poor coordination) and Type B (stimulus-driven).

FROM SPHERES TO SYSTEMS

Spheres consist of repetitive actions around an object or event to help disordered children learn new, organized ways of coping that help fill in their developmental gaps. Spheres are introduced by staff and may be more or less complex. When children can perform spheric actions unassisted they are referred to as *systems*.

THREE KINDS OF SPHERES LEADING TO SYSTEMS

Minisphere. The guiding of a child's behavior around a single event—for example, opening and closing doors, picking up and dropping objects, putting cups on cup hooks, or repetitively slicing clay—is known as a "minisphere."

Integrative sphere. Once various *minispheres* have been combined by staff and introduced as a connected series, such as climbing stairs in order to go down a slide or washing dirty dishes and placing them in a drying rack, they are referred to as "integrative spheres." Integrative spheres typically include several components.

Multispheres. Normal infants learn at about seven or eight months of age to shift their engagement from what they are doing (e.g., sucking a bottle) to something quite unrelated (waving a rattle) and can then return to the bottle, having kept the bottle's continued existence in mind. Many disordered children lack this vital capacity. Staff teach this capacity by first setting up different *minispheres* and then interrupting them in a way that enables the child to keep the one just left in mind even while engaged with another. The use of multispheres helps disordered children become comfortable with transitions.

GENERALIZING SYSTEMS WITH PLOP

PLOP is an acronym used to remind workers that before the child can generalize an action system learned at the Language and Cognitive Development Center (LCDC), he or she must learn to perform that system with P, different **p**eople; L, in different **l**ocations; O, with different **o**bjects; and, finally, P, when the object is presented from different **p**ositions. Once a child can deal with objects in this varied way it becomes highly probable that he or she will be able to generalize it both in the LCDC and at various other sites.

PRINCIPLES FOR EXTENDING SYSTEMS

Systems are expanded in two ways: Through the "principle of inclusion" and the "principle of extension."

The principle of inclusion states:

> Whenever the child, engaged by a figural property of an object or event, is concurrently stimulated by a background aspect of the situation, that background aspect becomes part of a total, engaging system. Subsequently, when only the background part of the system appears, the child compensatorily reacts to it as if it were the original, salient engaging property. (Miller and Eller-Miller 1989, p.155)

The principle of extension states:

> Whenever one engaging system acts upon a new property of an object or event...that property becomes an expanded part of the original system. The child then maintains the integrity of the newly expanded system when it is interrupted just as if it were the original system. (p.156)

SOME IMPORTANT MILLER METHOD® INTERVENTIONS

These interventions are designed to parallel normal development and in doing so to overcome developmental lags. In other words, we introduce and guide procedures, which in normal infants occur spontaneously, so that the normal developmental progression might be restored.

Multiple orienting. This strategy is important for children who tend to "use up" a particular *system*. To "revitalize" the fatigued system and to bring the children into better contact with the therapist or parent, he or she constantly "changes his or her mind" in a way that requires the child to constantly refer to him or her to determine what must be done next. For example, a child who is starting to "drift" within a particular action system requiring going up stairs across a board, down stairs, etc. is abruptly—while in the middle of the board—told to jump off or to reverse direction, and so forth.

Restabilizing. When a child is drifting out of contact, restabilizing strategies may be helpful in bringing the child back from his or her self-preoccupation. To restabilize a child you need to repeatedly and unexpectedly pluck at the child's shirt from front to back and side to side in a way which throws the child slightly off balance. In the course of "righting" or "restabilizing" himself or herself, the child becomes more aware of his or her own body and is therefore better able to relate to you. Restabilizing often works best when the child is elevated by standing on a chair or bench that brings the child to your eye level. The plucking should never be so vigorous that the child falls—merely enough to momentarily and unexpectedly cause the child to adjust his or her balance.

Mutual face-touching. When a child repeatedly demonstrates eye aversion and poor awareness of others, the use of mutual face-touching often proves helpful. Take both your child's hands in yours and begin, hand over hand, to have the child alternate between having one of his hands gently stroke your cheek and having you help him or her use the other hand to stroke his or her own cheek. This is done in a rhythmic fashion with you softly saying the child's name each time you help your child stroke his or her own cheek. Once this quiet, rhythmic alternation is established, you abruptly and unexpectedly break it by blowing on the child's hand. The dramatic contrast between a quiet and gentle rhythm and the abruptness of the blowing frequently induces a child to look intently at the adult—to determine what new strange event may be coming up next!

Restabilizing + mutual face-touching. When dealing with severe eye aversion, *restabilizing* followed quickly by *mutual face-touching* can be more effective in establishing meaningful eye contact than either strategy by itself.

Utilization. "Utilization" refers to a strategy—often introduced to help children emerge from tantrums—in which the teacher, therapist, or parent asks the child to repeat actions which were part of the child's tantrums. For example, if a child has been kicking and screaming, the teacher or therapist may tell the child to "kick" or to "scream" (but not at the same time). When the child responds to this request, a behavior which was initially an involuntary part of the tantrum becomes part of a system which is now linked to language. In other words the child becomes conscious of what he or she is doing. When that occurs, tantrums often disappear and the various actions are then performed more deliberately. Staff wishing to use utilization strategies must learn to distinguish between times it is appropriate to use it and when it is counterproductive.

Body schema. "Body schema" is a construct first introduced by Henry Head (1926), a neurologist, and later expanded by Paul Schilder (1951). It refers to the formation of a concept of the body that makes it possible to sit, stand, run, and jump, as well as to intend actions toward objects and people. While directly related to the body boundaries, the body schema extends beyond these boundaries, as when an amputee extends the notion of his body to include the prosthesis.

Zone of intention. The space within which a child on the autism spectrum can most effectively take in new information. Often this space is no more than 12 to 18 inches from the child's body. The task of the teacher or therapist is to be aware of the child's functioning zone of intention and to systematically expand it so that the child can take in information further away from the body.

Architecture. As used in the Miller Method®, the term "architecture" refers to the optimal relation between the child–object and person. A familiar example of poor architecture is when the teacher requires the child to put pegs in a pegboard but the teacher is standing while the child is seated and the pegboard is on the table. Improved architecture would be when the teacher is at eye level with the child, and the pegboard is between them at a height that allows the child to easily shift from peg board to teacher. Good architecture favors function; poor architecture impedes function.

Contagion. The tendency characteristic of poorly organized children to get "caught up" by the behavior of others. (In infant nurseries when one infant cries others also begin crying.) Deliberately established contagious situations are often used spherically (repetitively) to help establish *systems*.

Pacing. "Pacing" is a strategy that draws on the children's tendency toward contagion at early stages of development. Pacing is particularly important for children with *system-forming disorders* who have difficulty integrating or combining different components of a *system*. It consists of moving the child through the system quite rapidly so that the child has less opportunity to "lose" what he or she has just done. For example, when going up and down a slide placed at right angles to a set of steps, a child with system-forming disorder may well lose contact with where the steps are. Rapid pacing helps to correct this.

Narration. "Narration" is used in Miller Method® programs to help children connect what they hear with what they are doing. This is vital for developing receptive and expressive language as well as enhancing awareness of the self. The teacher or therapist "narrates" like a sports announcer what the child is doing while he or she is doing it. Vocal gesture is built into the narration in a way which expresses the worker's delight with the child: "Andrew is riding his bike" (or climbing, jumping, etc.). Narration is far more important to the child than saying, "Good job!"

Spontaneous expansions. "Spontaneous expansions" refers to the ability of the child to deviate from the original or "prescribed" way of doing things: For example, the child going down the slide on his or her back or side, head first, feet first, etc. Spontaneous expansions are important precursors of *executive function*.

Executive function. "Executive function" refers to the child's ability to act intentionally in his or her surroundings. It includes planning, problem solving, and making choices as to which action–object systems the child wishes to activate or combine in new ways. Children capable of executive function have moved beyond the stage where they are "captured" by their action–object *systems*.

Important programs. Two important programs used in the Miller Method are the Sign and Spoken Language Program (SSLP) to develop functional communication and the Symbol Accentuation (SA) Reading Program to develop both sight and phonetically based reading and writing. Both programs draw heavily on *system* concepts.

Note: Those seeking a more comprehensive discussion of cognitive-developmental systems theory—and the various programs generated by the theory—will find it in our previous book, From Ritual to Repertoire (Miller and Eller-Miller 1989).

Appendix B

Miller Diagnostic Survey for Children with Developmental Issues[1]

Child's Name . . . .   Parent's Name . . . .

Date of Birth . . . .   Date MDS Submitted . . . .

Diagnosis . . . .   E-Mail Address . . . .

Diagnosis By . . . .   Home Phone . . . .

Address: . . . .

Child's Program Orientation:

ABA . . . TEACCH . . . Miller . . . Greenspan . . . Other . . . .

If Other, specify . . . .

Parent Concerns . . . .

. . . .

. . . .

SENSORY REACTIVITY

1. Does your child respond to tickles with giggles and expressions of delight?

    Never ☐   Rarely ☐   Sometimes ☐   Often ☐   Always ☐

---

1   The Miller Diagnostic Survey (MDS), copyright © Arnold Miller 2001, is used with permission.

2. When you engage in rough physical play with the child (tossing him/her in the air, rolling him/her around, upside down, etc.) does the child laugh and, when you stop, seem to want more?

Never ☐ Rarely ☐ Sometimes ☐ Often ☐ Always ☐

3. If you make a loud noise (dropping a metal pot) behind the child does he/she start and turn toward the sound?

Never ☐ Rarely ☐ Sometimes ☐ Often ☐ Always ☐

4. When the child has a nasty fall, touches something hot, or is hit by someone, does he/she cry?

Never ☐ Rarely ☐ Sometimes ☐ Often ☐ Always ☐

5. Does he/she locate and touch the injured part?

Never ☐ Rarely ☐ Sometimes ☐ Often ☐ Always ☐

BODY ORGANIZATION
Gross motor

6. Does the child seek out things to climb (monkey bars, trees, etc.) as if "the higher the better?"

Never ☐ Rarely ☐ Sometimes ☐ Often ☐ Always ☐

7. When climbing over a fence the child knows which leg to bring over first.

Never ☐ Rarely ☐ Sometimes ☐ Often ☐ Always ☐

8. While walking with caregiver the child avoids stumbling over obstacles in his/her path.

Never ☐ Rarely ☐ Sometimes ☐ Often ☐ Always ☐

9. Does the child use the toilet to urinate or defecate?

Never ☐ Rarely ☐ Sometimes ☐ Often ☐ Always ☐

10. Does the child ride a tricycle (or bicycle) without support?

Never ☐ Rarely ☐ Sometimes ☐ Often ☐ Always ☐

11. Does the child ride his/her tricycle (or bicycle) from one place to another even when it means steering around an obstacle to get there?

Never ☐ Rarely ☐ Sometimes ☐ Often ☐ Always ☐

12. Does the child find his/her way from one place in the house (or apartment) to another (from bathroom to bedroom, from kitchen to bedroom, from downstairs to upstairs)?

    Never ☐   Rarely ☐   Sometimes ☐   Often ☐   Always ☐

13. When the child is about 50 yards from his/her home (with the home still visible) can the child find his/her way back to it?

    Never ☐   Rarely ☐   Sometimes ☐   Often ☐   Always ☐

14. When the child is about 50 yards from his/her home (with the home no longer visible) can he/she find his way home?

    Never ☐   Rarely ☐   Sometimes ☐   Often ☐   Always ☐

Fine motor

15. Can the child pick up small objects with pincer grasp (thumb and index finger)?

    Never ☐   Rarely ☐   Sometimes ☐   Often ☐   Always ☐

16. Does the child pull and turn a knob to open a door?

    Never ☐   Rarely ☐   Sometimes ☐   Often ☐   Always ☐

17. The child opens a jar with a top requiring two turns of the lid.

    Never ☐   Rarely ☐   Sometimes ☐   Often ☐   Always ☐

18. When the child performs a task (stacking blocks, hanging up a coat, putting toys away) his/her eyes focus on what his/her hands are doing.

    Never ☐   Rarely ☐   Sometimes ☐   Often ☐   Always ☐

19. Does the child stack blocks one on top of the other (at least three or four blocks)?

    Never ☐   Rarely ☐   Sometimes ☐   Often ☐   Always ☐

20. If the child stacks, does he/she attend to how well they are balanced while stacking?

    Never ☐   Rarely ☐   Sometimes ☐   Often ☐   Always ☐

21. Does the child hang his/her clothing on a hook in such a way that it stays?

    Never ☐   Rarely ☐   Sometimes ☐   Often ☐   Always ☐

Problem solving and tool use

22. Visiting a new setting with toys and devices to climb, the child soon begins to explore the various possibilities.

    Never ☐   Rarely ☐   Sometimes ☐   Often ☐   Always ☐

23. If you placed three chairs on the ground in different positions (one on its side, another on its back, and a third with its back up) and you asked the child to right (or fix) the chairs, could he/she do it?

    Never ☐   Rarely ☐   Sometimes ☐   Often ☐   Always ☐

24. Would the child place his/her hands in the proper position to gain the leverage required to right each chair?

    Never ☐   Rarely ☐   Sometimes ☐   Often ☐   Always ☐

25. The child opens a slide bolt or other door fastener to open a closet or screen door.

    Never ☐   Rarely ☐   Sometimes ☐   Often ☐   Always ☐

26. If the child wishes to get an out-of-reach object on a shelf—and there is a stool near the shelf—the child climbs up on the stool to get that object.

    Never ☐   Rarely ☐   Sometimes ☐   Often ☐   Always ☐

27. If the stool (or chair) is on the opposite side of the room, the child looks around to find it, brings it to the shelf, climbs up, and gets the object.

    Never ☐   Rarely ☐   Sometimes ☐   Often ☐   Always ☐

28. If the stool is in an adjacent room (out of sight), the child spontaneously finds it and brings it to the shelf to get the out-of-reach object.

    Never ☐   Rarely ☐   Sometimes ☐   Often ☐   Always ☐

29. The child cannot solve a problem at first but does so after seeing you model the solution.

    Never ☐   Rarely ☐   Sometimes ☐   Often ☐   Always ☐

30. Does the child pull a string attached to a toy either to bring it closer or to pull it along?

    Never ☐   Rarely ☐   Sometimes ☐   Often ☐   Always ☐

31. Does the child use a stick or other object to knock over a stack of blocks or other stacked items?

    Never ☐   Rarely ☐   Sometimes ☐   Often ☐   Always ☐

32. Does the child use a stick to get an object out of reach (ball or toy car) under the couch or behind something?

    Never ☐   Rarely ☐   Sometimes ☐   Often ☐   Always ☐

SOCIAL CONTACT
Aberrant social contact

33. The child avoids making direct eye contact with you.

    Never ☐   Rarely ☐   Sometimes ☐   Often ☐   Always ☐

34. The child is more interested in objects than people.

    Never ☐   Rarely ☐   Sometimes ☐   Often ☐   Always ☐

35. The child walks over people in his/her way as if they were objects.

    Never ☐   Rarely ☐   Sometimes ☐   Often ☐   Always ☐

36. If a stranger walks up to your child and holds out his/her hand, does your child take that hand and walk off with the stranger?

    Never ☐   Rarely ☐   Sometimes ☐   Often ☐   Always ☐

37. When you (the caregiver) follow the child through a swinging door, the child neglects to hold the door so that it doesn't hit you in the face.

    Never ☐   Rarely ☐   Sometimes ☐   Often ☐   Always ☐

Adaptive social contact

38. When three or four adults are sitting in a living room your child consistently tries to be closer to his/her mother or caregiver than to the others.

    Never ☐   Rarely ☐   Sometimes ☐   Often ☐   Always ☐

39. When the child's caregiver leaves him/her with unfamiliar babysitters the child becomes very upset and tries to stay with the caregiver.

    Never ☐   Rarely ☐   Sometimes ☐   Often ☐   Always ☐

40. When the child is hurt he/she comes to you, his/her caregiver, to make it better.

    Never ☐   Rarely ☐   Sometimes ☐   Often ☐   Always ☐

41. The child plays successfully with children his/her own age.

    Never ☐   Rarely ☐   Sometimes ☐   Often ☐   Always ☐

42. When the child ventures into new space he/she periodically returns to the mother or caregiver for refueling before venturing out again.

    Never ☐   Rarely ☐   Sometimes ☐   Often ☐   Always ☐

43. The child wants to be close to and spend time with one particular child rather than others.

    Never ☐   Rarely ☐   Sometimes ☐   Often ☐   Always ☐

44. The child plays "peek-a-boo" with his/her mother or caregiver (hiding and then suddenly reappearing).

    Never ☐   Rarely ☐   Sometimes ☐   Often ☐   Always ☐

45. The child looks over his/her shoulder at you with glee and excitement when you come after him/her saying "I'm going to get you!" or something similar.

    Never ☐   Rarely ☐   Sometimes ☐   Often ☐   Always ☐

46. The child plays a game of catch or ball-rolling with another in which one first receives the ball and then returns it.

    Never ☐   Rarely ☐   Sometimes ☐   Often ☐   Always ☐

47. The child plays a bowling game (or something like it) in which one child bowls and knocks down pins while another child sets them up until, after a time, they switch positions.

    Never ☐   Rarely ☐   Sometimes ☐   Often ☐   Always ☐

48. The child waits for someone to "take their turn" before he/she takes his/her turn.

    Never ☐   Rarely ☐   Sometimes ☐   Often ☐   Always ☐

49. The child shows by his/her behavior that he/she understands that some things are "mine" and that others are "yours."

    Never ☐   Rarely ☐   Sometimes ☐   Often ☐   Always ☐

50. When you play a game with the child to see who can be first to get a desired object under a cup, the child strives to pick up the cup rapidly in order to be first.

    Never ☐   Rarely ☐   Sometimes ☐   Often ☐   Always ☐

COMMUNICATION
Receptive

51. When you ask the child to show you either his/her mouth, nose, eyes, ears, or hair, he/she does so.

    Never ☐   Rarely ☐   Sometimes ☐   Often ☐   Always ☐

52. When you ask the child to point to *your* mouth, nose, eyes, ears, or hair he/she does so.

    Never ☐   Rarely ☐   Sometimes ☐   Often ☐   Always ☐

53. When you ask the child to point to any of these parts on a large picture, he/she does so.

    Never ☐   Rarely ☐   Sometimes ☐   Often ☐   Always ☐

54. If there is an object in front of the child (a block or toy) and you hold out your hand and firmly tap your palm as you say "Give!" the child gives you that object.

    Never ☐   Rarely ☐   Sometimes ☐   Often ☐   Always ☐

55. If you ask the child by word and gesture (pointing) to bring a familiar object (located six or seven feet away) the child does so.

    Never ☐   Rarely ☐   Sometimes ☐   Often ☐   Always ☐

56. When asked by word and gesture to bring a familiar object from another room the child does so.

    Never ☐   Rarely ☐   Sometimes ☐   Often ☐   Always ☐

57. Asked to get a familiar object from another room when that object is in an *unfamiliar* location as in "Bring the shoe on the table in the dining room" the child does so.

    Never ☐   Rarely ☐   Sometimes ☐   Often ☐   Always ☐

58. When the child is asked in a single sentence to bring two different things from another room, the child does so.

    Never ☐   Rarely ☐   Sometimes ☐   Often ☐   Always ☐

59. When you call the child to come to you the child comes.

    Never ☐   Rarely ☐   Sometimes ☐   Often ☐   Always ☐

60. When the child is doing something unacceptable and you firmly tell him/her to stop, the child stops.

    Never ☐   Rarely ☐   Sometimes ☐   Often ☐   Always ☐

Nonverbal communication

61. The child makes "call sounds" to get your attention.

   Never ☐   Rarely ☐   Sometimes ☐   Often ☐   Always ☐

62. The child babbles or jargons (which sounds as if he/she is saying something).

   Never ☐   Rarely ☐   Sometimes ☐   Often ☐   Always ☐

63. The child signals with gesture or sound when he/she is hungry or needs to go to the toilet.

   Never ☐   Rarely ☐   Sometimes ☐   Often ☐   Always ☐

64. When the child wants something he/she expresses this by pulling you by the hand toward the desired object.

   Never ☐   Rarely ☐   Sometimes ☐   Often ☐   Always ☐

65. The child points or uses other gestures to indicate what he/she wants.

   Never ☐   Rarely ☐   Sometimes ☐   Often ☐   Always ☐

66. When the child points or gestures to indicate a desired object, he/she looks at the object or event first and then at you.

   Never ☐   Rarely ☐   Sometimes ☐   Often ☐   Always ☐

Aberrant verbal communication

67. The child echoes words used by another.

   Never ☐   Rarely ☐   Sometimes ☐   Often ☐   Always ☐

68. The child utters words but does not direct them to a person.

   Never ☐   Rarely ☐   Sometimes ☐   Often ☐   Always ☐

69. The child confuses the terms "I" and "you" and may refer to himself as "you."

   Never ☐   Rarely ☐   Sometimes ☐   Often ☐   Always ☐

Adaptive verbal communication

70. The child uses single words to indicate his/her needs.

   Never ☐   Rarely ☐   Sometimes ☐   Often ☐   Always ☐

71. After you supply the first few words of a song or story, the child completes it.

Never ☐   Rarely ☐   Sometimes ☐   Often ☐   Always ☐

72. The child uses multi-word sentences to communicate his/her wishes.

Never ☐   Rarely ☐   Sometimes ☐   Often ☐   Always ☐

73. The child looks at you while using his/her words and waits for a reply.

Never ☐   Rarely ☐   Sometimes ☐   Often ☐   Always ☐

74. The child varies his/her sentences by changing subjects and verbs appropriately as needed.

Never ☐   Rarely ☐   Sometimes ☐   Often ☐   Always ☐

75. The child tells you about things that happened in school or elsewhere.

Never ☐   Rarely ☐   Sometimes ☐   Often ☐   Always ☐

76. The child tells you about things that happened in the past or that he/she expects will happen in the future.

Never ☐   Rarely ☐   Sometimes ☐   Often ☐   Always ☐

SYMBOLIC FUNCTIONING

77. Does the child match pictures to objects?

Never ☐   Rarely ☐   Sometimes ☐   Often ☐   Always ☐

78. If so, does he/she understand that it is possible to point to a picture to express his/her wish for that object?

Never ☐   Rarely ☐   Sometimes ☐   Often ☐   Always ☐

79. Does the child scribble on paper?

Never ☐   Rarely ☐   Sometimes ☐   Often ☐   Always ☐

80. Does the child complete a drawing of a face if the teacher or caregiver draws a circle with some of the facial parts put in?

Never ☐   Rarely ☐   Sometimes ☐   Often ☐   Always ☐

81. Does the child draw objects or people?

Never ☐   Rarely ☐   Sometimes ☐   Often ☐   Always ☐

82.   The child varies his/her drawings to reflect different things, people, or events that have impressed him/her during the week.

Never ☐   Rarely ☐   Sometimes ☐   Often ☐   Always ☐

83.   The child plays make believe with toys such as "driving" a toy car while making motor sounds or feeding a baby doll with a bottle.

Never ☐   Rarely ☐   Sometimes ☐   Often ☐   Always ☐

84.   Does the child's make believe play vary to reflect his/her changing interests and experiences?

Never ☐   Rarely ☐   Sometimes ☐   Often ☐   Always ☐

85.   Does the child count from one to five or from one to ten?

Never ☐   Rarely ☐   Sometimes ☐   Often ☐   Always ☐

86.   When asked does the child give you three, five, seven of a particular set of objects?

Never ☐   Rarely ☐   Sometimes ☐   Often ☐   Always ☐

87.   Does the child add and subtract numbers?

Never ☐   Rarely ☐   Sometimes ☐   Often ☐   Always ☐

88.   Does the child apply his/her knowledge of numbers in counting change from a purchase?

Never ☐   Rarely ☐   Sometimes ☐   Often ☐   Always ☐

89.   Does the child sight read single words (STOP, GO, DANGER, HOT) and know what they mean?

Never ☐   Rarely ☐   Sometimes ☐   Often ☐   Always ☐

90.   Can the child sight read sentences and show understanding of what he/she has read?

Never ☐   Rarely ☐   Sometimes ☐   Often ☐   Always ☐

91.   Does the child derive meaning from sounding out unfamiliar words?

Never ☐   Rarely ☐   Sometimes ☐   Often ☐   Always ☐

92.   Can the child write a letter to a friend or relative with only modest help?

Never ☐   Rarely ☐   Sometimes ☐   Often ☐   Always ☐

ABERRANT BEHAVIOR

93.   The child "twiddles" or spins certain objects that he/she comes across.

Never ☐   Rarely ☐   Sometimes ☐   Often ☐   Always ☐

94.   The child rocks, arm-flaps, or walks on toes.

Never ☐   Rarely ☐   Sometimes ☐   Often ☐   Always ☐

95.   When distressed the child hits self, bites hands, bangs his/her head.

Never ☐   Rarely ☐   Sometimes ☐   Often ☐   Always ☐

96.   In a new setting the child will either repetitively run in circles or run from one wall of the room to the other.

Never ☐   Rarely ☐   Sometimes ☐   Often ☐   Always ☐

SYSTEM FUNCTIONING

97.   The child is so drawn toward any new sound or visual change (something moving) that he/she needs to move toward it.

Never ☐   Rarely ☐   Sometimes ☐   Often ☐   Always ☐

98.   If, while stacking blocks, the stack falls down, the child needs to restore it.

Never ☐   Rarely ☐   Sometimes ☐   Often ☐   Always ☐

99.   When the child goes down a slide he/she seems to "forget" where the ladder is so he/she can climb up and slide down again.

Never ☐   Rarely ☐   Sometimes ☐   Often ☐   Always ☐

100.   The child has difficulty putting puzzle pieces in a puzzle or pegs in their holes because he/she looks elsewhere while his/her hands fumble to find where the object belongs.

Never ☐   Rarely ☐   Sometimes ☐   Often ☐   Always ☐

101.   When the child has an object in his/her hand and someone takes it, the child is distressed.

Never ☐   Rarely ☐   Sometimes ☐   Often ☐   Always ☐

102.   Given a similar but not identical object (perhaps a green balloon instead of the red one taken) the child rejects it.

Never ☐   Rarely ☐   Sometimes ☐   Often ☐   Always ☐

103. The child lines up blocks, animals, cars, etc. and resists anyone altering his/her arrays.

Never ☐   Rarely ☐   Sometimes ☐   Often ☐   Always ☐

104. The child does one or more of the following: Opens and closes doors, flicks light switches on and off, flushes the toilet, turns water faucet on and off.

Never ☐   Rarely ☐   Sometimes ☐   Often ☐   Always ☐

105. The child becomes upset if the usual seating arrangement around the table is altered or if you change the usual route to school or to the store.

Never ☐   Rarely ☐   Sometimes ☐   Often ☐   Always ☐

106. In a setting with toys and climbing devices, the child will wander from one toy or climbing device to another but never gets involved with any of them.

Never ☐   Rarely ☐   Sometimes ☐   Often ☐   Always ☐

107. The child tantrums when required to shift from one thing to another.

Never ☐   Rarely ☐   Sometimes ☐   Often ☐   Always ☐

Note: Responses to certain questions enable one to determine how disposed a child is toward a closed system disorder, a system-forming disorder, or some admixture. The higher the score on these questions the greater the child's disposition to fall into that category.

Questions emphasizing closed system disorders: 98, 101, 102, 103, 104, 105, 107.

Questions emphasizing system-forming disorders: 97, 99, 100, 106.

Once the MDS is completed by a parent or professional, a report may be obtained from LCDC by following instructions under the Miller Diagnostic Survey on the home page of www.millermethod.org.

Appendix C

Sam and the Boys

Arnold Miller, Ph.D.

An extended version of *Sam and the Boys* is available in book form,
with space for writing the letters related to sounds, from
Cognitive Designs, Inc., with or without the
Symbol Accentuation Reading Program.

SAM AND THE BOYS

Sam, the driver, was taking Joe and Bob from camp to the train station. When it was time to go Joe and Bob jumped into the back of the old car. Sam got into the driver's seat and turned on the motor.

The car said, **"Rrr...rrr...rrr"** but did not move. Everybody waited and looked worried.

Suddenly the sound changed from "Rrr..." to **"Rrrmm...rrmm...rmm."**

Smoke came out of the exhaust pipe and the car started to move. Everybody cheered "Hooray!" and waved goodbye to camp.

The road was narrow and bumpy with many rocks and holes.

Each time the tires hit a rock the boys heard a big "b" sound.

Sometimes there were three rocks in a row. When the tires hit them the boys heard, **"b…b…b."**

After one big bump the old car started to shake, so Sam stopped the car.

He got out, looked at this front tire, and slowly shook his head.

Then Sam told the boys to come out of the car. Joe came out first and helped Bob. Everybody looked at the front tire. It was getting flat.

"**Sh…sh,**" said Sam. "Listen and you can hear the air come out of this little hole in the tire." They listened and heard the sound. Joe said it sounded like "**Ffffff…ffff.**" Bob said it sounded like "**Ssssss…sssss.**"

When Sam put his finger over the hole the sound stopped.

When he picked up his finger the sound started again: "**Ffffff…ff…ffffff**" or "**Sssssss…ss…sssss.**"

"We better hurry and change the tire," said Sam, "or you boys will miss your train." So, everybody began to help.

While Sam jacked up the car, Joe and Bob took out the heavy spare tire and then rolled it over to Sam.

Then, while Sam put on the spare tire, the boys put the old flat tire in the trunk of the car.

Soon they were ready to go.

Sam started the motor which made the **"Rrrr"** and then the **"Rmmmm"** sound as the car started to move.

"Hooray!" shouted the boys. "Now we can catch the train!"

Sam was so happy he gave red and white striped candy canes to the boys.

"**Mm mmm,**" said Bob. "Good." "**Mm mmmm,**" said Joe. "It sure is good!"

This time Sam drove the old car very carefully around the holes and rocks. He didn't want to have any more flat tires.

This time the boys did not hear any "**b...b...b**" sounds from the tires bumping over rocks and holes.

Far away they could see the station. The train still had not come. They could catch it. But just then, as the old car went "rmmm" around a curve, they saw something blocking the narrow road. It was a big cow which had walked through a broken fence and sat down in the road.

Sam drove right up to the cow and blew his horn, first with a long blast **"Ooooooo"** and then with shorter blasts, **"Ooo…ooo…ooo."** The cow got up and looked at Sam and the boys.

She opened her mouth and said, **"Mooooo,"** then with shorter sounds like Sam's horn, **"Moo…moo…moo."**

Sam blew his horn some more, **"Ooooooo."** Every time Sam blew his horn, "Oooooo," the cow would answer, **"Mooooo."**

Sam started to get mad and the boys started to get excited.

"We'll miss the train, Sam, if that big, old cow doesn't move. **"Sh…Sh,"** said Sam. "Calm down and I will try to shoo that old cow off the road."

Then Sam got out of the car and said **"Shoo…shoo"** and waved his arms.

But all the cow did was say, **"Moo…moo."** Then Sam started to push the cow. Each time he pushed the cow he went, **"Oof…oof…oof."**

While Sam went **"oof,"** Bob climbed up on the roof.

He wanted to see if the train was coming.

"Get off that roof," said Sam, "before you fall off!"

Just then, Joe said, "Quiet…**sh…sh…** I think I hear the train."

Everybody listened and they heard from far away **"Ch…ch…ch…ch…ch,"** from the train.

"The **choo…choo** train is coming," cried Bob, "and we will miss it because of that old cow." From far away they heard the train whistle say, **"Toot…toot."**

"Foo," said Joe, "I am not going to miss that train. I will help Sam push that cow off the road."

"Me too," said Bob, "I will help too." And then all began to push and pull the cow.

"All together," said Sam. **"Oof…oof…oof,"** they went.

"**Moo…moo…moo,**" went the cow. "**Ch…ch…ch…toot…toot,**" went the train coming near the station. "**Shoo…shoo,**" said Sam to the cow.

But still she stood—with a pleasant look on her face—in the middle of the road.

"I have an idea," said Joe. "Maybe, if we scare the cow, she will walk off the road. We can all yell…**boo!…**together. Ready, get set…YELL!"

"BOO…BOO…BOO!" went everybody.

Still the cow just sat there swishing her tail and calmly saying **"Moo,"** once in a while. All the yelling did not scare her off the road.

Just when they thought the cow would never move and they would not be able to catch their train, a jet plane flew by.

It made such a loud **"Zoom"** and a **"boom"** as it went by that all the birds flew off the branches of the tree they were sitting on.

The noise made the old car shake and rattle. Sam and the boys looked up.

And the cow jumped straight into the air, then made a long **"moooooo"** as she ran lickety split for the barn.

Sam and the boys laughed and got back into the car. Sam started with a **"rmm"** and the old car got to the station just as the train pulled in.

Then the boys climbed aboard the train, waved goodbye to Sam and the old car as the train went **"ch...ch...ch"** and took them home until next summer.

THE END

FOR THE TEACHER

Sam and the Boys may be read in conjunction with children who have had training in lessons 16 through 20 of the Symbol Accentuation Reading Program. Alternatively, it may be read as an introduction to these lessons.

To help the children gain as much as possible from *Sam and the Boys*, the teacher reading the story should pause at appropriate places to provide the children with opportunity to make the relevant sound effects. The sounds in the order they appear in the story are as follows:

Rrrr

Rrrmm

B...b...b

Sh...sh

Ffff...Ssss

Ooooo...oo...oo

Moooo...moo...moo

Shoo...shoo

Oof...oof

Roof

Ch...ch...ch

Choo...choo

Toot...toot

Boo...boo

Zoom

Boom

Appendix D

The Language and Cognitive Development Center

BRIEF HISTORY

The Language and Cognitive Development Center (LCDC) has metamorphosed several times over the last 41 years. In 1965 my wife, Eileen Eller-Miller, a speech and language pathologist, and I, a clinical psychologist, started a private practice specializing in children with developmental and communication issues. This practice expanded rapidly. Wishing to become a research as well as a service center, we decided in 1971 to become a nonprofit entity and, at the same time, to apply for and become a Massachusetts Public Health licensed clinic. Three years later, we decided to add a school for children with developmental disorders to the clinic and, in 1974, LCDC became an accredited PL 766 school serving the same population.

The next significant change occurred 30 years later on June 18, 2004, when Mrs. Miller died after a long struggle with cancer. Prior to her death, my wife and I discussed the future of the LCDC. We both agreed that the center and its work should continue. After her death, I closed the school part of the program, sold our property in Jamaica Plain, Boston, and relocated the center's clinic program to Newton, Massachusetts.

Today, in our new center, with the sturdy support of Dr. Paul Callahan, an elite group of professionals, and a dedicated board of directors, the work continues. Below, I list and describe the LCDC's various programs.

THE LCDC'S PROGRAMS
Parent–child training (PCT)

Parents—after completing the Miller Diagnostic Survey—bring their children to the LCDC for three days of assessment and intensive work. The first day includes an Umwelt assessment of the child (see Chapter 3) while the second and third days consist of trial interventions to determine the most effective way of treating the child. Parents participate during all three days. At the end of the third day there is a family conference where we share our understanding. Typically, PCTs are conducted by Dr. Callahan, Kristina Chrétien, and myself.

Individual Miller Method® therapy

The center accepts a limited number of children for regular face-to-face treatment on a basis of one- to three-hour sessions per week. Usually, these children are from families who live within a 100-mile radius of the LCDC. Children accepted for treatment range in age from 18 months to 12 years.

Videoconferencing Miller Method® consultation

For the last ten years the LCDC has perfected methods for delivering consultation and treatment to schools and families remote from the center with the help of videoconferencing (VCO) technology. Recently, in addition to videoconferencing work with schools and families in six states, the LCDC has expanded its VCO capability to include families in Israel and the Alia Center for Early Intervention (for autistic children) in the Kingdom of Bahrain.

VCO sessions for schools range from one to four one-hour sessions per week. Sessions with schools include both clinical and classroom consultation. In clinical sessions the children are seen individually by on-site staff—a half hour per child—permitting LCDC senior staff to guide and train speech and language, occupational, and physical therapists as well as psychologists in the application of its approach. In addition, since many classrooms are wired for VCO, LCDC staff are able to observe and consult directly with classroom teachers, and offer suggestions about classroom management as well as the curriculum.

VCO is also a very effective modality for families treated by center staff because it allows us not only to see and hear but also to control the remote camera by zooming in, panning, and tilting so that we can access every aspect of the child's functioning and guide parents or therapists into proper applications. We are also able to exchange information back and forth through this exciting modality. This means that not only do staff working with the child at home get trained, but the family itself develops the sophistication that helps generalize the program from school to home.

Training workshops

Three or four times a year Dr. Miller with members of his staff conducts an intensive four-day training workshop in the Miller Method® approach. Workshops are conducted either live at the LCDC or by videoconferencing. Parents of special children may attend at a reduced rate.

This workshop is the first phase leading to certification in the Miller Method®. Certification entails closely supervised work with children with both closed system and system-forming disorders. The trainee must demonstrate skill in intervening appropriately with the children, and conducting and interpreting the Umwelt assessment as well as the Miller Diagnostic Survey. The training is completed only after a comprehensive examination on all facets of the approach. Details of the certification process are specified in the center's website.

Research

Ongoing research at the LCDC deals with ways of comparing various interventions to determine which are most effective for different children. The Miller Diagnostic Survey is an important tool in this research (see Chapters 3 and 11). Dr. Miller plans an outcome study of children who have attended the LCDC to determine factors which predict the best outcomes.

Information

Parents or professionals seeking further information on the LCDC's programs are invited to visit our website (www.millermethod.org) and to contact Dr. Paul Callahan on (800) 218 5232 or (617) 965 0045.

References

Acredolo, L.P. and Goodwyn, S.W. (1988) Symbolic gesturing in normal infants. *Child Development* 50, 450–66.

Baron-Cohen, S. (1995) *Mindblindness: An Essay on Autism and Theory of Mind. Learning, Development, and Conceptual Clarity.* Cambridge, MA: MIT Press.

Baron-Cohen, S., Tager-Flusberg, H. and Cohen, D.J. (2000) *Understanding Other Minds: Perspective from Developmental Cognitive Neuroscience.* Oxford: Oxford University Press.

Bettelheim, B. (1950) *Love is Not Enough: The Treatment of Emotionally Disturbed Children.* New York: Glencoe Free Press.

Blakeslee, S. (2002) A boy, a mother and a rare map of autism's world. *New York Times,* 19 November.

Bogdashina, O. (2003) *Sensory Perceptual Issues in Autism and Asperger Syndrome: Different Sensory Experiences – Different Perceptual Worlds.* London: Jessica Kingsley Publishers.

Brown, M. (1971) SEIMC's evaluation of the Symbol Accentuation Reading Program. Buffalo, N.Y.: Regional Special Education Instructional Materials Center, State University College.

Cook, C. (1997) Application of the Miller Method with preschool children with autism or pervasive developmental delay. Unpublished doctoral dissertation, Kent State University.

Cook, C. (1998) The Miller Method: A case study illustrating use of the approach with children with autism in an interdisciplinary setting. *Journal of Developmental and Learning Disorders* 2, 2, 231–64.

Gilman, S. and Newman, S.W. (1992) *Essentials of Clinical Neuroanatomy and Neurophysiology* (8th edn). Philadelphia, PA: F.A. Davis.

Goodwyn, S.W. Acredolo, S.P. and Brown, C.A. (2000) Impact of symbolic gesturing on early language development. *Journal of Nonverbal Behavior,* 24, 2, 81–103.

Grandin, T. and Scariano, M.M. (1986) *Emergence: Labeled Autistic.* Novato, CA: Arena Press.

Greenspan, S.I. (1997) *Infancy and Early Childhood: The Practice of Clinical Assessment and Intervention with Emotional and Developmental Challenges.* Madison, CT: International Universities Press, Inc.

Greenspan, S.I. and Wieder, S. (2000) Developmentally appropriate interactions and practices. In S.I. Greenspan (ed.) *The Interdisciplinary Council on Developmental and Learning Disorders' Clinical Practice Guidelines* (Ch.12). Bethesda, MD: Interdisciplinary Council on Developmental and Learning Disorders.

Head, H. (1926) *Aphasia and Kindred Disorders of Speech.* London: Cambridge University Press.

Howlin, P., Baron-Cohen, S. and Hadwin, J. (1999) *Teaching Children with Autism to Mind-read: A Practical Guide.* Chichester: John Wiley and Sons.

Kanner, L. (1943) Autistic disturbances of affective contact. *Nervous Child* 2, 217–50.

Kanner, L. (1971) Follow-up study of 11 autistic children originally reported in 1943. *Journal of Autism and Childhood Schizophrenia* 1, 119–45.

Kellogg, R. (1970) *Analyzing Children's Art.* Palo Alto, CA: Mayfield.

Konstantareas, M.M. (1984) Sign language as a communication prosthesis with language impaired children. *Journal of Autism and Developmental Disorders* 14, 1, 9–25.

Konstantareas, M.M. (1987) Autistic children exposed to simultaneous communication training: A follow up. *Journal of Autism and Developmental Disorders* 17, 1, 115–31.

Konstantareas, M.M., Oxman, J. and Webster, C.D. (1977) Simultaneous communication with autistic and other severely dysfunctional children. *Journal of Communication Disorders* 10, 267–82.

Lewin, K. (1935) *Dynamic Theory of Personality.* New York: McGraw-Hill.

Lovaas, O.I. (1987) Behavioral treatment and normal education and intellectual functioning in young autistic children. *Journal of Consulting and Clinical Psychology* 55, 3–9.

Luria, A.R. (1981) *Language and Cognition.* New York: Wiley.

Marko, K. (1968) Symbol Accentuation: Application to classroom instruction of retardates. In *Proceedings of the First International Congress for the Scientific Study of Mental Deficiency, Montpellier, France* (pp.773–5). Surrey, England: Michael Jackson Publishers.

McNeil, D. (1970) *The Acquisition of Language: The Study of Developmental Psycholinguistics.* New York: Harper & Row.

Messier, L.P. (1970) Effects of reading instruction by Symbol Accentuation on disadvantaged children. Unpublished doctoral dissertation, Boston University.

Miller, A. (1959) An experimental study of the effect of sensorimotor activity on the maintenance of the verbal meaning of action words. Unpublished doctoral dissertation, Clark University.

Miller, A. (1963) Verbal satiation and the role of concurrent activity. *Journal of Abnormal Social Psychology* 3, 206–12.

Miller, A. (1968) Symbol Accentuation: Outgrowth of theory and experiment. In *Proceedings of the First International Congress for the Scientific Study of Mental Deficiency, Montpellier, France* (pp. 766–772) Surrey, England: Michael Jackson Publishers.

Miller, A. (1970) Report on Symbol Accentuation with learning disabled children. Informal report from the Reading Department of the Wellesley Public Schools, Wellesley, MA.

Miller, A. (1991) Cognitive-developmental systems theory in pervasive developmental disorders. In J. Beitchman and M. Konstantareas (eds) *Psychiatric Clinics of North America: Vol. 14: Pervasive Developmental Disorders.* Philadelphia, PA: W.B. Saunders Press.

Miller, A. (2000) *Where is Angela?* Video documentary. Cognitive Designs: www.cognitivedesigns.com.

Miller, A. (2005) Heinz Werner: Catalyst for a new way of understanding and treating children on the autism spectrum. In J. Valsiner (ed.) *Heinz Werner and Developmental Science.* New York: Kluwer Academic/Plenum Publishers.

Miller, A. (2006) Teaching to children's reality. *Autism Quarterly*, Starfish Publishers.

Miller, A. and Miller, E.E. (1968) Symbol Accentuation: The perceptual transfer of meaning from spoken to printed words. *American Journal of Mental Deficiency* 73, 200–8.

Miller, A. and Miller, E.E. (1971) Symbol Accentuation: Single track functioning and early reading. *American Journal of Mental Deficiency* 76, 1, 110–17.

Miller, A. and Miller, E.E. (1973) Cognitive-developmental training with elevated boards and sign language. *Journal of Autism and Childhood Schizophrenia* 3, 65–85.

Miller, A. and Eller-Miller, E. (1989) *From Ritual to Repertoire: A Cognitive-Developmental Systems Approach with Behavior-Disordered Children.* New York: John Wiley.

Miller, A. and Eller-Miller, E. (2000) The Miller Method: A cognitive-developmental systems approach for children with body organization, social, and communicative issues. In S.I. Greenspan and S. Wieder (eds) *ICDL Clinical Practice Guidelines: Revising the Standards of Practice for Infants, Toddlers, and Children with Developmental Challenges.* Bethesda, MD: Interdisciplinary Council on Developmental and Learning Disorders.

Miller, A., Shore, S. and Rankin, N. (2006) The Miller Method: Establishing and assessing gains among children with autism spectrum disorder. Submitted to *Journal of Genetic Psychology.*

Miller, E.E. (1970) The effect of the Symbol Accentuation Reading Program with 10 psychotic children. Unpublished report to the League School of Boston.

Mukhopadhyay, T.R. (2000) *Beyond the Silence: My Life, the World and Autism.* London: The National Autistic Society.

Piaget, J. (1948) *Language and thought of the child.* London: Routledge and Kegan Paul.

Piaget, J. (1954) *The construction of reality in the child.* New York: Basic Books.

Ross, H.S. and Kay, D.A. (1980) The origins of social gains. In K.H. Rubin (ed.) *Children's Play: New Directions for Child Development* (Vol. 9). San Francisco, CA: Jossey-Bass.

Schilder, P. (1950) *Image and Appearance of the Human Body.* New York: International Universities Press.

Schmahmann, J.D. (1994) The cerebellum in autism: Clinical and anatomic perspectives. In M.L. Bauman and T.L. Kemper (eds) *The Neurobiology of Autism.* Baltimore: The Johns Hopkins University Press.

Shlien, J.M. (1963) Phenomenology and personality. In J.M. Wepman and R.W. Heine (eds) *Concepts of Personality.* Chicago: Aldine.

Shore, S. (2000) *Beyond the Wall: Personal Experience with Autism and Asperger Syndrome.* Shawnee Mission, KS: Autism Asperger Publishing Company.

Sousa, D. (2001) *How the Special Needs Brain Learns.* Thousand Oaks, CA: Corwin Press.

Spitz, R. (1945–46) Hospitalism. *Psychoanal. Stud. Child.* I., 53–74; II, 113–117. New York: International Universities Press.

Stern, C. and Stern, W. (1928) *Monographien über die seelische Entwicklung des kindes 1. Die Kindersprache. Eine Psychologische und Unersuchung* (4th rev. ed.). Leipzig: Barth.

Trevarthen, C., and Hubley, P. (1979) Secondary intersubjectivity: Confidence, confiding, and acts of meaning in the first year of life. In A. Locke (ed.) *Action, Gesture, and Symbol.* London: Academic Press.

Uexküll, J. von (1957) A stroll through the worlds of animals and men. In C.H. Schiller (ed.) *Instinctive Behavior, Part I.* New York: International Universities Press.

Uzgiris, I. and Hunt, J. McV. (1980) *Assessment in Infancy: Ordinal Scales of Psychological Development.* Urbana, IL: University of Illinois Press. (Original work published in 1975.)

Vygotsky, L.S. (1962) *Thought and Language.* Cambridge, MA: MIT Press.

Warr-Leeper, G., Henry, S. and Lomas, T.C. (1997) The effects of Miller Method intervention on functional communication: Multiple case studies for children with severe communication disorders and hearing impairments. Unpublished honours study.

Werner, H. (1948) *Comparative Psychology of Mental Development.* Chicago, IL: Follett.

Werner, H. and Kaplan, B. (1963) *Symbol Formation: An Organismic Developmental Approach to Language and the Expression of Thought.* New York: Wiley.

Wing, L. and Potter, D. (2002) The epidemiology of autistic spectrum disorders: Is the prevalence rising? *Mental Retardation and Developmental Disabilities Research Reviews,* 8, 3, 151–61.

Subject
Index

Author Index